P9-AOF-125

BROTHERS OF DOOM

By Hoffman Birney

GRIM JOURNEY
EAGLE IN THE SUN
ANN CARMENY
BROTHERS OF DOOM

In collaboration with Charles Kelly

HOLY MURDER

FRANCISCO PIZARRO

From the Original Painting in the Palace of the Viceroy

BROTHERS OF DOOM

The Story of the Pizarros of Peru

BY

HOFFMAN BIRNEY

G. P. PUTNAM'S SONS

NEW YORK

COPYRIGHT, 1942, BY HOFFMAN BIRNEY

To

L I L I Á N

Whose ancestor, Juan de la Torre
was one of the "Men of Gallo" and
a founder of Arequipa

AUTHOR'S NOTE

These pages represent an attempt to reconstruct at least a semblance of the lives and the times of as colorful a group of individuals as this world has ever known; an attempt to fill a portion of the gaps in those textbooks which dispose within the space of one short chapter of all those events between 1492 and the establishment of Jamestown and Plymouth and which dismiss as briefly the achievements of all those whose native tongue was not English.

There is little that is original here. I have discovered no hitherto unknown source material, nor have I consulted any texts which have not been referred to many times before. If I have at times differed with my betters—with Prescott and Markham and Means—it is because it has been my privilege to travel over much of the territory where the Pizarros and their companions marched and fought, to follow the trails which they must have traveled because none other exist in the land, and to cross the passes which they must have crossed because only at those points could the ramparts of the cordillera be surmounted. It has been my good fortune to do much of that traveling by air—a method of transportation of which Prescott never dreamed and of which later historians beheld only the beginnings. I have flown the length and the breadth of Peru many times; from Cuzco to Lima and from Lima to Iquitos on the Marañon just above the mouth of the Napo, which Gonzalo Pizarro followed so painfully. From half a mile above the Napo jungles one can appreciate truly and fully the boldness of the venture to discover the Land of Cinnamon.

I have always believed that footnotes should be used most sparingly and that chapter notes and extensive biographical references serve only to confuse the reader or to impress him, perhaps, with the author's profound erudition and with the tremendous scope of that author's researches. I pretend to no such learning, nor has my reading extended beyond the facilities of the National Library in Lima, the New York Public Library, and the Library of Congress. A list of the major works consulted is given herewith:

Anonymous. [There can be little doubt that the author was Francisco de Xeres.] *La Conquista del Peru*. Seville, 1534. The original is one of the rarest of all books on America. A copy is in the National Library in Lima, another in the New York Public Library. The latter was reproduced in facsimile and translated by Joseph H. Sinclair in 1929.

Cabello de Balboa, Padre Miguel. *Miscelánea Antartica*. The original manuscript has vanished, and even the date of its writing is unknown although it was probably written during the period 1566—*circa* 1603 when Padre Cabello was in Peru. An eighteenth-century copy is in the New York Public Library.

Cieza de Leon, Pedro de. *Primera y Segunda Partes de la Chronica del Peru*. Both parts, translated and edited by Sir Clements Markham, were published by the Hakluyt Society, London, in 1864 and 1883.

Garcilaso de la Vega, El Inca. *Primera Parte de los Comentarios Reales de las Incas.* Lisbon, 1609. [Also Antwerp, 1615.] Markham translation: London, Hakluyt Society, 1869 and 1871, two volumes.

Herrera y Tordesillas, Antonio de. *Historia General de los Hechos de los Castellanos en las Islas y Tierra Firme del Mar Oceano.* Madrid, 1601-1615. Four volumes. The work went into many subsequent editions and was drawn upon heavily by all seventeenth- and eighteenth-century compilers of accounts of travel and exploration. I do not have the bibliographical references of English translations, if any have been made.

Lopez de Gómara, Francisco. *Primera y Segunda Partes de la Historia General de las Indias.* Saragossa, 1553 [and Madrid, 1849]. See above.

Markham, Sir Clements R.
A History of Peru. Chicago, 1892.
The Incas of Peru. London, 1910.

Means, Philip Ainsworth. *Ancient Civilizations of the Andes.* New York, 1931. Unquestionably the most scholarly and the most comprehensive volume ever written in English on this subject. One of the few books mentioned in this bibliography which is available—by the simple method of purchase from the publishers—to the average reader. *Fall of the Inca Empire.* New York, 1932. The title is somewhat misleading. The first four chapters cover an all-too-brief account of the Conquest.

Oviedo y Valdes, Captain Gonzalo Fernandez de. *La Historia General de las Indias.* Madrid, 1535 and 1557.

Pizarro, Pedro. *Relación del descubrimiento y conquista de los Reynos del Peru.* Lima, 1921. Edited by Drs. H. H. Urteaga and C. A. Romero.

Prescott, William H. *History of the Conquest of Peru.* New York, 1847. In spite of all that has been said and might be said in criticism, still foremost among all works in English on this subject.

Sarmiento de Gamboa, Captain Pedro. *Historia de las Incas.* Translated and edited by Sir Clements R. Markham. London, Hakluyt Society, 1907.

BROTHERS OF DOOM

Chapter One

THEY WERE FOUR, and in all of history no four brothers have known lives more full. Hernando, Francisco, Juan, and Gonzalo Pizarro—to list them in the order of their birth rather than of their fame—and of the four only Hernando, the eldest, could boast of legitimate birth and only he died a natural death. Fame laid her accolade upon them all. They knew glory and wealth and the honors that generous monarchs, well paid for their generosity, could bestow; and the dark star which ever guided their destinies led them from fame to infamy, from wealth to poverty, to the dungeon, the daggers of assassins, the warclubs of Indian enemies, and to the headsman's block.

They were brothers by virtue of the easy recognition of an era when bastardy was not a shameful thing and birth in wedlock was of importance only in such matters as succession to a title or to establish lawful inheritance of property or estates. The four were sired by one man, Gonzalo Pizarro, a swashbuckling officer of infantry who spent many of his years of service in Trujillo in the province of Estremadura, Spain. He married an *hidalga*, the Doña Isabel de Vargas, who bore him his eldest son, Hernando, "legitimate by his

3

pride as well as by his birth." The year of Hernando's birth has been given as 1460. It was probably a decade later, at least, since it is of record that he was living in 1560 when he was released from the fortress-prison of Medina del Campo. The year of Hernando's birth is of no more material importance than is the date—given variously as 1471, 1475, and 1478—when Francisco Pizarro was born to one Francisca Morales, a woman of the people and a bedfellow of Don Gonzalo's.

That same Francisca has also been named as the mother of Juan Pizarro, born during the last decade of the fifteenth century, and of the fourth brother, Gonzalo, born in 1506. This is scarcely probable. Had she been only sixteen years old in 1478—latest of the dates given for her son Francisco's birth—she would have been forty-two in 1506. We know, too, that she was married to one Alcántara who was—for the record, at least—the father of her son Francisco Martín de Alcántara. That the four Pizarros were sired by Don Gonzalo is quite certain, but it is more probable that Juan and the younger Gonzalo were born of a union other than that which produced Francisco.

It is not strange that those dates are largely conjectural. The brothers were men, full grown, before they strode into the pages of history as the destroyers of one of the world's greatest empires and the conquerors of the richest domains in the western world. Even legend speaks of the boyhood of only one, Francisco. We read that he was miserably poor and that he found employment as a swineherd, that he was so starved as to seize for himself food intended for the beasts, and that in extremities of hunger he drew his own sustenance from the hot dugs of the sows he tended. He was a foundling,

4

say other apocryphal tales, and was abandoned by his mother on the steps of one of Trujillo's churches so that she, unencumbered, might follow her soldier-lover. Of only one thing can we be certain: there was no time for schooling during those years when the peasant boy fought for the privilege of living. Francisco Pizarro, marked by fate to be the head of Spain's richest colony and the familiar of kings, never learned to read or write. In later years he was able to grip a quill and inscribe, boldly, the flourished rubric with which Latins have always decorated their signatures, but the name itself was written by the hand of his secretary.

Hernando, the eldest brother, was well educated for the times. Don Gonzalo may have neglected his children of the left hand, but his legitimate issue was trained to carry on the traditions of the name. There is considerable evidence that Hernando, after an education in Spain and Italy, served as an officer in the armies of Ferdinand and Isabella, an assumption substantiated in some measure by his later exploits in Peru.

His younger brothers, too, were Francisco's superiors in education, which tends to support the theory that they were not born of Francisca Morales. Both Juan and Gonzalo could read and write, but they, like Francisco, were miserably poor: ". . . poor, and as proud as they were poor," says a contemporary, "and their greed for wealth was equal to their poverty."

One thing all of the four possessed to bulwark that pride and to make that poverty endurable. To each of his offspring, Gonzalo Pizarro bequeathed a tall, straight body, superb physical strength and powers of endurance, a natural skill with sword and lance, and lean, patrician features. Bastards

5

they might be, but to outward seeming they were hidalgos—sons of somebody. In the years of their fame they were described in considerable detail by contemporary writers; portraits were painted of both Francisco and Hernando. We can look upon those pictures, pen and brush, and see strong men with the broad shoulders and narrow flanks of the horseman, with brilliant dark eyes—perhaps too closely placed—and with full red lips beneath sweeping mustaches. They wore beards, the pointed or forked beards of the sixteenth century, and all were quite bald at brow and temple. Steel helmets, worn almost daily over many years, produce such a baldness.

They were alike in many ways, those Brothers of Doom: in appearance and strength and immunity to disease and—with some reservations in the case of Hernando—in character. All were loyal, but their loyalty was first to themselves, then to God, church, and king. All were cruel and ruthless and proud and of deathless ambition and utterly fearless, but the cavalier who did not possess those qualities did not long survive. They should be judged, if judgment is to be rendered, by their times and the standards of those times, by the century which gave to the world the Spanish Inquisition, the Borgias, and the conquest of the Indies.

Those were gaudy days, those closing decades of the fifteenth century and the opening years of its successor; earth will never know their like until another Columbus returns to tell of interstellar conquests and of the course to other planets. Today's world is old and weary; its every corner is known, its every people ethnographically charted. Three of the Pizarros were born in a world that was as flat as the paper upon which these words are written, a disk of a world surrounded by Ocean, into which the too-adventurous mariner was doomed to plunge. A world in which the matchlock was but slowly superseding the bow, when the art of printing had been known to Europeans for less than half a century; a world in which life was abundant and incredibly cheap. Witches rode the skies at night, to be exorcised by charms and talismans, to be destroyed by torture. Feudal rights were still held and still confirmed. Landowners, according to their degree, could exercise the high justice, the middle, and the low; the right of the seigneur was as firmly established as the authority of king or pope—as many a girl, wailing or smirking as she rode to her husband's door, could testify. Messer Giovanni Boccaccio had been dead for a century, but the tales he had written lived and were told and retold and laughed at right merrily. The concept that women could be virtuous or constant was regarded as a quaint jest. A woman was known by the number and the rank of her lovers; a man by his conquests, his mistresses, and the children he had sired. There was no stigma in illegitimacy when the children by the left hand vastly outnumbered those by the right, nor is there the slightest foundation for assuming that Francisco Pizarro was known contemptuously as the Bastard of Estremadura. In a day when all men and most women sinned there was none to hurl that particular stone.

Cruelty was as familiar to the young Pizarros as the hot sunlight on the red-brown hills of Estremadura. Jews were herded into their ghettos like impounded cattle, and shrieking children stoned bearded rabbis on the streets. Learned doctors argued and quibbled over points of law, of land tenure, of inheritance, of crown and feudal rights, and of contracts, but the concept of law as controlling impartial

7

justice had yet to be born. Law was savage and unspeakably cruel. The guilt of the accused was taken for granted, and confession was hastened by the lash and the rack and the *escalera*—the torture by water which took the name of the ladderlike instrument to which its victims were lashed. The condemned were punished publicly. Women were exposed naked to the gibes of the populace or, naked, flogged at the cart-tail about the town. The nursing child of a woman condemned to death shared the mother's fate. Animals were solemnly tried, condemned, and executed. Boys and girls were familiar with brandings, with the sight of human heads stuck on pikes, or of a man's body—quartered like a beef— being exhibited at the town gates or on the four sides of the plaza. Castration, dismemberment, mutilation, the *garrote,* and the stake were as familiar as the procession of the Mass or the priest's chants.

Cruel, bestial, lusty days, untrammeled by justice or science or education. Sore and swollen eyes were still treated by application of the eyes of a crab, plucked from its living body. "For a fever take the ripe foot-shank of a dead black hound and hang it on the arm, and it will shake off the fever." Blood from incised wounds was staunched with a hot iron, but the cauterization was aided by an incantation which mentioned the name of Longinus, the soldier who, according to tradition, pierced with his spear the side of the crucified Christ.

Such was the Spain—and the world—into which Francisco Pizarro was born a few years after Ferdinand V of Castile and Leon married, in 1469, Isabella of Aragon, sister of Henry IV. Henry died five years later, and Spain emerged as a nation in which the seeds of empire were even then germinating. Ferdinand V became Ferdinand II, and the little principalities of Aragon, Sicily, Sardinia, Naples, Castile, and Leon were welded into a single state under the joint rule of Ferdinand and Isabella—a captious, jealous, suspicious man and a truly great woman, one of the most remarkable women of all time. Theirs was an harmonious partnership, marital, religious, and political. They repelled the Portuguese invasion of the western frontiers and with it the claims of Alfonso V that his niece was the legitimate issue of Henry IV and Juana of Portugal (which she was not!) and hence should replace Isabella upon the throne of Aragon. They expelled the Moors from Granada and the Iberian Peninsula, further consolidating their rule, and they established, albeit slowly, a stable and united government over a sadly lawless land.

In those days justice suffered and was not to be done upon the malefactors who plundered and tyrannized in the towns and on the roads [writes Hernando del Pulgar, who, as one of Isabella's secretaries, should know of what he spoke]. None paid debts who did not want to do so, none was restrained from committing any crime, and none dreamed of obedience or subjection to a superior. What with present and past wars, people were so accustomed to turbulence that he who did not do violence to others was held to be a man of no account.

The paragraph is worth re-reading. It could well serve as an epitaph for Gonzalo Pizarro, who died on the headsman's block in the Valley of Sacsahuana, two thousand Spanish leagues from that Toledo in which del Pulgar wrote.

Citizens, peasants, and men of peace were not masters of their own property [del Pulgar continues], nor could they have recourse to any for redress of the wrongs they suffered at the hands of governors of fortresses and other thieves and robbers. Every

9

man would gladly have pledged to give the half of his property if at that price he might have purchased security and peace for himself and his family.

Atahualpa, Sapa Inca of Ttahua-ntin-suyu, the Land of the Four Sections, was to pay for security and peace for himself and his people with a ransom so vast that even the gold-hungry Spaniards led by Pizarro could not believe its reality. Nor could they wait for the whole of that ransom to be paid; they seized that which was in hand and—considerately—strangled the Inca ruler instead of burning him alive.

In the Spain of the Pizarros' youth, corruption in high places was taken for granted. Nepotism ruled the church; popes referred openly to their sons and daughters; cardinalates and bishoprics—and the income from those was princely —were placed on the auction block and given to the highest bidder. The throne was despotic, and favoritism and despotism have run ever on a coupled leash. Favorites obtained virtually all public appointments, graft was universal, and bribes or political pressure dominated the courts.

"There was often talk in towns and villages of forming brotherhoods to remedy all these evils," says del Pulgar, "but a leader was wanting who would have at heart the justice and tranquillity of the kingdom."

Cruelty, ruthlessness, despotism, and corruption. Francisco Pizarro was a child scarcely walking when Isabella first listened to the plea of Alonso de Ojeda, Prior of the Dominicans of Seville, that the Office of the Holy Inquisition be established in Spain to purge the land of heresy; he was but three years older when the pious sovereigns yielded and delegated the institution of that holy office of savagery, hypocrisy, and cruelty to Pedro Gonzalez de Mendoza, Car-

dinal of Spain, and a Dominican friar named Tomás de Torquemada, then a man of sixty and onetime father confessor
to the Infanta Isabella. There is no act of savage slaughter
for which Francisco Pizarro was responsible in Peru but can
be paralleled by the record of the Inquisition in Spain where
the boy Francisco must have witnessed—or at least listened
eagerly to the talk of those who had witnessed—the long-
drawn-out ceremonies of the *Auto-de-Fé,* the Act of Faith,
which ended with the application of the torch to the fagots
piled about the feet of the unrepentant heretic.

That atmosphere was breathed by the Brothers of Doom
throughout their formative years. Outwardly, at least, all of
them were devout sons of the church, for it was an era when
any accusation of heresy, however made, led to the burning
field at La Dehesa or—if the accused were more fortunate
—to public exposure and scourging and shame.

You are to be whipped in procession about the city on each of
the six Fridays now following and on the first Friday of each
month for the next year, being naked to the waist, bareheaded,
and barefooted; and are to fast on each of those Fridays; and are
disqualified for the rest of your life from holding office, benefice,
or honorable employment; and from using gold, silver, precious
stones, or fine fabrics in your apparel; and should you at any
time relapse into error or fail to perform any part of the penance
imposed, you will be considered an impenitent heretic and be
abandoned to the secular arm . . . *Christi nomine invocato!*

Such was Spain and the world as the fifteenth century
drew to a close; the Spain to which—on the fourth day of
March, 1493, and to the little port of Palos from which he
had sailed just seven months and one day earlier—Christo-
pher Columbus returned with the glowing words that the

earth was indeed round and that by sailing ever to the westward he had reached the most eastern lands of Asia.

*

The half century which followed was the most momentous in all the history of the world. There had been earlier discoveries, but none to parallel that of Columbus. In the main, the extension of European civilization since the days of Alexander had been but a gradual thrusting back of frontiers, an extension of marginal territories. Navigation was coastal, a cautious progress from headland to headland, rarely out of sight of or contact with the land. Even in reaching Asia, the Portuguese navigators had skirted the continental shores for all the long distance around Africa. Too, they returned with little that was not already known; Oriental trade had been established for many centuries over the overland routes.

Columbus died believing that his Indies were indeed Asiatic, but Spain, racing to empire, knew that a new world lay a thousand leagues to the west. It was new in all things. New people and trees and animals and birds and fruits; mysterious jungle-covered mountains from whose flanks great rivers dashed to the sea. Columbus sailed on his second voyage with three large ships and fourteen caravels—a brilliant contrast to the gloom which surrounded his first embarkation—and with him sailed the flower of the manhood of Spain, grandee, priest, soldier, and gold-hungry adventurer. Within twenty years the world learned more geography than during the preceding twenty centuries; within twenty more that knowledge was doubled. World horizons, so widened by Columbus's original discoveries, expanded tremendously

12

when the great navigator attained the South American mainland at the mouth of the Orinoco and named those coasts the Tierra Firma. He clung to his Asian delusion, although the size and volume of the mighty river seemed to identify a great continental land mass which could be no part of the geographers' Cathay.

Only Columbus and a mere handful of his immediate followers were explorers; all others were gold seekers. The Great Admiral sought gold too, but only for the sake of the favors it might purchase from an avaricious king; his search was for a new trade route to the Spice Islands, to the lands of Prester John and to the Indian Ocean; a trade route which would shatter the commercial supremacy of the Portuguese, who had rejected his dream of a westward passage and whom he hated. Seeking that grail, he followed the southern coast of Cuba to a point from which a day's sailing would have carried him around the western tip of the island and into the open sea, but he turned back and declared Cuba a peninsula, the eastern extremity of the territories of the Grand Khan. Further exploration took him to within sight of the Honduran coastline where he gave Cape Gracias á Dios its name and continued southward to Portobello, northernmost point of the present Panamá, in search of the strait which would open the way to the lands which Marco Polo and Sir John Mandeville had described. The strait was not there, but Columbus died believing that the rich coast —the Costa Rica—which he called Veragua was indeed the Aurea Chersonesus from which King Solomon had drawn his wealth of gold.

Utter delusion, of course, yet bear with these tales a little longer, for in the small store of gold which Columbus

13

obtained from the Indians of the Mosquito Coast was the genesis of epic legends; of El Dorado, the Golden Man; of Zenu, where the rivers bore gold in such quantities that the natives stretched nets across the streams to trap the larger nuggets; of Dobayba and—in truth—of the golden verities of Mexico and Peru. Those who followed Columbus—and Francisco Pizarro was of that number—cherished neither his delusions nor his ambitions. They left their homes in Spain, they crossed the Western Ocean, and they set about the conquest of the Indies with a single objective—gold. Gold which after deduction of the King's Fifth would purchase luxury in their native land. Gold which would pay their debts. Gold. No matter where it might lie; they would go to it. Gold; nor did it matter how deeply it might be stained with the blood of peaceful natives. Torture the Indians until they revealed the hiding places of their hoards; hold their head men for ransom; flog them into seeking more and more and yet more; enslave them; hunt them down with savage dogs if they attempted escape; burn the rebellious to discourage other rebellions—but get the gold which the king expected and demanded from his new, strange lands beyond the sea.

The last few years have seen many efforts to stress the Conquistadores' achievements as explorers and colonizers at the expense of their earned reputations as greedy, brutal, and utterly ruthless gold seekers. We are told—not always with entire truthfulness—that the priest and the husbandman marched with the fighting men. We are reminded that cathedrals and schools rose swiftly from the ruins of Cuzco and of Tenochtitlan and that the University of Lima antedated by nearly a century the founding of Harvard and of William and Mary. Would the fate of Aztec and of Inca have

14

been different, we are asked, if the treasure houses of Mexico and Peru had been located within access of the Massachusetts Bay Colony or of Jamestown.

Such whitewashing is as ridiculous as it is unsubstantiated by fact. Ferdinand of Spain was bankrupt, and only gold would restore his credit and assure that his kingdom would not break up into the minor principalities of which it had been formed. Every license granted for voyages to or explorations within the New World speaks of gold and specifies the terms upon which the loot of the new lands should be divided. Dozens of letters from the king to his governors acknowledge gratefully the receipt of gold, speak sharply or regretfully of failures to deliver the promised wealth, or mention tales of new sources which might be investigated. Grandee and peasant, hidalgo and common soldier starved and fought and died for gold. That they conquered a world in its search was incidental, as were such secondary ideals as the extension of empire or the propagation of the faith. The New World, from Florida to Patagonia, was conquered long before the ideals of Las Casas or Cabeza de Vaca approached realization.

Many men hitherto unknown were to crowd one another for place on history's pages within the first decade of the sixteenth century. The names of some are still with us— Juan Ponce de Leon, for example, remembered for his quaint faith in a fountain of youth which he sought in the land he named Florida, less famed for his conquest of the island of Boriquen, east of Hispaniola. He built there the town of Caparra, and he called its harbor Puerto Rico, which in time supplanted the native name for the island. He had a dog, did Juan Ponce, a dog named Berezillo which was trained to

15

pull down and kill fleeing Indians and whose services in battle were worth those of several men-at-arms. Berezillo died from the wound of a poisoned arrow, but he left a son, Leoncito, the Little Lion, who was larger and fiercer than his sire. Leoncito passed into the hands of another hidalgo, Vasco Nuñez de Balboa, and he crossed the mountainous isthmus of Darien and—with that master and a hard-bitten adventurer named Francisco Pizarro—stood upon the shores of the Great South Sea.

Ponce de Leon is remembered, but only the larger histories have place for others with equal or greater claims to fame: Rodrigo de Bastides, first to explore the Colombian coast; the treacherous rebel Francisco Roldan; and Alonso de Ojeda, kinsman to the prior of the Dominicans who introduced the Inquisition into Spain and one of the most vividly colorful personalities in the entire record of the conquest of the Indies. A veteran of Columbus's second voyage, Ojeda made two expeditions on his own account to the Tierra Firma—an impecunious Florentine merchant named Amerigo Vespucci sailed on one of them—and finally landed on Hispaniola where quarrels and resultant lawsuits stripped him of all his possessions and left him heavily in debt. His reputation, however, was that of a daring navigator and a first-class fighting man, and he had friends in high positions in the Spanish court. One of those friends was Bishop Don Juan Rodriguez Fonseca, the implacable enemy of Columbus, and it was through the bishop's influence that Ojeda obtained the assignment to lead another and still more important expedition to Veragua, there to establish a colony and to obtain the gold which the Indians of that hostile coast possessed in such quantity.

Veragua promised rich returns, and a rival for leadership arose in the person of Diego de Nicuesa, "an accomplished courtier of noble birth who had filled the post of grand carver to Don Enrique Enriquez, uncle to the king." He was also "versed in the legendary ballads or romances of his country and was renowned as a performer on the guitar." His other qualifications for leading an expedition into hostile lands are less clear, but Ferdinand—ever ready to avoid an issue—split the region into two parts and awarded one to each man. The line ran from north to south through the middle of the Gulf of Urabá—the present Gulf of Darien, which bites deeply into the Colombian coastline in the extreme southwest corner of the Caribbean Sea. All to the west of that line was declared to be Veragua and was awarded to the former grand carver; the lands to the east as far as Cape de la Vela near the mouth of the Gulf of Venezuela was given the name of New Andalusia and turned over to Alonso de Ojeda. Each man was to enjoy the title of governor, each was to erect two fortresses in his district, and the crown modestly laid claim to only one-tenth of the profits from any mines to be discovered during the first year. After the fourth year the royal commission was to be the customary 20 per cent.

There was jealousy and quarreling, of course. New Andalusia was virtually unknown territory while several expeditions had confirmed the Great Admiral's report that Veragua was rich. Ojeda, who would fight without waiting for a hat to drop, challenged Nicuesa to a duel. Don Diego accepted the challenge but suggested that they might as well have something worth fighting for—such as a side bet of five

17

thousand castillanos[1], the winner to take all. There was no duel, since Ojeda would have found some difficulty in raising five castillanos, let alone five thousand, for such a purpose. Still, there were those in Hispaniola who were willing to finance the expedition to New Andalusia, and the most liberal contributor was one Martín Fernandez de Enciso, a lawyer of Santo Domingo. By virtue of a legal degree he was entitled to be called El Bachiller—literally, the Bachelor—Enciso, a Spanish professional title which can prove only confusing when translated.

Bickering and financial difficulties may have delayed but did not halt the work of preparing the two expeditions. Nicuesa was first to depart, with seven hundred men and six horses. A few days later—on November 10, 1509—the two ships and two brigantines of Ojeda's command left the harbor of Santo Domingo and squared off for the southwest in obedience to the signals of the veteran pilot Juan de la Cosa. On board were three hundred men and twelve brood mares. History is silent as to whether or not a stallion was included in the complement. A soldier named Hernando Cortez had intended to sail with the expedition but was prevented—and spared for the conquest of Mexico nine years later—by a leg injury. Among the three hundred, however, was a distant kinsman of Cortez, a veteran man-at-arms who was then about thirty-five years old—Francisco Pizarro.

[1] Little effort will be made in this narrative to approximate the value of such monetary units as the castillano, the maravedi, the gold crown, and others mentioned in the sources. The dollar of 1941 is a far more acrobatic coin than that to which Irving and Prescott and Sir Clements Markham tried to peg sixteenth-century exchange. It is sufficient to say that five thousand castillanos would prove an attractive purse for a heavyweight championship bout; the ransom of 1,326,539 *pesos de oro* which **Pizarro** obtained for the Incan leader Atahualpa would build a battleship!

18

Chapter Two

THIS IS THE TALE of four brothers who destroyed an empire and gave to Spain the richest of her colonial possessions, but the story of the next eighteen years can be of but one of them. In 1510 Hernando Pizarro may have been serving with the armies of Spain in Italy, Juan was a boy of fourteen or fifteen, and Gonzalo had just reached his fourth birthday. The three were quite unknown and were so to remain until a day in the summer of 1528 when their brother Francisco was to return to his native province of Estremadura and enlist them under his banner. Those eighteen years cannot be passed over either in the life of the man or the chronicle of the times through which he lived.

Francisco Pizarro steps from obscurity on that November day of 1509. Not immediately does the light of historical knowledge beat strongly upon him. He is still a shadowy figure, one of many soldiers who participated in the attempts to establish outposts of Spain on the Tierra Firma, and the most that can be said is that he was upon the stage which later he was to tread as the leading character in a drama second to none in the conquest of the New World.

There is no known record of how or when or in what

capacity Francisco Pizarro crossed the Western Ocean or of his services prior to joining the Ojeda expedition. It has been said—entirely without authority—that Ojeda found him on the dock in Cadiz, apparently endeavoring to thumb a ride to the west. That is purest—or rankest—speculation. He is not mentioned in any of the accounts of Ojeda's first voyage, 1499-1500, or of the second, launched in 1502, which ended with the commander's being stripped of his authority and being taken in chains to Santo Domingo. It was Juan de la Cosa, the pilot, who made the journey to Spain in 1508 and there skillfully pleaded Ojeda's cause and obtained for him the commission to settle New Andalusia. Ojeda himself remained in Hispaniola, destitute but hopeful, and it is far more probable that he there encountered Pizarro and enlisted him for the expedition to the mainland. There is no need of adding to the legend which cloaks the early years of the conqueror of Peru. He was a common soldier, that is certain, and as such he joined the rush with which the young manhood of Spain enlisted in the many expeditions which followed upon Columbus's return from his second voyage. He may, for all we know, have been one of the many who crowded upon the admiral's ships for that triumphant second voyage. The names of but a handful of those have come down to us, and it is rather apparent that Pizarro was a veteran of considerable experience. He may have achieved some noncommissioned rank, the equivalent of corporal or sergeant, perhaps, but he was not an officer. Definitely he was not. No table of organization for the colonial forces in 1510 has been preserved, but the equivalent of commissioned rank was accorded only to gentlemen—to *hijos de algo*, to men whom birth entitled to the use of *de*, to knights of one of the many Spanish orders. It was they who rode the horses, those beasts which so terrified the Indian peoples from New Mexico to Chile; it was they who were entitled to place on the narrow quarterdeck. The common soldiers roosted where they could find space forward of the mast or—when the tropical rains swept the ships—crowded into the stinking hold. Francisco Pizarro was one of them.

He learned much on that expedition of Ojeda's, did Francisco Pizarro, much that he was to remember and turn to account in the years which lay before him. He was no stranger to the smashing, utterly merciless warfare which the Spaniard ever brought to the many native groups of the Caribbees and the Tierra Firma, but this adventure was to sate even the most bloodthirsty of fighting men. The little fleet first approached the South American mainland between two long islands which lay parallel to the shore. The site was to become one of the best harbors on the north coast, and there, in 1533, Pedro de Heredia was to found the city of Cartagena, but Ojeda and his followers saw only a sandy peninsula extending into a shallow bay, the dense tropical growth of the marshy foreshore, and the darker ridges of the Turbaco hills beyond. De la Cosa had seen the place before, and he warned Ojeda that the natives would fight on sight. He urged the commander to continue to the westward, to the Gulf of Urubá, where the Indians were less hostile.

Alonso de Ojeda was not one to listen to advice, however good. No Indian could be quicker to fight than was he, none could be more confident of victory. Pizarro may have been one of the original force which landed, met a group of natives, and charged their village. A number of Indians were killed, eight particularly stubborn fighters being disposed

21

of by setting afire the hut in which they had taken their stand. Sixty or seventy prisoners were sent to the ships, destined to be sold into slavery in Hispaniola. Pizarro, if he was a member of the landing force, returned to the harbor with those prisoners. Ojeda and Juan de la Cosa, with seventy men, pushed on boldly into the jungle to a village which we are told was named Yurbaco, which makes obvious the derivation of the name of the hills where the more wealthy of the citizens of Cartagena have built their homes. There the little band fell into a skillfully planned ambush, and only two of the seventy escaped. One—and there is no authority for the assumption that he was Francisco Pizarro —seems to have managed to return to the ships where he told his companions that Juan de la Cosa had died miserably under a rain of poisoned arrows. He could not have reported that all the attackers of Yurbaco had perished, or the ships would have departed immediately from that inhospitable shore. Instead, the fleet remained for many days, and throughout that time a zealous search was conducted for any who might have survived the Yurbaco massacre. One man at last was found hiding like a hunted capybara among the tangled roots of the mangroves in the swamps. His clothes were in rags, he was almost dead from hunger and exhaustion; but he was a grandee of Spain, and he had not cast aside his long rapier or the small round shield which was worn on the left arm. By the blazon on that shield the searchers recognized their commander, Alonso de Ojeda.

It was at that dramatic moment that the ships of Diego de Nicuesa entered the harbor. The chroniclers do not say what he was doing so far to the east of his territory of Veragua, but all are unanimous in agreeing that old feuds

22

were forgotten. They delayed only until Ojeda had regained some of his strength, and then four hundred men marched upon the village. Their orders were simple. None, young or old, man or woman, should be spared. Horses were employed, too, the first of these animals to be used in battle on the American mainland, and the doomed Indians of Yurbaco were the first of many to be terrified by the sight of beasts more huge than any they had ever known, beasts with iron-shod hooves which crushed brown bodies, beasts which bore on their backs men in gleaming armor who shouted the old Spanish battle cry of "Santiago! Santiago!" as their red blades rose and fell.

Hundreds were killed or driven back to perish in the flames of the huts, which had been fired in the first attack, nor were any prisoners taken. When dawn came the victorious Spaniards looted the settlement of what must have been a large amount of the pale gold of the north coast. *Guinin,* the Indians called the metal which was so easily fashioned into ornaments, and the name was soon corrupted into "guinea" gold and thus distinguished from the yellower, more desirable metal of Veragua. Nicuesa and his men shared seven thousand castillanos. How much fell to Ojeda's followers is not mentioned, but it is certain that the vengeance taken for Juan de la Cosa was profitable as well as pleasant. In the course of the sacking of Yurbaco, incidentally, the rotting body of the veteran navigator was found where the Indians had tied it to a tree.

Nicuesa set sail for Veragua, and Ojeda's little flotilla journeyed more slowly to the south and west along the Colombian coast. After considerable search for the mythical River Darien, said to be rich in gold, the commander followed the advice which had been given him by de la Cosa and chose a site for a town on a headland at the eastern entrance to the Gulf of Urubá, which was within the geographical limits set for New Andalusia. He called the place San Sebastián "in pious hope that the honor thus paid the saint who was martyred by means of arrows would protect him and his men from similar missiles."

The saint did not appreciate the tribute, for the brief existence of the settlement was a story of continual warfare with the natives. There were few pitched battles—American Indian warfare was ever a system of furious raids, of ambushes, and of swift retreats—but dusky archers lurked everywhere in the thick vegetation, and the Spaniards knew that a slow and agonizing death followed inevitably upon the slightest scratch from the bone points of the long arrows. Ojeda promptly dispatched one of the ships to Hispaniola with a letter urging his friend and partner, Enciso, to join him immediately at the new settlement with additional men and arms and provisions.

Many chapters could be written of the events of those long weeks during which the garrison waited behind the stockade of San Sebastián for Enciso. Incidents given merely passing mention by the chroniclers could be lengthened into sagas of battle, of fear, and of despair in which the grim soldier Francisco Pizarro could be given a leading role. There can be no question that he did take part in those engagements, but his name is not mentioned. He may have seen Ojeda wounded by an arrow and have stood by while the commander ordered certain grisly surgery with red-hot plates of iron to cauterize the wound. We are told that Ojeda endured with composure an ordeal so painful that an entire barrel of vinegar was used to soak the cloths in which his feverish body was wrapped. The raging fire consumed the cold poison, says the Reverend Bishop Bartolomé de las Casas—and what present chronicler would question the word of the Apostle of the Indies?

A minor incident, that of the wounding of Ojeda, and quite inconsequential to a biography of Francisco Pizarro and his brothers, but it shows the stuff of which the Conquistadores were made. In that day and in those lands there was a chance that the strong might survive; there was no doubt of the fate which awaited the weakling or him who vacillated. The steel of Francisco Pizarro was bred in him, but it was tempered during those months at San Sebastián. Throughout his career he was as merciless to himself as to others; he was forbearing only when expediency and opportunism dictated such a course. There at San Sebastián he must have shown marked ability to command and have risen above the level of the common man-at-arms, for when Ojeda left the settlement to return to Hispaniola he named Francisco Pizarro as commander in his absence.

Ojeda's departure was enforced. He had not yet completely recovered from his wound—or its treatment—when a sail appeared on the lonely sea and a vessel cautiously entered the bay and dropped anchor. Those of the garrison, weary of strife and desperately short of provisions, hastened to welcome Enciso, but the lawyer was not one of the seventy men aboard the craft. It was commanded by one Bernardino de Talavera, and his crew was a choice lot of footloose adventurers, knaves, debtors, and ordinary criminals from Hispaniola. The ship which Ojeda had sent had arrived at that island, and there had been much talk of the rich store of gold and Indian slaves which it had brought. Enciso busied himself with preparations to sail, but Talavera decided to steal a march on the lawyer and declare himself in on a portion of the rich spoils of New Andalusia. He recruited his gang, stole a vessel at Cape Tiburon, and blithely set out to the southward. None aboard was a skilled navigator, but with a maximum of good luck and a minimum of good management they found their way to San Sebastián. Talavera quickly appraised the desperate need of the colonists and coldly demanded cash—gold—for the provisions with which his ship was laden.

Ojeda accepted the terms and paid. He rationed the food obtained from Talavera and—when his men protested that the allowance was insufficient—told the garrison that all must pull tight their belts until Enciso arrived. But the lawyer did not appear, and finally, with stores again running low, Ojeda offered to return to Hispaniola in Talavera's vessel, there determine what was delaying his partner, and return with supplies and reinforcements. He named Pizarro as commander and gave him letters confirming the order, letters which Francisco could not read but which were to prove of some value. Wait fifty days, Ojeda said, and if I have not returned or if Enciso has not come, abandon the settlement and sail for Santo Domingo in the two brigantines which remain.

Pizarro and his men waited. The fiftieth day passed, but no sail had appeared. Only seventy men remained of the three hundred who had sailed from Santo Domingo in November of 1509, but even seventy were too many for the frail craft which were anchored below the headland. Thirty, perhaps, could crowd upon each of the brigantines, and

Pizarro waited with grim certainty that the wait would not be long. The four horses which remained were killed—poor, patient beasts—and their meat salted for the voyage of more than eight hundred miles. Finally—there was none who recorded the date or the number of the survivors—the two vessels set out, keeping such close company with one another that a few days later, when a sudden squall lashed the Caribbean, those on Pizarro's ship saw a mighty wave sweep over the other craft and founder it. The ocean was still an abiding-place of terror, and there were those on the surviving vessel who swore that it was no wave but a great monster out of the deep which had risen and crushed their consort. Their tales were repeated quite solemnly by contemporary historians.

Pizarro then abandoned the plan of returning to Hispaniola. His vessel may have been injured in the storm, food and water may have been insufficient for the long voyage, or he may have lost confidence in his navigators. His reason was probably an excellent one, for none other could have turned him back toward the Tierra Firma which had treated them so harshly. He gained the mainland at the harbor where Ojeda had met defeat, the site of the future Cartagena; and he found—one may imagine his amazement—a vessel at anchor there. The commander of the craft was the lawyer, Martín Fernandez de Enciso.

He will hold a brief space in these pages, will Enciso, along with that other ill-starred incompetent, Diego de Nicuesa, the grand carver. More prominent will be another man, a soldier as tough as Francisco Pizarro although of gentler birth and less obscure origin, whose entrance into history is identical with that of Pizarro. Vasco Nuñez de

Balboa was his name, and he too was an insignificant subordinate marked for deathless fame. Some, quibbling on a point of questionable accuracy, have referred to him by his patronymic and called him Vasco Nuñez. He is Balboa, however, to every schoolboy, and there is considerable evidence that he was known by that name—his mother's—during his life. The "rule" of Spanish nomenclature that a man shall be known by the first of his surnames is one often broken. Nuñez was, and is, a common Spanish name, and it is quite possible that the man chose his mother's name for the sake of clearer identification. Only the Spanish-born can pierce the mysteries of Spanish nomenclature or comprehend a system under which three full brothers will be known, respectively, as Henrique Garcia, Pedro Garcia-Salazar, and Manuel Salazar y Fuentes.

The province of Estremadura has well been called the Cradle of the Conquistadores. Cortez, the Pizarros, Valdivia of Chilean fame, Sebastián de Benalcazar, the conqueror of Ecuador, Hernando de Soto, Diego de Almagro, Alvar Nuñez Cabeza de Vaca—all were natives of that province. Balboa, too, was born there in Jeres—old Xeres[1]—de Caballeros *circa* 1575 and was about the same age as Francisco Pizarro. Knowledge of his activities is fragmentary prior to his appearance with Enciso, but he came to the New World in 1500 with Rodrigo de Bastides and apparently remained in Hispaniola when Bastides, after being shipwrecked on that island, was arrested by Francisco de Bobadilla and returned to Spain in chains. Bastides, in spite of his mis-

[1] The modern form of Spanish words has been followed throughout this narrative. Jeres for Xeres, Trujillo for Truxillo, and Cajamarca for the older form of Caxamalca.

adventures, gained a fortune from his expedition, and Balboa's share may have been sufficient to support him for a time in Santo Domingo. He obtained a grant of land at Salvatierra, where the mountains march down to the sea between Santo Domingo and Punta Palenque, and appears to have attempted farming for a time. He failed in that endeavor and in 1510, when Enciso was assembling his expedition, was deeply in debt and a very short jump ahead of his creditors—and jail. He stowed away on Enciso's ship, we are told, by concealing himself in a cask which was carried aboard with other stores. When the vessel was well out at sea he left his hiding place and appeared before Enciso. The chroniclers would have us believe that the lawyer was furious and promised to maroon the unenlisted recruit on the first uninhabited island that was sighted. There are no islands in the Caribbean between Hispaniola and the northern coast of South America, as Enciso probably knew, and circumstances indicate that his anger was for the record only, a salve for his legal conscience, and that Balboa's stowing away was what might be called an inside job. He had his arms and equipment with him, and we read a little later in those same chronicles of his dog, Leoncito, son of Ponce de Leon's famous Indian killer. By inference, the dog came aboard with his master. The stowaway was not punished, and Enciso seems to have been rather pleased to enroll a veteran of the Bastides voyage, who knew something of the region to which the expedition was bound.

A singular—one might well say unique—feature of the Bastides expedition had been its considerate treatment of the Indians. The natives of the Tierra Firma had actually been regarded as possessing some proprietary rights in the

29

land, and that investment of good will had paid enormous dividends. Juan de la Cosa, who had been Bastides' pilot, had urged similar forbearance upon Ojeda, but that bull-headed individual, veteran of the slaughters in Hispaniola, preferred the role of conqueror and had paid therefor with the loss of nearly a third of his fighting men in a single engagement. It is more than possible that Balboa, a Bastides veteran, counseled Enciso to adopt a temperate attitude, for the lawyer and his men kept their rapiers sheathed, parleyed with the natives, and were treated with the utmost friendliness by the same Indians who had fought so bitterly with Ojeda a few months before. Amicable trade relations were established, provisions and fresh water were obtained, and there was no interference while the Spaniards made necessary repairs to their ship.

At this juncture Pizarro's brigantine entered the harbor, and the lawyer-sailor-soldier learned that San Sebastián had been abandoned. Enciso decided to see the settlement for himself, but he made one stop on his southwesterly course. To explain why that stop was made will be a digression, but there will be many such in the course of this tale. Pizarro and Balboa were among those present, and the incident unquestionably made a sharp impression on their minds and affected their own courses in similar situations.

The Indian peoples of the American mainland were not fools. Early in the history of the Conquest they learned—a lesson of desperation!—that when they fought these strange, fair-skinned invaders they were killed; when they received them hospitably their meager stores of food were devoured, their shrines demolished by fanatic priests, and their women seized by officers and soldiers no less fanatical, though their zeal was of the flesh rather than the spirit. The game was a losing one no matter how *los Indios* played it, but they learned promptly that there was one infallible method of persuading the unwelcome visitors to move on. The Indians could not understand the Spaniards' eagerness to obtain the useless metal gold—good for nothing but the fabrication of ornaments—but from the southern Andes to the Rockies the tribesmen took skillful advantage of that greed. The Conquistadores would rush after any rainbow sobeit they were told that a pot—or preferably a couple of hogsheads—of gold lay at its ending, and so the Indians of Yurbaco told Enciso and his followers of Zenu.

"Go to Zenu," said they, "if it's gold you seek. Zenu is only twenty-five leagues from here. There—ah, there is the source of all the gold which we possess. The mountains abound with it. It is so plentiful that the people of that region stretch nets across the rivers to catch the larger nuggets that are carried down by the floods. Much escapes, of course, but the nets retain all that any man needs. All who live in this region bear their dead to Zenu and bury them there with all the golden ornaments which were theirs in life."

Balboa was to hear similar tales in Darien. Francisco Pizarro was to listen to them on the Pacific coast of Colombia and Ecuador. They were told to Cortez in Mexico; they sent Diego de Almagro to Chile. The rather conservative reports of Alvar Nuñez Cabeza de Vaca, when he reached Mexico in 1536 after his long overland journey from the region of the present Galveston, were speedily magnified by the austere viceroy Antonio de Mendoza into the legend of the Seven Cities of Cibola where the streets were paved with gold and the houses decorated with emeralds and other gems.

Five years later, in 1541, the tale of gold beyond the horizon was told to Francisco Vasquez de Coronado by the conquered Indians of New Mexico and sent him careering across the Texas Panhandle, Oklahoma, and Kansas in search of the wholly mythical Quivira where—again—gold and gems were to be had for the labor of picking them up from the ground.

Oviedo tells in his *General History of the Indies* of meeting in Spain the Indian slave Francisco Chicora, so named by his owner, Lucas Vasquez de Ayllón, for the land of Chicora—the present North Carolina—where he had been made prisoner in 1520. Francisco Chicora's stories set marks for future Munchausens and Gullivers: tales of scaled men and of tailed men, of giants and of how they were made, of vast stores of gold and silver and precious stones. The Indian glanced contemptuously at a ring which Oviedo wore—we have the cynical historian's word that it was set with a flawless pearl weighing twenty-six carats—and declared that in his country men would scarcely go to the trouble of picking up so insignificant a bauble. His stories accomplished their purpose, it may be remarked. He and several of his tribesmen were returned to their native land as guides and interpreters for an expedition led by Ayllón. Five hundred men landed from six ships near Cape Fear in 1526—and Francisco Chicora and his fellows promptly vanished into an interior where there were neither giants nor tailed men, gold nor pearls.

Men are ever eager to believe the unbelievable whether it be a legend older than history or a clever tale born of a wily native's desperation. The Spaniards transplanted bodily from the Old World to the New the story of the Amazons, the

32

warrior women *a mazones*—without breasts—because they amputated the right mammary that it might not interfere with the wielding of sword, bow, or lance. Their habitat was set first in the Windward Islands, moved to the Tierra Firma, and pushed steadily inland by the extending fringe of exploration to survive, at last, in the name of the world's mightiest river system and tropical forest. El Dorado, the Golden Man, has lived in one form or another from Arizona to Argentina; the name of Quivira remained on maps until the dawn of the nineteenth century.

And let the mocker beware. Our own times and our own land have seen the Atlantic beaches trenched again and again for the very questionable treasure of William Kidd; a dozen expeditions have sailed to inhospitable Cocos Island and there searched for the "loot of Lima," the existence of which is little less mythical than Zenu or the Amazons.

So Enciso departed from Yurbaco and sailed to Zenu and took possession of the land in the names of God our Lord and their Catholic majesties under power of the decree given to the sovereigns by His Holiness, Pope Alexander VI. A lengthy ritual, performed with pomp and ceremony, with display of the banners of Castile and Aragon and of the Cross of Christ; a ritual which must have delighted the legal-minded Enciso but which, interpreted, prompted one of the caciques[2] of Zenu to remark that the pope must have been drunk to give away lands which belonged to others and the king crazy (loco) to accept the gift.

Enciso and his men netted no gold from the swift streams of Zenu, nor did he discover the cemetery with its wealth of

[2] With the possible exception of llama, no word is more generally mispronounced than cacique, translatable as chieftain or headman of a village or tribe. Yáh-ma, please, instead of láh-ma; and kah-theé-kay, not kah-seék.

33

mortuary offerings. The caciques showed him a choice collection of the skulls of their enemies, impaled on poles set about the village, and told him his own head and those of his men would be added to those trophies if he did not withdraw. The lawyer replied with a charge, and the Indian ranks broke before the onslaught of the men in armor. One of the defiant caciques was taken prisoner; two Spaniards died in agony after receiving superficial wounds from poisoned arrows.

The two vessels sailed on, only to meet disaster as they rounded the headland at the entrance of the Gulf of Urubá. The ship under Enciso's command struck a rock and swiftly broke up. Pizarro's brigantine was able to save all those on board, but virtually all the foodstuffs and supplies, together with all the horses and swine, were lost. Ashore, they found that the Indians had burned the stockade fort which Ojeda had built.

In that more than critical situation Balboa remarked that the Bastides expedition had made a landing on the western shore of the gulf and found there a region quite suitable for settlement and peopled by tribesmen who did not use poisoned arrows. The country was drained by a river which the natives called Darien, and there was said to be gold in the hills.

His suggestion was adopted immediately. Although the chroniclers do not say so, we may assume that there was some preliminary exploration and that the tiny brigantine made a number of trips across the twenty-five miles between San Sebastián and the settlement to which Enciso gave the grandiloquent name of Santa Maria de la Antigua del Darien. It was on the western shore of the gulf, a little less than halfway between the Caribbean and the head of the bay, and therefore beyond the limits of New Andalusia and within the boundaries set for Veragua, assigned to Diego de Nicuesa, erstwhile grand carver. Neither Enciso nor any under his command seem to have paid any heed to that geographical detail, later so important. They stepped ashore, accepted the challenge of Zemaco, cacique of the region, and advanced to battle. Zemaco was soundly trounced, and the Enciso forces proceeded right merrily to plunder all the villages in the vicinity. The loot amounted to some ten thousand castillanos.

Even by today's monetary standards—and in today's expressive phraseology—that wasn't hay. The share of the humblest sailor or man-at-arms amounted to the equivalent of some five hundred dollars, and the little band was jubilant. There were other villages to be sacked, other Indians to be enslaved, and other squealing women and girls to be dragged to the thatched huts of Antigua. *Sin duda,* there was gold enough and women enough for all; *sin duda,* this was an excellent spot for a settlement, and they toasted Vasco Nuñez de Balboa who had brought them thither. It was then that Martín de Enciso cracked the whip.

He was neither the first nor the last legal-minded man to prove tactless and incompetent when catapulted into a position of authority. The veteran Ojeda might have given his lusty followers their heads for a month or so, knowing that easy conquest, women, and loot would dim memories of friends who had died at Yurbaco, of the poisoned arrows and slow starvation at San Sebastián, of the miserable death which had overtaken half the company when Valenzuela's brigantine had foundered. Thereby the course of the history

35

of the Conquest might have been changed—but Enciso was not a veteran of many battles and sieges, nor could he command such veterans. He read the laws and regulations which the crown had laid down for the expedition, and he sternly forbade all private trading for gold. Death was the penalty for violation of that edict—and the men who stood in the ranks with Pizarro and Balboa desired neither to die nor to have their private rights interfered with. They growled, as soldiers have ever done and ever will do, and the impoverished Balboa promptly capitalized upon that discontent. Not yet—nor for many years—was the star of Francisco Pizarro in the ascendant. It had barely appeared above the horizon when he squatted over a mess kettle in a thatched hut between the sea and the jungle and cursed Enciso for a shark-faced lawyer who desired for himself all the gold that might be wrung from this land of Darien. If Ojeda were only here—but Ojeda, shipwrecked, was floundering through the marshes along the southern coast of Cuba and was doomed never again to sail toward his province of New Andalusia. There was no Ojeda, but there was the stout hidalgo Vasco Nuñez de Balboa, who could read and write, who knew the terms of the king's writ as well as did Enciso, and who could match with craft the unpopular orders of the *alcalde mayor.* It was Balboa who pointed out that the lawyer was quite without authority since he and all his men were actually trespassers upon land allocated to the province of Veragua and to Diego de Nicuesa.

We must skip prodigiously over the details of the political warfare which followed. Enciso was deposed, stripped of all authority, but permitted to remain in the settlement. Allegiance was pledged to Nicuesa, governor of Veragua, and a ship sent to the westward to find him and invite him to locate his seat of government at Antigua. The grand carver was found on the northernmost point of the Panamanian isthmus where he had landed from one leaky ship constructed from the wreckage of the other vessels of his squadron. "In the name of God," he said in despair, "let us stop here." No trace of the original settlement remains in the little village thirty miles northeast of the Caribbean entrance to the Panamá Canal, but it still bears the Name of God— Nombre de Dios—given it on that day by Diego de Nicuesa.

Nicuesa was starving; only sixty men remained of the seven hundred who had sailed with him, and he leaped at the opportunity presented by the ambassador from Antigua. A bit of food must have picked him up to a remarkable degree, for even as a potential administrator he was less tactful than the deposed Enciso. He talked loudly of his policies and of the penalties for private trading for gold, and reports of those words were borne to Antigua in advance of his coming. It was then that Vasco Nuñez de Balboa set foot upon the path which was to lead him to deathless fame and to an ignoble death. The colonists, under Balboa's leadership, first refused the governor permission to land and finally— after weeks of quarreling—banished him. A death sentence would have been more merciful. He was given a leaky brigantine and some stores and on the first day of March, 1511, set sail for Hispaniola with seventeen men who remained loyal to him. Neither ship nor crew were ever heard from again.

Enciso was treated more kindly. He had friends and loyal followers who saw clearly that Balboa's leadership could be regarded legally as only a rank usurpation of authority, and

37

these won for the lawyer permission to return to Spain and there lay the circumstances of the case before the throne. A caravel, small but seaworthy, was assigned to Enciso, and he made the long voyage to Hispaniola, thence across the Atlantic, without mishap. Balboa must have sensed that his own position was a ticklish one, for he sent two deputies with the lawyer. One, Zemudio, was to go all the way to Spain and there plead Balboa's case; the second, Valdivia, was sent to Santo Domingo for the ostensible purpose of obtaining supplies and reinforcements. Privately he carried a letter and a sizable bribe to be presented to Miguel de Pasamonte, royal treasurer of the Indies, as a bid for his favors and influence.

Francisco Pizarro remained at Antigua. He was an illiterate soldier, neither diplomat nor navigator, and there was no place for him on Enciso's caravel. The chronicles are silent as to what part he took in the factional quarreling which preceded the departure of Nicuesa and Enciso, but his own actions, through the months and years which followed, are the strongest evidence that at no time did he proclaim himself openly as a follower of Balboa. The fleeting glances we obtain of him, the very casual mention in the chronicles of his activities in the tumultuous history of Darien, give us in truth a measure of the man. Courage, ambition, and greed were his; but those were qualities which were absent from none of the Conquistadores, or a continent would not have been added to the lands of Spain within a few decades. He was cruel, as were all who bore the banner of the lion and the lilies, but not with the sadistic delight in cruelty of the Teuton or the Hun. Latin cruelty is impersonal, oriental. The truly ingenious devices for the infliction of agony upon

38

human beings will be found in the museums of northern Europe. He has been called perfidious in his treatment of such associates as Almagro, and perhaps the word is well chosen. It is certain that there was in him no sense of gratitude toward those with whose help he climbed to fame. Much of that can be seen in the shadowy outline of the man in Darien, as can also his inflexible pertinacity. Once he was determined upon a course, neither years nor leagues of unknown sea nor jungle nor mountains nor huge armies of Indian foes could turn him aside. One more characteristic must be noted: through all his life he was loyal to his king. Had he lived he would probably have condemned his rebel brother Gonzalo to the block.

The ambassador Valdivia returned with no more supplies than a single light brigantine could carry. The message he bore from the treasurer Pasamonte to Balboa must have been unsatisfactory for he was promptly dispatched on a second voyage to the seat of government. The brigantine was wrecked off Jamaica, and Valdivia and thirteen men, in a small boat, were finally driven ashore upon the Yucatete coast. They were captured, and all but two were sacrificed upon the Mayan altars. One of those two, Geronimo de Aguilar, lived for seven years among the coastal tribes, learned the Mayan speech, and was finally rescued by Hernando Cortez when that captain, most intrepid of all military leaders of all time, touched at the island of Cozumel. Aguilar served as interpreter on the immortal expedition to Mexico and rose eventually to the position of *regidor* of the conquered city.

Thus, by long and tenuous threads, are the histories of all the conquests linked. Francisco Pizarro, a soldier in the ranks, learned the art of war and the duties of command from Ojeda and Balboa; the wily Pedro Arias Davila taught him a ruthless diplomacy which he used well when he too was a governor. When he moved to the conquest of Peru his co-leader was Diego de Almagro, a veteran of Darien, who was sent to the headsman's block on Pizarro's order. In the ranks of that conquest was one Hernando de Soto, who was shocked by the cruelty with which the Indians of Peru were treated but who learned so well the lesson of cruelty that his later march across our southern states to the Mississippi stands almost alone as a saga of barbaric savagery by those who conquered in the name of Christ. Cortez, prevented by an injury from sailing with Ojeda, did not conquer Mexico until he had first defeated, both in battle and in diplomacy, Panfilo de Narvaez, who—for his testimony against Cortez when that captain was tried for his deeds and his misdeeds by the Council of the Indies—was rewarded by the granting of his petition to explore and colonize the vast region then known as Florida. With him, treasurer of the expedition, was Alvar Nuñez Cabeza de Vaca, fated to learn humility during eight years of captivity and of wandering from Texas to western Mexico, doomed to fail miserably when—in Paraguay—he endeavored to put into practice those lessons of humility and of fair dealing toward a conquered people. Cabeza de Vaca's accounts of the northern lands were directly responsible for the expeditions which first explored the American southwest. The preliminary search for the Seven Cities of Cibola was undertaken by Friar Marcos de Niza, who, as a priest with Pizarro's forces, had witnessed the treacherous slaying of the ransomed Inca Atahualpa. The most prominent applicant for leadership

40

of the military expedition which followed in the footsteps of the friar was Pedro de Alvarado, lieutenant of Cortez and conqueror of Guatemala, who possessed "almost a lust for murder." We will read later of his attempts to chisel in—no better term exists—on the conquest of Peru. Command of the Cibola expedition was given, however, to a comparative newcomer to the Indies, Francisco Vasquez Coronado, whom no historian has condemned as possessing a lust for murder. There is no murderous lust in ordering that no prisoners be taken alive or in approving, if not actually directing, the erection of two hundred stakes and the burning thereat of the captives of Tiguex on the upper Rio Grande.

The men of Darien and Veragua fought with Cortez in the shadows of the pyramids of Tenochtitlan; the veterans of Mexico went on to Guatemala and to Peru. Friar Marcos, who watched Atahualpa die under the *garrote* in Cajamarca, was the first white man to look upon Hawikuh in New Mexico; soldiers who had fought at Cuzco followed Coronado across the Staked Plains. Their trail is on the lands of this hemisphere from Chile to Kansas and is everywhere the same; a trail marked by the sword and the stake and the *garrote* and by thousands upon uncounted thousands of slaughtered natives whom neither Spain nor Rome regarded as human. Magnificent in their courage, in their dauntless acceptance of any odds, but let us see the Conquistadores as they were and not through the eyes of those who, four hundred years later, would picture the Spanish Conquest as one of cultural penetration.

Chapter Three

THE NAME OF FRANCISCO PIZARRO begins to appear regularly in the chronicles after the expulsion of Nicuesa in 1511. It is an exaggeration to say—as has been said—that he was second in command to Vasco Nuñez de Balboa; but he soon qualified as a subordinate military leader who could be relied upon, and he marched upon all the various expeditions and sorties which Balboa launched in order to bring the land of Darien firmly under his control. A potential conqueror was made of the soldier Pizarro during those years when the Spaniards struggled to establish a permanent colony on the shores of the Caribbean. He who knew much of fighting learned more. He who had known hunger and thirst and privation experienced those trials anew and learned a greater endurance. There in Darien he tasted the fruits of victory and of defeat, and he found there his Quest —the Grail toward which he set his eyes and to the search for which he dedicated himself until he found it in Cajamarca nearly a dozen years later. Not at once but in tiny morsels of information obscured by legend he learned of a nameless land far to the south where gold was the commonest of metals, so abundant that men fashioned it into plates and goblets and ate and drank therefrom. The story differed in no wise from many others which had been told the unwelcome intruders upon the Tierra Firma—it was Zenu and Dobayba and Quivira—but Francisco Pizarro believed in it, and he clung to that belief.

First of the tales was told by Panciaco, son of Comagre, who was cacique of a "province"—actually a region of tribal domination—which bore his name. Comagre was fourth or fifth of the neighboring caciques to be subdued and seems to have been a cut above them both in character and in military strength. He is said to have been able to muster three thousand warriors, and Balboa, with eighty men, approached him in friendship rather than with war drums beating the charge. Pedro Martyr devotes considerable space to a description of the chieftain's huge dwelling, of his storerooms, and of the food, palm wine, and maize beer which were set before the hungry Spaniards. Comagre was impressed not at all by the bearded strangers. He declined to be terrified and regarded them, says Martyr, as "wanderers who lived only by their wits and by looting." Disdainfully, he made Balboa the very handsome gift of four thousand ounces of gold, and his opinion of the white men was not changed by the brawl which promptly broke out over the division of the loot. His son, Panciaco, equally disgusted, struck the pan from the scales and scattered the gold on the ground.

"If this is what you so prize," he exclaimed, "I can tell you of a land where men eat and drink from golden vessels and where that metal is as cheap as is iron with you!"

He continued with history-making words. From the summits of the mountains of Darien, he said, one could see a vast ocean. The streams which flowed into it carried incredible wealth of gold, and its shores were ruled by kings who ate from golden platters. How far were these lands? Many days' journey, and the intervening country was peopled by savage tribes, many of which were cannibals. An expedition of at least a thousand men would be needed.

Panciaco was a bit vague, as well he might be. Very probably he had himself climbed to the crests of the interior mountains of Darien and had seen the limitless expanse of the Pacific, but of what lay beyond he could repeat only tales and rumors which had come to him and his people through many months. From Darien to Cuzco, capital of the Incan Empire, the airline distance is more than sixteen hundred miles; it is more than six hundred to Quito, then the northernmost province of the Land of the Four Sections. Between are mountain, jungle, marsh, and rivers in a succession of obstacles as formidable as can be found anywhere on earth. There was, of course, no direct commerce between the Andean highlands and the villages of the Caribbean coast. Intertribal trading in the Americas was developed on no such vast scale. Panciaco's tale of the Golden Empire had reached him through tribesmen who, journeying far, had met men of other tribes who, in turn, had encountered wanderers from still more remote lands. It is leaping at conclusions to say, as have some, that the young warrior told Balboa of Peru; there was no such direct information in his repetition of old tales which had become almost legends. There was definite truth, however, in his account of the great sea which lay beyond the mountains, and this confirmed what the Spaniards themselves had long credited. They knew that this land was not Asia but it must lie very

44

close thereto; and if the strait which Columbus had sought did not exist, at least the sea was there, and Balboa determined then to seek it.

Space forbids our histories—the histories which you and I studied in school and which our children are studying today—from saying more than that on September 26, 1513, Vasco Nuñez de Balboa discovered the Pacific Ocean. That is all. His name is retained and, later, cemented in memory by Keats's immortal error which credited "stout Cortez" with the discovery. Few of us remember the year, still fewer know that with Balboa marched the future conqueror of Peru, the illiterate, stubborn, vain Francisco Pizarro.

Nor do those histories tell that the discovery of the Pacific was hastened by months, if not years, by sheer political expediency; the same brand of politics which, working in reverse, long delayed the conquest of Peru. Balboa's worst fears regarding his status in the eyes of the king were confirmed when word came from his friend at court, Zemudio, that the glib lawyer Enciso had argued the case only too well before the throne. The king regarded Balboa as a high-handed usurper, if not a murderer who had sent Diego de Nicuesa to a miserable death. A royal summons had been issued recalling Balboa to Spain where Enciso—a devil's advocate indeed—would appear against him; a new governor was to be appointed over Veragua and New Andalusia and this province of Darien.

So far, however, the information was confidential and unofficial, and Balboa knew well the character of his king, the avaricious, jealous, petty-minded Ferdinand. A great exploit—a deed which would bring new luster to the crown and promise new wealth to the monarch's chronically empty treasury—would restore any man to favor. There was but one such exploit open to Balboa, and he set out to discover the Great South Sea.

Not with the thousand men which Panciaco had declared essential. There were not half that number of Spaniards upon the mainland of the American continent in 1513. The commander mustered one hundred and ninety-six of the tough veterans of Darien and sailed in a brigantine and nine dugout canoes to Coyba, a few miles to the west along the isthmus, where he added an unspecified number of Indian "allies"—for which you may read the word slaves. A few of the Spaniards were armed with the matchlock, the arquebus, earliest of the ancestors of today's military rifle with the exception of its still more primitive forebear, the hand cannon. The matchlock was just beginning, in 1513, to supplant the crossbow as a projectile weapon for infantry. It was heavy and incredibly clumsy, fired by a device which was merely a mechanical adaptation of the hand and fingers which had applied the glowing wick to the touchhole of the hand cannon. The wheel-lock, first of the truly mechanical ignition systems, was still in the experimental stage; the flintlock's unknown inventor was still unborn. The crossbow was a far more accurate weapon than the arquebus, but it was silent; it inspired no such terror among savage foes as did the bellowing roar of the matchlock, the sudden cloud of white smoke, and the flash of orange flame. Indians, one and all, believed that the thunder and the lightning were servants of the white man, and they fled before the fire power as they did from the equally terrifying horse.

Balboa took no horses. A few appear to have been in Antigua at that time, but the mountains and jungles of the isthmus were impassable for them. His only animal allies were dogs, a pack of those beasts which the Spaniards bred and trained for Indian fighting. They are usually called bloodhounds, but that translation conveys a wholly erroneous impression. Today's bloodhound is a patient, superlatively gentle creature, bred and trained only to follow a scent. The *podenco* or *sabueso* of the Conquest was a totally different beast, more like a bull mastiff or a huge boxer than any other dog alive today. He was trained to attack at command and to leap for the throats of the Indians. Las Casas, that priest who was centuries before his time as a crusader for the humanities, has described how those dogs were trained and how—for sport—the holders of encomiendas[1] in the Indies rode gaily to hounds with the shrieking natives as their quarry. It is in connection with the expedition to the South Sea that we read first of Leoncito, Balboa's favorite, and so indomitable a fighter that he was awarded a soldier's full share of any booty taken.

No man can set down with any degree of accuracy the course followed by Balboa and his men, but our present knowledge of the Panamanian interior, made possible only within the last few years by aerial mapping, permits a very fair approximation of the dogleg route. From Coyba—later Acla, by which name it still appears on the maps as a Tule or San Blas Indian village—Balboa went northwest, then west, across the broken lands of the divide between the headwaters of the Bayano and the Chuchunaque rivers.

---

[1] The word cannot be translated briefly. An encomienda was more than a grant of land, for an encomendado held, not only the land awarded him, but all natives living upon his fiefment. Their souls—after baptism— may have belonged to God; their bodies and the labor thereof were the absolute property of the landowner.

Somewhere in the geographical center of Darien, close to the foot of the mountains known variously as the Serrania de Maje, the Cordillera de Porras, or the Coastal Range, was the village of Quaraquá, a cacique of high local repute as a fighter. His legions wilted, however, before the first bellowing volley from the matchlocks. The Spaniards and their allies pursued, the savage dogs did their bit, and we are told that the chieftain and six hundred of his warriors were slain. A considerable amount of gold was taken in the sacking of Quaraquá's village where the Spaniards recuperated from the fighting and where new guides were drafted from among the prisoners—proof that the coastal Indians knew little of the interior. Some men, wounded in the fighting, were sent back to Coyba to join those who had been left to guard the ships. Sixty-seven of the original one hundred and ninety-six remained for the venture. The Spaniards were entertained during their stay with Quaraquá by watching the cacique's brother and several subchiefs or priests being torn and devoured by the dogs. These men were dressed in long robes of white cotton [?]; they appeared effeminate to the superlatively masculine Spaniards and were suspected of being homosexual perverts.

The mountains rose steeply—as do all the mountains of Panamá—from behind the village. From the summit of those jungle-clad hills, Balboa was told, the sea was visible. He had heard the same story before, on the Caribbean coast, and had not yet seen the ocean, but this tale must have been convincing, for when the climb was almost completed he ordered his men to remain where they were while he, alone, advanced to the summit. There, in very truth "silent upon a peak in Darien," he gazed on the Pacific; then called or

48

signaled to his followers to join him. The priest, Andres de Vara, raised his voice in the *Te Deum Laudamus,* in which Balboa and the trail-weary soldiers joined, but the commander had other words for them.

"Be loyal to me," he appealed, "and by Christ's favor you will become the richest Spaniards who have ever come to the Indies!"

His words were applauded, of course, and of those men some remained loyal to the last, although we know nothing of the wealth they gained. Another, never conspicuous by his loyalty to Balboa, became the richest of them all. He was Francisco Pizarro.

The highest peak in the coastal range, called on most maps Mount Darien, is usually pointed out as the scene of that discovery. It may well have been, for on that 26th day of September, 1513, Vasco Nuñez de Balboa stood either upon that summit or one close to it. That can be fairly well demonstrated without discovery of the cairn which Balboa built at the site, the cross which he ordered made from "a fair and tall tree," or the names of his king and queen, which were cut deeply into the bark of another tree.

Had the first sight of the Pacific been from a point any considerable distance to the west of Darien Peak, Balboa would have reached the coast on the shores of the Bay of Panamá rather than on those of San Miguel Bay which is directly south of that summit. Nor could his vantage point have been far to the eastward of the dominating mountain of the coastal range. Had it been, any approach to the sea would have been checked by the bottomless marshes which extend for miles to the north and south of Darien Harbor, the inner basin of San Miguel Bay. In September, when the

49

rainy season has not yet begun to wane, those marshes would form a barrier more formidable than the mountains, yet none of the scouting parties seem even to have skirted them. There is some mention of muddy or marshy ground in the chronicles, but the reference seems to be to nothing more than tidal flats.

Four hundred and twenty-five years after Balboa I flew from the Canal Zone city which bears his name to San Miguel Bay. From a thousand feet above the jungled hills we could trace the courses of the many rivers, still nameless, which flow from the coast range to the sea. The rivers are quite impassable, but between them, at a number of points between the Negro village of Chimán and San Miguel Bay, are ridges along which a party of sturdy men might hack a path from the mountains to salt water. Two such ridges are very noticeable approaching the northern shore of the bay; a third ends in the headland which marks the northern entrance to that gulf, and all of them run almost directly north to the main coastal range just east of Darien Peak. The thesis can never be proven, but I firmly believe that the first white men to reach the waters of the Pacific followed the second of those ridges.

The scouting parties did not set out immediately to cut a way from the summit of the coastal range to tidewater. There was a spot of fighting to be done first, this time with a cacique named Chiapés. The arquebusiers went to work, the fighting dogs dashed through the smoke and ripped the throats from the fleeing Indians, and Chiapés bought peace with no less than five hundred pounds of gold. Balboa made the village of Chiapés his headquarters and sent out three parties, each of twelve men, to determine the best route

50

to the sea. The commanders were Alonso Martín, Juan de Escarray, and Francisco Pizarro, but only the first was successful. Martín gained the northern shore of the bay and there found two dugout canoes. He stepped into one and floated for a few minutes, thus earning the place he claimed in history: that of being the first European to embark upon the unknown ocean.

There follows a slight but not particularly important discrepancy in the chronicles. The scouting parties must have returned to headquarters and reported, and we read that Balboa, with twenty-six Spaniards and some Indians, set out for the coast on September 29. So large a party could not have bettered to any great extent the time of two days which Martín had required for the same journey, yet Balboa named the great bay San Miguel because it was discovered upon St. Michael's Day—which happens to have fallen upon September 29. Such errors—most of them inconsequential—are not rare when one compares the early narratives. There is another, much disputed, in regard to the precise date upon which Francisco Pizarro first set out for Peru.

With all that ceremony which Latins love, Don Vasco took possession of the sea—"and lands and coasts and harbors and islands and all thereto annexed"—in the names of their Catholic Majesties Ferdinand and Juana[2], "now and

[2] Spain was not yet an empire or even a united kingdom. Isabella died in 1504 and left no male heirs. As early as 1502 the Cortes of Castile and Aragon recognized Juana, daughter of Ferdinand and Isabella, and her husband, Philip the Handsome, founder of the Habsburg dynasty, as their future rulers. Castile had not recognized the rights of women to rule, and there was violent opposition when, after Isabella's death, Ferdinand ignored the rights of Philip and endeavored to seize that crown for the insane Juana. Philip died in 1506, and since the mad Juana was quite incapable of reigning there was little opposition to the regency of Ferdinand. Juana's name appeared on all public documents, however, until her death in 1555, only

51

for all time, as long as the world endures, and unto the final day of judgment of all mankind."

Big words. Words as arrogant as the hidalgo who uttered them; words born of pride of blood and of race and of color and creed and caste; the Spanish pride which is quite incomprehensible to those of colder blood. Francisco Pizarro, man-at-arms, stood and listened and doffed his steel helmet or padded cap—a soldier of that day may have worn either —when the priest Vara raised his voice in prayer and thanksgiving to the Father, the Son, and the Holy Ghost. He was not hidalgo, this man Pizarro, who is but a shadow moving through the history of the conquest of Darien, nor would he ever be. He was to become—could he then have dreamed it?—a knight of the Order of Santiago and a marquis of Spain. The loot of an empire was to buy him the right to wear the coat of arms of the man who had casually sired him and to quarter thereon the eagle and pillar of Aragon, the rampant lion of Castile, and the llama—a creature as yet unknown to Europeans. He was to be given the rights and privileges of an hidalgo, but hidalgo he would never be and he knew it. Was there jealousy, then, of this Balboa, this "son of somebody" who had won to command and who had ordered his followers to remain behind that he might, alone, be first of his race to gaze upon the Great South Sea? Only in the deeds of Francisco Pizarro can the reply to that question be found. Jealousy and envy and distrust are as Spanish as pride and amazing courage. Pizarro, greatest of the Conquistadores in his contribution to Spain's empire, had all those qualities.

a few months before the abdication of her son, Charles I, who succeeded to the Spanish crown on the death of Ferdinand in 1516, although he was not formally recognized by the Cortes until 1518.

The company remained on the Pacific coast for several months, then fought its way back across the isthmus by another and even more difficult route through the tangled mountain systems of Darien. To tell of that fighting and of the loot taken would be repetitious. Both gold and pearls were taken, and Balboa named the Pearl Islands in the Gulf of Panamá when they were pointed out to him as the source of the prizes. Túmaco, the cacique who told of the Pearl Islands, did more. He confirmed the story of Panciaco of a land, far to the south, where gold was as common as dirt and where the people had domesticated pack animals. The description—probably twice interpreted before reaching Balboa in the halting Spanish of an Indian who had been taught a little of that tongue—was inadequate. Túmaco took a handful of clay and shaped a four-legged beast, long of neck, which the white men variously declared to be a deer, a tapir—they had encountered tapirs in the Darien jungles —or even a camel. Whether Francisco Pizarro hazarded a guess we are not told. He and those with him were the first of their race to hear even thus indirectly of the llama, the burden beast of the Andean highlands.

They fought and defeated Poncra, a cacique who declared he had no knowledge of the source of the gold which the Spaniards took in his village. Even torture—and those men knew well how to employ the *garrucha*, the Italian *tratta di corda*, the ordeal by water called the *escalera*, and hot irons— did not cause him to alter his statements, and he and three of his subchiefs were thrown to the dogs. Much later a specious attempt was made to condone that barbarity by describing Poncra as a creature deformed both in body and

53

soul, a physical monstrosity who was guilty of gross perversions.

Tubanamá was more amenable. His village was captured in an unbelievably bold night attack, and he was told that he would share Poncra's fate unless gold was forthcoming—a threat which produced six thousand crowns' worth of the metal from the cacique's subjects. His son was taken to Darien that he might be taught the language of the conquerors, and eighty women—less willing hostages—were added to the train. Throughout the conquest of the New World, women were spoils of war second only to gold and silver. The dilution of the Indian blood began in 1492 and was ably continued by those who carried Spain's banner into Mexico, Central America, and Peru. Balboa had his Fulvia, Cortez his Marina, and the line of the Pizarros was carried on by the marriage of Hernando to his niece Francisca, child of Francisco Pizarro and the Doña Inez Huaylas Ñusta, an Incan woman who deserves the title of princess by which she is known in the chronicles. She was the daughter of Huayna Capac.

Balboa returned to Santa Maria de la Antigua in January of 1514, and there was an end to exploration and conquest. The scene shifts to Spain where the king had appointed a new governor for the lone colony on the Tierra Firma. The man chosen was Don Pedro Arias Davila, a grandee with a distinguished record as a soldier and a courtier and with the backing of the shrewd Juan Rodriguez de Fonseca, Bishop of Burgos, who was "as thorough-going in patronage as in persecution." The new governor had every qualification to rule a new colony in a new world save those of tact, generosity, honor, and simple common sense in dealing with men who had pulled the whiskers of death and laughed. The history of the New World would have been vastly different had a man of larger soul, with less of arrogance and of envy, been appointed to rule over Darien and to inquire into the charges brought against Balboa by the lawyer Enciso. Those charges would in all probability have been dismissed, Balboa would have been permitted to carry out his plan to sail to the southward along the western coast, and the first Spanish landing in Peru would have been made in—let us say—1517 or 1518 when the Inca Huayna Capac was living and less spent by sexual excesses, and a decade before the Land of the Four Sections was rent asunder by civil war.

But Pedrarias Davila, as his name has been contracted, was made governor, and he sailed for the lands which had now been given the grandiloquent name of Castillo del Oro, Golden Castile, on April 12, 1514. He had with him two thousand of the flower of Spanish chivalry, packed like the proverbial sardines upon fifteen vessels. Within a week of that sailing, Pedro de Arbolancha, friend and ambassador of Balboa, arrived in Spain with news of the discovery of the Great South Sea. More, he brought with him the Royal Fifth of all the treasure collected by Balboa and an additional gift for the monarchs of the pearls which had come from the shores of the new ocean.

Vasco Nuñez de Balboa knew his king. Gold would open instantly the heart of Ferdinand the Catholic, and overnight the lawless and rebellious usurper, the murderer of Diego Nicuesa, became an explorer and discoverer second only to the Great Admiral himself. The land rang with his praises, and the king—eventually, for Spain was quite incapable of swift action—appointed him *Adelantado* of the South Sea and Governor of the provinces of Panamá and Coyba. The word *adelantado* has no precise equivalent in English. It is in no sense synonymous with "admiral," as it has been translated, nor does the word "governor" convey its full significance. An *adelantado,* early in the sixteenth century, held both political and military authority. He was a "fore-governor," if an awkward word may be coined, who entered little-known lands and consolidated royal jurisdiction there. Spanish policy was never calculated to grant any man a free hand. Balboa was given a full measure of royal praise along with his sonorous titles, but the letter granting those titles made clear that he was subordinate to Pedrarias, who —lest he in turn wax fat with pride of power—was ordered to consult with Balboa in all matters of importance. Only hatred, jealousy, and envy could result from so bungling an attempt to award joint powers while dividing authority; but hatred, jealousy, and envy were well established long before 1515 when those tardy letters finally reached Antigua.

Hatred and envy were inevitable. Balboa had made an excellent beginning toward the establishment of a permanent colony, and had all those qualities calculated to make an efficient and popular commander of a far-flung outpost. He was a rough, tough soldier, who could send Indians to the torture, loose the dogs on recalcitrant caciques, or order a man-at-arms given fifty or a hundred lashes for mutinous speech; yet he fought like a madman—or a Spaniard; when there was loot he shared generously with his men, and he set them a lusty example in surrounding himself with a harem of Indian maidens. The cacique who yielded to him was assured of decent, almost generous treatment so long as he did not hold out on any gold which he might possess or get silly notions as to the possible consequences to the race of an ever-increasing crop of halfbreed children. There were some two hundred houses in the settlement, a beginning had been made in agriculture, and so complete was Spanish domination of the region that a lone white man could go anywhere in perfect safety. For all that Vasco Nuñez de Balboa was directly responsible, and the war-proven veterans of Antigua knew it and adored him.

Such was the situation when Pedrarias anchored offshore during the last days of June, 1514. He made his official landing on June 30, and few more striking contrasts can be found than in the ceremonial pageant with which the new arrivals took possession of the capital city of Golden Castile. On the one side were the little legion of veterans. Their body armor and casques were dented and scarred; such remnants of European garments as remained to them were faded, tattered, and patched. One may doubt if a single whole pair of boots remained in Antigua; the veterans of Yurbaco and San Sebastián and Nombre de Dios were shod with fiber sandals made for them by their Indian women. They stood behind the red-bearded, reddish-haired Balboa, whom they had followed from hell to breakfast and return and at a word would follow again. They surveyed with the critical, amused, and contemptuous eyes of seasoned soldiers the popinjay courtiers and gallants who were less than three months from the effete surroundings of the Spanish court. Their eyes may have quickened momentarily when they saw Pedrarias' wife, the Doña Isabella, walking beside her husband. It had been many months since any of them had seen a woman of their own race—but the Doña Isabella was a middle-aged woman, counting nearly thrice the years of the brown-skinned maidens of Antigua.

We may be sure they doffed their caps and bent their knees when they saw the new Bishop of Darien, Juan de Quevedo, in the splendor of his episcopal robes. Their own priest, Andres de Vara, had only rags for vestments; the cross which swung at his waist had been broken and repaired with a lashing of sinew, but Padre Andres had crossed the mountains with them and had stood upon the shores of the southern sea. A bishop he might be, this Franciscan, de Quevedo, but he and all those other wide-eyed newcomers who followed Pedrarias Davila had still to prove their mettle and their worth.

The two thousand young men who marched in the train of the new governor had been prepared to follow Gonsalvo Hernandez de Cordova to Italy when Ferdinand, jealous of the Great Captain, countermanded the orders for the advance on Naples. The hidalgos found themselves equipped for a war which had been denied them by a monarch's whim. Many of them, the historian Oviedo tells us, had mortgaged their estates in order to purchase all the gorgeous trappings considered essential for a gentleman who rode to the wars. They could not return to Madrid and Seville and Trujillo and face their creditors, and they fought for places in the expedition to Golden Castile. All had heard tales of Zenu and of Dobayba and of El Dorado. All believed that gold, in lumps, could be picked up off the ground in the fabulous lands beyond the sea—and the gathering of shining lumps of gold was labor to which even a *caballero* might stoop without losing caste. Two thousand men, and there is no record that any one of them was a veteran of any expedition to the New World. Not one had heard the scream of a jaguar or the hoarse bellow of the crocodiles of the jungle rivers; not one had ever seen a poisonous snake comparable with the huge bushmaster or the equally deadly, if smaller, fer-de-lance; not one was acquainted with hardship or toil.

They died. While Pedrarias—whose capacity for petty jealousy was as great as that of his master Ferdinand—squabbled with Balboa, the cavaliers died. They had expected to reach a city, a worthy capital of a golden province, and they found a collection of thatched huts on the marshy banks of a muddy river which flowed sluggishly through a deep valley. They landed in June. The rainy season was at its height, and the gay knights were drenched by the torrential tropical downpours, then steamed by the intense sun. They were driven to madness by the bites of insects to which the veterans had become inured; they died from snakebite and of jungle fevers and from hunger.

The old soldiers, the "Men of Darien," let them die. Nothing in these new lands was cheaper than life, and the veterans felt only contempt for the lily-handed popinjays of the court, who were too caste-proud to work even when life itself depended upon labor. Seven hundred died within a month, and the jungles of the Atrato delta absorbed their bones and the body armor which they wore to the grave. Some bought a brief respite from death. They bartered their finery—their velvets and silks and their engraved armor—with the men of Darien for a few loaves of Indian bread or for mandioca flour and melons from the little gardens which were tended by the Indian women. The tropic-hardened old-timers— Francisco Pizarro, Blas de Etienza, Juan de Escarray, and

59

their like—traded with the fever-racked and famished new-comers; then, when they had nothing more to trade, let them die. Pedrarias, frightened by the terrific mortality, permitted one shipload of his cavaliers to depart. Some joined Diego Velasquez in the colonization of Cuba, then under way by the usual method of exterminating the native population. A few stayed in Hispaniola, and the remainder returned to Spain, "broken in health, in spirits, and in fortune."

There is little to show that Pedrarias worried much more over the fate of the new colonists than did Pizarro and the men-at-arms. The new governor was himself sick, and be-tween bouts with malaria or some other tropical disease he was kept busy with his active rivalry and still more active jealousy. He tried, with some approach to legality, to convict Balboa as a usurper and the murderer of Nicuesa. Balboa beat that case and worked with equal zeal to foil the crotch-ety Pedrarias and to earn for himself new laurels as the great-est discoverer since Columbus. He planned another crossing of the isthmus, this time from the more northern harbor of Nombre de Dios, with the object of establishing a permanent settlement on the shores of the new ocean. Pedrarias fore-stalled him by sending four hundred men under Juan de Ayora to explore the regions which Balboa had already penetrated. The only result of that was to make irreconcil-able enemies of all those caciques with whom Balboa had established reasonably friendly relations. Balboa sneered, and the governor promptly placed him in command of an-other expedition—to discover and to conquer the reputedly rich province of Dobayba with its golden temple. At the last minute Pedrarias wavered. After all, Dobayba might be as rich or richer than it was reputed in legend, and Balboa might find it and thus win fame which would completely eclipse his political superior. He nominated Luis Carillo, one of the new officers, as co-leader with Balboa and bade them godspeed as they set forth up the river which we now know as the Atrato.

The accounts of that first recorded exploration into the interior of South America are fragmentary. The golden temple and the rich mines were not found, and contemporary historians went into few particulars of the failure. The party ascended the Atrato to a point not far from the mouth of the Murri River, almost a hundred miles from the sea in an air line. With a bit of luck and the crossing of the Cordillera Occidental, they might have reached the Pacific at a point many leagues to the south of the Gulf of San Miguel, but that luck was not with them. The Indians of the region made a daylight attack from scores of canoes upon the Spaniards. Carillo was killed, Balboa wounded, and a hundred of the Europeans either fell beneath the hail of arrows or were drowned. Balboa rallied the survivors, beat off further attacks, and retreated overland to Antigua. He and his followers blamed the dead Carillo—and divided authority—for the failure. Nothing much was done about it. Spanish policy and Spanish disposition were ever to shrug failure aside and to wait for new successes to wipe out even its memory; but in studying the history of Darien it is here that one first perceives the defection of the veteran Pizarro from the ranks of Balboa's adherents. It could scarcely have been a foresight of things to come, a conviction that in the long run the king's men were bound to win. No such political vision was to characterize his conduct in the years which lay ahead. Nor was he of sufficient stature in the colony for any record of his conversations with the governor to have been passed on to the historians. Such conversations must have been held, however, for Pizarro was allied from this time forward with the governor's faction and he was rewarded as richly as an illiterate man-at-arms, a commoner, *un hijo natural,* could expect.

First of those rewards was his assignment as second in command to Gaspar Morales on another trans-isthmian expedition. This was in 1515, and the letters certifying Balboa as *Adelantado* of the South Sea, Governor of Panamá and Coyba, had reached Antigua. Leadership of any such expedition was rightfully Balboa's, but the *adelantado-gobernador* was consistently and skillfully blocked by the wily Pedrarias, who had forgotten more of political chicanery than the bluff soldier would ever know.

Pizarro now had an opportunity to put into practice those lessons he had learned, and he took full advantage thereof. Morales, fresh from the Spanish court and quite inexperienced in Indian warfare, could have been no more than nominal head of the little band of sixty men. Pizarro led them to the Pacific without incident, established friendly relations with a cacique named Tutibra, and obtained four canoes as transport to the Pearl Islands, the exploitation of which was the objective of the expedition. Half of the men were left behind at Tutibra's village, the others paddled across the twenty-five miles of water which—at the closest point—separates the archipelago from the mainland. They landed eventually on the largest island of the group, named Isla Rica by Balboa, now Isla del Rey.

There followed one of the miracles encountered on every page of the history of the conquest of the New World: the

62

miracle of why the little force of white men was not oblit-
erated by the warriors of Isla Rica. The explanation, like
that of sundry other miracles, is quite obvious. It was not
Saint James—the "Santiago!" of the Spanish battle cry—
nor prayers to Our Lady nor to God which brought victory
to Pizarro and Cortez and Alvarado and all the others of
the long list of conquerors who faced a hundred times their
number of well-armed foes. Fear of the unknown, the mysterious, the terrifying defeated the Indians of Isla Rica as it
was to vanquish the warriors of Mexico and Peru. Fear
of white-skinned strangers whose long swords flashed like
lightning and—like lightning—brought death to all they
touched; fear of the thunder of the matchlocks and of death
which struck from a distance through sudden clouds of
smoke; fear of the men and the dogs, equally savage, who
charged from out of those smoke clouds and slew and slew
and slew until the sword arms tired and the black dogs were
crimson. This is the true story of the Conquest.

Defeated, the cacique of Isla Rica made peace on the
victor's terms. He pledged eternal friendship, pledged to
deliver one hundred pounds of pearls annually to that king
whose vassal he had now become, and made a token payment of a basketful of pearls which included at least two
of almost unbelievable size. Verbally, he did a bit more. He
confirmed in some measure the tales which the Spaniards
had already heard of the mysterious land far to the south,
beyond the sea, where gold and silver were dross. Herrera,
historian of the Indies, may be correct in his assumption
that it was there, on Isla Rica, that the idea of his Quest
was born in Francisco Pizarro.

So far, good, but the little band left its luck behind on

Isla Rica. The remainder of the story of the expedition would be but a repetition of clashes with hostile tribesmen, of desperate fighting in the swampy lowlands to the east and south of San Miguel Bay, of ghastly cruelties inflicted on the vanquished, and, finally, of a return to the Caribbean coast in which every step was contested by their now thoroughly aroused enemies. They reached Antigua, and the tale of their sufferings caused infinitely less comment than the baskets of pearls, to which they had clung throughout the anabasis.

Verily, said the men of Darien, the coast of the Great South Sea promises far more than these shores. Gold is there, we know, and now pearls have been added. It is from there, too, that we must embark on any voyage to the mysterious land which we have been told lies to the southward.

Those words were the death knell of the Caribbean colonies. Antigua was to be given back to the jungle within eighteen months; Acla, its successor as the seat of government, was to endure only until 1519 when Pedrarias Davila established the original Panamá, the ruins of which still stand a few miles to the east of the present city at the Pacific portal of the Panamá Canal.

There is little of Francisco Pizarro in the tale of those few years. Even the historian Oviedo, then at Antigua, finds reason to mention him only once. We may assume, if we wish, that he was content to relax into the inconspicuous role of an old soldier—he was about forty years old—and to perform such routine garrison duties as might be assigned a trusted veteran. He may have engaged in a few more battles, since the administration of Pedrarias was marked by almost constant minor warfare with the Indians, but it is quite certain that he did not accompany the most historic of the expeditions undertaken at the governor's command—that of Francisco Becerra, who set out with one hundred and eighty men to find the elusive Zenu where gold could be netted. The group was ferried across the Gulf of Urabá and from there set out into the interior. Months later, one Indian boy made his way back to Antigua, sole survivor of the expedition, whose single contribution was to eliminate the name of Zenu from the histories.

Nor was Pizarro more than a bystander in the long game of politics which ended with the downfall of Balboa. Possibly the action was a bit too fast for a man who could neither read nor write; or, like many another subordinate, he figured that politics had best be left to politicians. Indeed, the whole affair was one of power politics of the most sordid variety. Pedrarias Davila seems to have been kind to his family, but no other redeeming feature can be found in the man. After many months of bickering with Balboa, of thwarting him in every project which he desired to undertake, he embraced the *adelantado* in a sudden gesture of friendship —"there is enough of gold and fame in this land for all"— and offered him the hand of his daughter in marriage. The good Bishop Quevedo, himself no amateur in the political game, suggested that move to the governor. Balboa accepted, and Pedrarias assured him that the first ship which sailed for Spain would bear a summons for the seventeen-year-old *doncella* to set out for Darien. In the meantime there was man's work to be done—and the brown Fulvia, daughter of the cacique Careta, to lighten the hours when a man took surcease from toil. Up the coast, a few leagues beyond the entrance to the gulf, was a new settlement named Acla, built at or near the village in the province of Coyba whence Fulvia had come. Balboa was charged with the task of completing the building of this outpost, and there he set about one of the most stupendous undertakings in the history of America. In comparison, Darien was not to know its like for four hundred years when the canal was cut from the Caribbean to the Pacific and Columbus's dream of a strait that would offer a shortcut to the Spice Islands became a reality. At Acla, Balboa and his men cut trees from the jungle, hewed them into the knees, strakes, and other timbers necessary for four brigantines, and transported those knocked-down vessels bodily across the isthmus, there to be assembled, rigged, and launched. Two were finally completed and were the first European craft to float on the waters of the Pacific. Balboa sailed them to the Pearl Islands and then for a distance of twenty leagues to the east of the Gulf of San Miguel.

He turned back from what appears to have been merely a shakedown cruise for ships and men, but further voyaging —perhaps even to the land of gold in the south—was undoubtedly contemplated when he heard a rumor that a new governor was on the way to replace Pedrarias. The possibility of so important a change in the colony's affairs called for investigation, and he sent Andres Garabito, a trusted friend, to survey the situation at Acla and report thereon. There was truth in the rumor. Lope de Sosa had indeed come from Spain but had been stricken on the long voyage and had died aboard ship in the harbor of the colony he was to govern. There was considerable excitement in Acla, of course, and the conduct of Garabito is extremely difficult to understand. He may, while pretending friendship, have hated Balboa for many months because of the manner in which the leader had halted Garabito's advances toward the favorite Fulvia. Oviedo—a born gossip and hence none too accurate although always delightful—tells that story and then hints that the emissary may have been a mischief maker or a fool. At any rate, long before Balboa left Acla, Garabito had written a letter warning Pedrarias that the *adelantado* was a trifler who had no intention of doing right by the governor's daughter when that maid arrived from Spain. Balboa had lived so long in the tropics, said Garabito in effect, that he had lost all preference for the fair-skinned maidens of Castile. He was a gentleman who preferred brunettes, such as Fulvia and her tribal sisters. And—if that were not enough for the proud and jealous governor—Garabito talked glibly in Acla of Balboa's plans to set up another colony with himself at its head. Arrested and threatened with torture—the one followed inevitably upon the other in Spain and her possessions—the man enlarged upon those statements and named Hernando de Arguello as financial backer and certain of Balboa's officers as accessories to the plot.

Pedrarias did not move to arrest the man he hated, then camped upon the Pacific and awaiting the return of his emissary. Instead, he forwarded a friendly letter requesting Balboa to return to Acla to discuss plans for the expedition to the south. The *adelantado* obeyed. He returned with the messengers and left on the Pacific the major portion of those who were his most devoted supporters. More, he refused to believe those messengers when, nearing Acla, they warned him that the governor planned to arrest him and exhume all the old charges and a few new ones. Therein lies strong evidence that Balboa's own conscience was quite clear. He refused to turn back as the messengers suggested, and on the outskirts of Acla he was halted by a squad of soldiers and informed by their leader that he was under arrest. Francisco Pizarro headed that detachment. He gave the necessary orders and stood by while the fetters were riveted upon his former leader's wrists and ankles. The discoverer of the South Sea was taken in chains to the settlement and there cast into prison.

The trial of Vasco Nuñez de Balboa has never been listed among the great trials of history, but it merits a place there as an example of the travesties upon justice possible under Spanish jurisprudence. He was charged with treason by conspiring to set up a new nation, quite independent of Spain, beyond the mountains. And lest that be insufficient, the old accusations of usurpation of power and responsibility for the death of Diego Nicuesa were exhumed and laid before the *alcalde mayor*, Gaspar de Espinosa, who was trial judge and jury.

Death, of course, was the penalty for those crimes, but actually Balboa was fighting for his life against the jealousy and hatred of a wily and incompetent politician to whom every man of action was a possible rival. That is as certain as is the fact that Pedrarias, at every stage of the proceedings, had the trial judge under his thumb and refused to permit that weak official even to consider a verdict which would have spared the life of the *adelantado*. Full responsibility for the unjust fate accorded one of Spain's most gallant soldiers must be laid upon Pedrarias Davila, but no one is wholly justified in hanging upon that stout peg the conclusion that verdict and sentence were regarded by the men

68

of Acla as a gross miscarriage of justice. The attitude of the average citizen must have been that Balboa was guilty or that political strife between high officials was none of his business. The Balboa faction could not have been as strong as has been represented. Certainly it was not articulate or inclined to action.

The trial consumed many days. How many we are not told, but between arrest and execution there was ample time for a revolutionary movement to get under way and for a messenger to have crossed the isthmus and enlisted all or part of the three hundred men there in a *putsch* to free the *adelantado*. None can call Oviedo an unprejudiced and dispassionate historian. His dislike of Pedrarias as an individual and as a political leader is as clear as his admiration for the gallant bearing of the doomed Balboa. His gossipy history is spiced throughout with his own prejudices, and he was quite capable of omitting mention of evidence which was presented to the court and which was common knowledge in Darien. Balboa despised and distrusted the governor; it is quite possible and even probable that he gained recruits for his projected voyage to the south by promising the conquest of new regions where he, and not the unpopular Pedrarias, would rule.

Certainly there was no frenzied protest in Acla when the verdict was announced. No mobs stormed the stockaded prison when the public crier shouted that the hidalgo Vasco Nuñez de Balboa was guilty of rebellious conspiracy and he and four others were to die. The execution was a public spectacle, of course, and was attended with all the ghastly —and pious—mummery, all the horrid formalities which custom demanded on such occasions. The scaffold was a stout platform sufficiently elevated to afford all spectators an uninterrupted view. The doomed man mounted it and there made formal confession of his sins and received absolution and the final sacrament. He could make a public address if he wished, nor did custom permit the interruption of those last words, no matter how protracted. Some were spared the ignominy of that last parade and public display. The last rites of the church were given them in the decent privacy of the cell, and the condemned was there strangled right speedily by means of the leathern collar—*el garrote*—which is still employed for capital punishment in some Latin countries. The court's decree was then carried out by bearing the body to the scaffold and there, publicly, striking the head from the shoulders.

No such grim mercy was granted Vasco Nuñez de Balboa. He walked through the bright tropic sunlight to the scaffold in the plaza, he heard the crier call upon all to witness the punishment inflicted upon a traitor; and he stood beside the headsman and—"in a great voice"—declared that the charge was false and that he had always been loyal to his king. Then, calmly, he laid his head upon the block. Three of his subordinate officers—Botello, Valderrabano, and Muños—followed him and died in like fashion and with similar courage. None can say that the Spaniard does not know how to die. Then—and Oviedo tells us that night had already fallen, so protracted had been the ceremonies—Hernando de Arguello was led to the block. His crime was that he had given Balboa financial aid when the appropriation from crown funds had been insufficient for the building of the brigantines and that he had written a letter—intercepted by Pedrarias

—which urged the *adelantado* to embark immediately on his voyage to the south.

We read that the people of Acla implored the governor to spare Arguello, declaring that God had hastened the nightfall to halt this last deed of vengeance. The reply of Pedrarias, as recorded by Oviedo, was that he would die himself rather than spare one of the conspirators. The thud of the ax upon the block told those who stood about the plaza that Arguello was dead. A good color-story, that, but somewhat tarnished by the same reporter's other color-story telling how Pedrarias was ashamed to show himself before the men he had expedited to death but remained hidden in a near-by house and watched the gory spectacle from a peephole in the wattled walls. He must have been quite sure of his position, that governor, for he declared the estates of the dead forfeited to the crown and challenged the Balboa faction by ordering the severed heads to be stuck on pikes and left on display for several days in the plaza.

It has been said that Francisco Pizarro commanded the guard which surrounded the scaffold on which Balboa died. The statement is as unsupported as other legends with which his early career has been embroidered by ignorance. He was present, however, and it is quite probable that the fate of his former leader taught him that nothing better could be expected by anyone who set himself above the faraway but still omnipotent King of Spain.

Acla may still be found upon the maps. The jungle marches almost to the sea along the Caribbean, but the army and navy planes from the Canal Zone fly above the huts of a small village of San Blas Indians on the narrow beach.

71

Once or twice a year a trading vessel drops anchor offshore, and the Indians exchange coconuts for fishhooks and machetes and cotton prints. White men are given sullen permission to land—Panamanian Negroes never!—but they must not enter the houses or attempt any exploration of the thick jungle, and they must return to their ships before darkness falls. Those Indians—and their ancestors included Careta and Ponca and Panciaco and Balboa's Fulvia—do not like white men. They shake their heads in pretended ignorance of the question when asked if anything resembling the ruins of ancient buildings are hidden in the jungle roundabout or if old weapons or tools are ever found when they plant their corn. Probably not, even if the Indians chose to tell the truth. The houses built by the Spaniards at Acla were of no more permanent form than the thatched huts which stand there today, and no metal would endure for four centuries in a region with an annual rainfall of nearly a hundred inches. The Indians of Acla have never heard of Vasco Nuñez de Balboa, discoverer of the Great South Sea, whose bones rotted peacefully in the soil whereon they walk; nor do they know that another conqueror, Francisco Pizarro, served his novitiate and learned the fundamentals of conquest in their land of Darien.

Chapter Four

FRANCISCO PIZARRO had been in the New World about ten years when Balboa died at Acla in 1517. Another decade was to pass before he strode into the front ranks of the great conquerors. He vanishes, so far as history is concerned, with the meager mention that it was he who placed Balboa under arrest and brought him in chains to Acla. We know only that after the seat of government was moved to Panamá in 1519 he received a veteran's reward of a few acres of land near the new capital. It was a *repartimiento*, literally a "division," which probably meant that other soldiers had similar holdings in the vicinity. We are told that he became a small farmer—which is to say that the Indians who lived on his acres raised sufficient crops to support themselves and their master. Any surplus was sold in Panamá, and the product of those sales gave him a few crowns for clothing and wine and other necessities. If he dreamed of further adventuring, of conquest in that land of gold of which occasional rumors still reached the colonists, he told no one of those ambitions.

Nor is there any record of his participation in the expeditions presently sent out by Pedrarias Davila and which resulted in the conquest of the more western regions of Panamá and of the lands which we know now as Costa Rica and Nicaragua. Pushing steadily northward, those Conquistadores met in Honduras the legions which Cortez, after the conquest of Mexico, had sent to the south. Not until 1522 did Pedrarias manifest any interest in the southern sections of his province or in further exploration of the coast which Balboa had discovered. Knowing him, we cannot believe that he advanced any funds for the project, but he at least gave permission for a sea expedition headed by Pascual de Andagoya. This rather futile excursion got no farther than Puerto—or Punta—de Piñas, some thirty-five miles south of the Gulf of San Miguel and within the limits of the present Panamá. To the Spaniards it was the province of Biruquote, derived from the name of a cacique, Birú. A river which drained the region was also called Birú, and the origin of the name Peru has never been better explained than by the theory that it is derived from that of the cacique, river, and province. Documentary reference is made to "those kingdoms called Peru, which lie beyond the gulf [the entire Gulf of Panamá, embraced within the crooked arm of the isthmus] and the crossing of the seas of the other coast" as early as March of 1526, many months before any Spaniards had even approached the Land of the Four Sections.

Andagoya's health was not good—he died shortly after his return from his abortive expedition—and he did not enjoy the prospects of stiff opposition from hostile Indians and even more hostile jungles. He returned to Panamá with few trophies save new tales of the golden land to the south. It was then that the fire began to burn again in the breast of the veteran Pizarro. He too had heard those tales; he too

74

had fought in the swamps of Biruquote; and within the space of a few months he had acquired two partners—one active—and the permission of the governor to embark on a new expedition. In return for his signature on the *permiso,* which was all he contributed, the unselfish Pedrarias was to receive only 25 per cent of the booty. Twenty per cent—the King's Fifth—went automatically to the crown; the partners could repay the costs of the expedition and reward themselves from the remainder.

Francisco Pizarro, Diego de Almagro, Hernando de Luque. Those were the partners. Three obscure individuals who were to participate in the loot of an empire; three men who never fully trusted one another, though they swore loyalty, each to the others, "by God our Lord and by the Holy Evangelists." Two were old soldiers, although less is known of Almagro than of Pizarro. His birthplace may have been in Estremadura, although it has been said that he took his name from the hamlet where he was born, Almagro, which is in New Castile, east of Estremadura. He was nameless— another bastard who carved for himself a niche in history— and naturally not entitled to the "de" with which his name is written. He may have come with Pedro Arias Davila or as a member of one of the later levies of troops with which Spain from time to time supplied her colonies. His reputation as a fighting man—and he was a good one!—was probably earned in the conquest of Costa Rica and Nicaragua; it is remotely possible that he was a veteran who had fought with Cortez in Mexico or with Alvarado in Guatemala. The truth is that he was quite unknown until he bobbed up in Panamá in 1523 and there listened to Pizarro's tales and was stirred to dreams of conquest. Like any lusty man-at-arms, he had a woman, an Indian girl of Panamá, and to them at just about this time or perhaps a year or two later a son was born. Almagro, whatever his faults, loved with all the tenderness of which a rough soul is capable the baby who was to become known as Almagro el Joven—Almagro the Lad—and play a brief, tragic, and pathetic role in the tragic history of Peru.

The other partner was Hernando de Luque, Vicar of Panamá. He would be a monsignor today, and was a man of education and of considerable influence in the colony. Most certainly, he was not the parish priest in the vicinity of Pizarro's holdings. It was he who conducted the various interviews with the suspicious and covetous Pedrarias and who—then and later—found the funds without which the project could not have continued.

Two vessels were available in the harbor of Panamá, and there could be no better evidence of Pedrarias' disinterest in maritime exploration than the fact that the larger was one of the brigantines built by Balboa and used by him in his limited navigation of the Panamanian coast. The ship was refitted, and Francisco Pizarro sailed with about a hundred men in mid-November of 1524. The tale of that first voyage is one of failure. To tell it would be merely to transfer to the Pacific coast of Colombia the story of the miseries and privations of San Sebastián and Veragua. Men died of disease in the pestilential marshes, they died of starvation in the camp Pizarro named Port of Famine, they died in the incessant bitter fighting with the Indians of the region. A small store of gold was taken, and the Spaniards heard more tales of mighty nations to the south and of a ruler who called himself Child of the Sun. They encountered a deserted village inhabited by cannibals, as inspection of the stew pots proved, and became convinced that only with a much larger force could they hope to conquer these hostile lands. Pizarro turned back and holed up at Chicamá, a short distance from Panamá, and sent the treasurer Nicolas de Rivera to bear to Pedrarias the small amount of booty which had been taken. Pizarro, it is quite obvious, had no fear of the jungle or of savage warriors, but his courage was not equal to facing the governor and telling him a story of failure.

Diego Almagro had the courage which his chief lacked. He too had sailed to the south, touching at all those points where Pizarro had been but never catching up with the other party. He too had fought with the Indians, and one of those battles had cost him an eye. He was now Almagro el Tuerto, the One-Eyed. Also, he had captured considerably more gold than had Pizarro and had advanced somewhat farther to the south, having turned back from Punta Chirambirá— still within the limits of the present Colombia and a long distance from Peru and its treasures. Almagro found Pizarro at Chicamá, and we are told that the two there pledged loyalty to one another and swore never to abandon their project of conquest. Quite possibly each was sincere at the moment; it is equally possible that Almagro even then was plotting a *coup* which would elevate him to the status of a co-commander. At any rate, he had that status when the second expedition set out to the southward.

He did not gain that diplomatic victory immediately or easily. There was little of the gambler in Pedro Arias de Avila. He counted the roll of the dead and balanced those casualties against the small quantity of gold taken and the story of jungles and swamps and mountains where no settlement could hope to prosper. He needed every fighting man he could muster to garrison the province to the north and to extend the conquests there; and he coldly vetoed Almagro's petition that he and Pizarro be permitted to recruit more men and assemble the supplies for a second voyage to Peru. Luque, the vicar, finally induced the governor to amend that decision. The priest was a man of vision, and he considered the ever more factual accounts of the great empire to the south as of far greater value than the meager amount of gold taken from the coastal Indians. He put pressure on Pedrarias—possibly no more than the pressure of his own adroit arguments—and the governor finally consented to further exploration. He was skeptical, however, for he sold out his own share in the possible returns for a thousand *pesos de oro*. In the *permiso* as drafted Diego Almagro was named as of equal rank with Pizarro, a clause which "sowed seeds of permanent distrust in Pizarro's bosom" and may well have inspired him to engineer exactly similar trickery at the Spanish court a few years later.

This was late in 1525 or quite early in 1526, for on March 10 of the latter year the three partners signed a contract "In the name of the Most Holy Trinity, Father, Son, and Holy Ghost, three separate persons in one true God; and of Our Lady the Most Holy Virgin . . . to discover and conquer the lands and provinces of those kingdoms called Peru." Two proxies, Juan de Panes and Alvaro del Quiro, signed for Pizarro and Almagro, neither of whom could write but who made the sign of the Cross with their fingers as their proxy signatures were affixed to the document. Further to solemnify the proceedings, Father Luque administered com-

78

munion and broke the holy wafer into three portions, one for each of the partners.

Aside from that administration of the sacrament the entire transaction might have been one for the acquisition and partition of acreage which lay within sight of the bell towers of Panamá Cathedral. None of the three had approached within five hundred miles of the most northern limits of the Land of the Four Sections; their knowledge of the empire of the Inca was limited to the thrice-told tales of jungle tribesmen; yet they calmly agreed to conquer that empire and to divide its lands and the loot therefrom. Small wonder that Luque, for his faith in that dream of conquest, was punningly called Hernando the Mad, there being considerable similarity between the words loco, or crazy, and Luque.

Two other points are conspicuous in that document.[1] Throughout its text, Pizarro is referred to as "Captain"; Almagro is merely named without title. Secondly, the necessary funds had already been advanced—gold ingots to the value of twenty thousand pesos—and Luque was named as having contributed that capital. Not until many years later was it revealed that the good prelate was but a straw man in the transaction. The twenty thousand pesos was advanced by none other than Gaspar de Espinosa, who had been *Alcalde Mayor* of Antigua and Acla and in that capacity had tried and sentenced Balboa. No satisfactory explanation has ever been advanced of why Espinosa desired to remain

[1] The text of the famous contract was first printed in the *Annales* of the Licentiate Fernando Montesinos. who did not reach Peru until about a century after the conquest. It appears, in Spanish, as Appendix VI of Prescott's *Conquest of Peru*. The only complete translation of which I am aware is the excellent one made by John dos Passos for Shay's *Incredible Pizarro*.

79

a silent partner. At a guess, he feared the ridicule which would be his portion if the skeptical citizens of Panamá learned that he had contributed so large a sum for the pursuit of the will-o'-the-wisp, Peru. Let it be said here, however, that his investment was returned to him several thousandfold and that the two partners Pizarro and Almagro fulfilled all their pledges to Hernando de Luque, who died while the conquest was yet incomplete. It may well be that Luque, distrusting both the veteran soldiers but Pizarro the more, was thinking of Espinosa as well as of himself when he wrote into the contract the many solemn pledges that the loot would be equally divided.

The story of the second expedition, which sailed from Panamá in November of 1526, can be told as briefly as that of the first. This time the two ships sailed together. On board were 160 men, many of them equipped with firearms, and several horses. Bartolomé Ruiz de Estrada was pilot, and with him to plot the course the expedition set boldly out to sea and did not land until it reached Almagro's "farthest south," the mouth of the San Juan River. There Pizarro landed with some fifty or sixty men-at-arms; from there Almagro returned to Panamá for additional recruits and supplies, and Ruiz, with the larger brigantine, continued southwesterly along the coast to the present Esmeraldas in Ecuador, more than two hundred and fifty miles beyond Punta Charambirá. There, at Esmeraldas, Ruiz and his men became the first Europeans to meet with subjects of the Sapa Inca, the Emperor of Peru. They encountered what we are told was a "sailing raft," a *balsa* from Tumbez, on which a number of Peruvians, men and women, were making a coastal voyage. The veteran pilot visited that raft and made shrewd observations of its construction, of the large squaresail and of the movable keel—naught else than a centerboard—which enabled the navigator to beat to windward. He saw the exquisite textiles of Peru and learned that the cloth was woven from the fleece of llamas and similar animals, which were abundant in the land from which the raft had come. Gold and silver were as common as wood in the palaces and temples there, he was told. Several of the Peruvians transferred to the Spanish craft, apparently as willing prisoners since there is nothing to indicate that the encounter was not in all respects a friendly one. The Spaniards were ever zealous in obtaining such volunteers, who could be used later as interpreters.

Ruiz sailed on as far as Cabo Pasado, just south of the Equator, and from there returned to Punta Charambirá and Pizarro. Within a few days Almagro arrived from the opposite direction with some recruits and a considerable store of fresh supplies which went far toward restoring the spirits of Pizarro's crew, who had experienced starvation and all the other miseries which marshy jungles and hostile natives could hand out to them. The two ships, each with a fairly complete complement, sailed south as far as Tacamez, the present Atacames, Ecuador. The city, say the chroniclers, was one of some three thousand houses, and an army of ten thousand warriors waited ashore and forced Pizarro and a small party into precipitous retreat to the boats. The leader had landed in the hope of a peaceful conference with the natives. We must regard a bit skeptically the Spanish estimate of the number of their opponents. There was ever a tendency toward exaggeration, particularly under circumstances which dictated a strategic withdrawal of the would-be invaders.

The council of war which followed must have been marked

with bitter disputes. There was unity on only one point: that a far stronger force must be assembled before any such well-defended cities as Tacamez could be conquered. The final decision—what need to repeat the tale of arguments so bitter that at one point Almagro and Pizarro were about to draw swords on one another?—the final decision was that Pizarro, as before, would remain behind, this time on the island of Gallo, some twenty miles to the north and as far again offshore, while Almagro again returned to Panamá.

On that rocky island the career of Franciso Pizarro reached its nadir. His men were miserable, discontented, and mutinous. One of them, Juan de Sarabia, a native of the leader's own Trujillo, had smuggled a letter into a bale of cotton which Almagro was bearing north as a gift to the governor's lady. The expedition, said Sarabia, had failed, and he begged the authorities to send a vessel to rescue the few survivors who might be found upon the island. That the situation was desperate and mutiny imminent is better illustrated by the fact that Pizarro after a very short time burned his bridges by sending the remaining vessel, with a number of the malcontents, northward. Those who remained preserved their lives by eating crabs and other shellfish picked up on the shores.

Almagro returned to Panamá to learn that Pedrarias was no longer governor of that province. He had been replaced by Pedro de los Rios, a newcomer to the Indies, who would listen neither to Almagro nor the suave Luque. The letter sent by Sarabia had no little influence upon the new governor, for the doggerel verse which ended it was quoted to everyone and sung in all the taverns of Panamá. Quoted by

82

every historian of the period, it has been well, if somewhat freely, translated by Prescott:

> Look out, Senor Governor,
> For the drover while he's near;
> Since he goes home to get the sheep
> For the butcher, who stays here.[2]

That was enough. The new governor sent two ships to the Island of the Cock. They were commanded by Pedro Tafur, who was ordered to bring Pizarro and all his men back to Panamá. Luque and Almagro found among the crews of those ships a man who would carry secret instructions to Pizarro. We are not told who read Luque's letter to the illiterate leader, but he was urged to stand fast at any cost. His partners were working diligently, and in a short time Almagro would join him with the men and supplies necessary to continue the conquest of the land of gold.

It was then that Francisco Pizarro first showed the spark— no, the fire!—of greatness. He had been a commander, he now was to reveal himself as a leader. With his sword he drew from east to west a line in the sandy beach. To the north, he said, lay Panamá and poverty; to the south was the unknown land of Peru with its incalculable riches. Choose!

He stepped across the line, to the south, and thirteen men followed him. Their names should be recorded in any account of the conquest of the Inca Empire, for they were the true conquerors of Peru. Francisco Pizarro was no longer a young

[2] *Pues senor Gobernador,*
Mirelo bien por entero
que allá va el recogedor
y acá queda el carnicero.
Called by Means the earliest-known Spanish-Peruvian "poem."

83

man. He was well past fifty when on that day in 1527 he challenged his miserable, half-starved men to choose between the comforts—the obscurity—of Panamá and further miseries. Had none supported him he must, perforce, have returned with Pedro Tafur. It is inconceivable that at his age, opposed by the governor, he could have mustered another expedition. Another would have been the conqueror of Peru. Pizarro would have lived out his years on his little plantation; the brothers who were to share his destiny would never have seen the New World.

He stepped across the line, and thirteen men followed him and thereby sealed each his own destiny. They were:

Pedro Alcón	Alonso de Molina
Alonso Briceño	Martin de Paz
Pedro de Candia	Cristobál de Peralta
Antonio de Carrión	Nicolás de Rivera the Elder
Francisco de Cuellar	Domingo de Soraluce
Garcia de Jarén	Juan de la Torre

Francisco de Villafuerte

Those were the Men of Gallo, the men whose descendants still point to that title as to a patent of nobility greater than the Order of Santiago or of the Fleece. Names other than those here given have appeared on lists of the Men of Gallo. Some have given their number as sixteen—accepting all the names which appear on all the lists. Others have insisted that Bartolomé Ruiz de Estrada, the pilot, should be included as one of the loyal few; but although he was among those who crossed the line which Pizarro drew he sacrificed the highest distinction by returning to Panamá with Tafur in order to hasten aid to those who remained on the island.

84

The list here given is that compiled by Dr. Carlos A. Romero, who made a critical analysis of all the early accounts and chronicles and published his findings in the *Historical Review*, of Lima, in 1919.

For Francisco Pizarro, it was the Day of Gallo, for on that day he attained, although not immediately, the turning point of his fortunes. The steel of Darien was given the final test of its temper on that island off the Ecuadorian coast. It was found good, and from that day forward his star was in the ascendant.

His first act was to leave Gallo with the thirteen men who had cast their destinies with his. He built a boat of some kind—its description as well as the source of the materials used have not been handed down—and navigated it to the larger island of Gorgona, sixty miles to the north of Gallo and only some fifteen miles off the coast. It was there, some months later, that Ruiz found him. The pilot had had his troubles, for Governor Rios had been infuriated by the defiant action of Pizarro and the Thirteen. Only after long negotiation on the part of Ruiz and the diplomatic Luque did the governor at last consent to send a ship with sufficient men to navigate it but none to carry out wild dreams of conquest. Ruiz was to command that ship—another diplomatic victory—but he bore strict orders to Pizarro that he must return to Panamá before six months had passed.

Two men, too ill to be moved, were left on Gorgona in the care of friendly Indians. The remainder embarked with Ruiz and set out upon what was in all truth a pleasure cruise, an idyllic interlude in the dark history of conquest. They were too few, too weakened by the long months of privation even to think of warfare; and they sailed to the south, past Taca-

85

mez and past Ruiz' landmark of Cabo, and entered the Gulf of Guayaquil and landed at Tumbez, now Tumbes, which by some stretching of geographical limits may be said to be on the southeastern shore of the gulf. Prescott, historian rather than geographer, would have us believe that the Gulf of Guayaquil was a land-locked harbor and that the main Andean ranges, including the splendid peaks of Cotopaxi and Chimborazo, were in full view of those upon the ship. Prescott, God rest his scholar's soul, never saw the lands of which he wrote so well. Both Cotopaxi and Chimborazo are more than two hundred miles from Tumbes, nor is there a harbor in the Gulf of Guayaquil until a ship passes behind Isla Puná and gains the shallow waters in its lee.

Tumbez, then as now, stood upon the border. To the north was the "kingdom" of Quitu or Quito which the Inca Huayna Capac had conquered a few years before; to the south was the Land of the Four Sections—Peru. Tumbez was the most important of the northern coastal cities. It marked the northern limit of the ancient Chimu lands and took its name from one Tumbe or Tumba, who was driven to America from the Old World after the Deluge—unless the chroniclers are in error. There was a temple there, presumably to the Sun God of the Inca people, and in connection one of those establishments which the Spaniards were to designate as "convents" dedicated to the "Virgins of the Sun." Dormitory were a more fitting description than convent; to classify the residents as virgins is to approach the utmost in misunderstatement.

Pizarro and his fellows were welcomed most hospitably by the people of Tumbez. Several of the "chiefs" were invited to board the vessel where they listened eagerly to the account of their own countrymen of the superiority of the Spaniards, whose visit, they said, was entirely a peaceful one. These interpreters seem to have been some of those Peruvians taken by Ruiz from the sailing raft he had met a year before. We are not told whether they had been quartered in moderate comfort in Panamá or whether they had endured the long months of misery on Gallo and Gorgona. Such minor characters as Indian interpreters—and the Conquistadores had many of them—were not considered worthy of mention by the chroniclers.

Food was brought to the ship. Game and fish and all the vegetable products of the "bountiful vale of Tumbez." There, too, the conquerors saw the first living specimens of that beast of which they had heard tales in Darien so long before. Several llamas were brought to the shore where the Spaniards examined them and promptly called them "little camels"—a term which is zoologically far more accurate than that of Peruvian sheep.

There were other wonders. The visitors saw their first Inca noble and observed how the lobes of his ears had been stretched by the insertion of large disks of gold. They referred to him as the *"orejon"*—"big ears"—and as *orejones* the members of the Inca caste were known for years. Alonso de Molina landed and was taken for a tour of the city. His story of the wealth of the temple was not believed, and Pedro de Candia was sent to check on him. Candia's report far surpassed that of his companion. The building was "tapestried," he said, with plates of gold and silver, and attached to the "convent" was a garden in which the fruits, flowers, and vegetables were wrought of the same metals in wonderful simulation of the genuine.

The Spaniards obtained some raw gold and a number of golden vessels and ornaments, but by legitimate process of barter and not by armed conquest. Then they sailed on to the south, to be received everywhere with the same warm hospitality displayed by the people of Tumbez. Within a few leagues they rounded Cabo Blanco and passed beyond the zone of equatorial jungles and marshes and were off the arid coastal deserts of northern Peru. The friendly people paddled out to meet the strange vessel with gifts of fruit and vegetables grown in the fertile valleys of the infrequent rivers, and the word of the coming of the mysterious white men passed from village to village far more swiftly than the brigantine could travel.

They passed Chan-Chan, once capital of the Chimu kingdom, which the Prince Tupac Yupanqui had conquered for his father, Inca Pachacutec, about a century before, and where within a few years Diego Almagro was to found a settlement and name it for Trujillo in Estremadura. The explorers may have landed there, as they did at many points along the coast, but the landing party brought back no such tale of riches as were to be found at Tumbez. With each league they sailed farther along the coast of the lands ruled by the Sapa Inca, and they heard again and again of the power of that monarch and of the golden glory of the capital city far beyond the mountains.

The point from which Pizarro turned back is most uncertain, but the brigantine must have reached the neighborhood of the present village of Patevilca, 125 miles north of Lima, and very possibly sailed as far as Chincha, the same distance south of the capital. The expedition touched at Tumbez on its return, and Alonso de Molina and at least one

88

other, at their own request, were left there to learn the language and customs of the country. It might be mentioned that those pioneers died or were killed. Conflicting stories were told Pizarro when he next reached Tumbez, one of the most probable being that the visitors were slain for attempting to divert to their own uses a couple of the Inca's Chosen Women, the Virgins—more or less—of the Sun.

Several Peruvians were taken aboard the brigantine that they might be taught Spanish and serve as interpreters in the conquest which was now a certainty. Among them was a youth named Felipe by the Spaniards and generally called Felipillo. He developed into as treacherous and vindictive a young rascal as can be found in the history of the Indies.

Would that the full tale of the Conquest were as free from bloodshed and cruelty, from envy and treachery and distrust and hate, as the story of that peaceful cruise of a force too small in numbers even to dream of warfare and the loot which would follow victory. In that voyage the doom of the Sapa Inca and his people was sealed. The Spaniards had seen the land and the wealth of its temples; hatchets and other tools—much admired by the natives—had been exchanged for golden vessels and the matchless textiles of Peru. These, with Felipillo and his fellows and a few llamas, were brought to Panamá as proof of the tale told a dozen years before by Panciaco in Darien. There was a land of gold far beyond the southern horizon, and the loot thereof would be greater than that of Mexico and all the other colonies which had been added to the crown.

Strangely enough, Governor Rios declined to get excited. More, he flatly refused to permit another expedition. He had no intention, he said, of depopulating Panamá in order to

89

build up new lands, nor would he see more men sacrificed for the sake of a few Peruvian sheep and some odds and ends of gold and silver. Pizarro, Almagro, and Luque had exhausted their capital, nor could they solicit more funds or enlist men for their venture without the official sanction of the governor. They determined to go over Rios' head—as far over as was possible—and let the king himself hear the story of Peru. Pizarro was selected for that mission. It has been said that Almagro, small of stature and disfigured by his empty eye socket, would not have made a prepossessing ambassador; that Luque, educationally much better qualified, could not obtain leave from his duties as vicar; and that Pizarro, who was trusted by neither of his partners, was sent to Spain because none other was available. It is quite certain that Luque and Almagro did not trust Pizarro, and that the dour Francisco reciprocated that distrust to some degree, but the choice was really determined by the fact that of the three he alone had actually set foot on Peruvian soil and had first-hand information of the Land of the Four Sections.

He and Pedro de Candia, a Man of Gallo, sailed from Nombre de Dios and reached Seville in June or July of 1528. The financial wizard Luque found somewhere fifteen hundred ducats for the expenses of the journey, and Pizarro took with him Felipillo and several other Peruvians, two or three llamas which miraculously survived the voyage, and—most important—all the textiles, the golden vases and bowls, and the other tangible results of the coastal expedition. It may have been the sight of the gold—for Charles I was no less covetous than his grandfather Ferdinand—or it may have been the forthright manner in which the grim old man-at-arms told his tale which carried the day, but the rulers of

Spain and the Council of the Indies approved a *capitulacion*
—a contract, if you will—which awarded the loot of an
empire to two illiterate soldiers of whom it is inconceivable
that anyone at the court had ever before heard and to a
minor member of the priesthood.

Not immediately, of course. Not even with reasonable
dispatch. Governmental red tape is not speedily unwound,
and the policy of the Spanish court was ever to make haste
with exceeding slowness. Charles had done a bit of fighting
himself. He had whipped the French at Pavia and was more
interested in becoming a European emperor than in adding
new and unknown transatlantic colonies to the realm. He
expressed unqualified approval of Pizarro's petition and
passed the responsibility to the Council of the Indies with—
we cannot doubt—private instructions to give the would-be
conqueror anything and everything except money. Then he
took off for Italy to kneel before Clement VII and receive
from the pontiff the crown of Emperor of Rome.

It has been said that Pizarro found an advocate to plead
his cause—a lobbyist—in the person of Hernando Cortez,
just returned from Mexico. There is a nice little story which
tells how Pizarro met Cortez, a fellow-Estremaduran and a
distant kinsman, in the shrine of La Rabida, whither Francisco had gone to pray. He there recognized Cortez, whom
he could not have seen for eighteen years, and the conqueror
of Mexico emptied his purse in his kinsman's palm, telling
Pizarro that he'd find use for all the ducats before he even
received an audience from the king. The tale adds color to
a chapter of political machinations and delays; there is no
law forbidding one to believe it. There is more color and
infinitely more truth in the final historical appearance of

Martín Fernandez de Enciso. The lawyer had been hanging around Toledo for years, vainly endeavoring to chisel for himself some sort of political appointment in the Indies. He had lost money in Ojeda's expedition to New Andalusia and considered that he had claims against any and all of the Men of Darien. He met Pizarro at the dock, slapped an attachment of some sort on him and his possessions, and had him held in the debtor's prison. The future conqueror was not behind the bars for long. Word of the news he bore was carried to Toledo—could Pedro de Candia have been the messenger?—and orders for his release were promptly forwarded to Seville. Enciso, we may presume, was charged with the costs of the writ of attachment. Exit the lawyer, biting his nails.

That was the last prompt action which Pizarro was to encounter in many months. He was finally compelled to petition Charles's consort, Isabella, to the effect that his scanty funds were almost exhausted and that he would be in no condition to enjoy his concessions unless they were made without delay. The queen urged the council to make an end of quibbling, and on the 26th of July, 1529, she signed for her husband and the mad Juana, his mother, whose regal rights were still respected, the document which gave Francisco Pizarro all that he had asked and much, much more.

Peru was given the name of New Castile, and Pizarro was granted the right of its "discovery" and conquest. He was to hold the title and rank of Governor, Captain General, *Adelantado*, and *Alguacil Mayor* for life; was awarded an annual salary—payable from future receipts—of seven hundred and twenty-five thousand maravedis; and, further, could dispose of the conquered Indians and their lands according to the laws governing the award of encomiendas. He was but one step short of being a Viceroy of Spain.

There were still more honors. A royal *cédula* bearing the same date as the famous *capitulacion* named Francisco Pizarro a Knight of the Order of Santiago; another, on November 14, granted him the right to wear and display the coat of arms of Gonzalo Pizarro, who had sired him so casually more than half a century before. A second grant of arms was made on Janury 19, 1536, and—that the tale of his honors might be here completed—he was created a marquis on October 10, 1537. Before that year was out (December 22) he was given his third and final grant of arms. This one bore the coronet of a marquis as its crest, and its blazonry included seven heads, bound one to another by a golden chain, to symbolize the seven caciques he had conquered. In the center of the oval thus formed was the Inca "Atabalipa"— Atahualpa— also chained and with his hands dipping into a treasure chest. "Thus did the King heavily, if unconsciously," says Philip Ainsworth Means, "underscore the mercenary character of the Conquest."

There were other awards. Almagro was named "commander of the fortress of Tumbez" with an income of three hundred thousand maravedis and was declared to be henceforth an hidalgo. Father Luque was elevated from the vicarate to the purple. He was appointed Bishop of Tumbez and Protector of the Indians of the new province, and was to receive a thousand ducats yearly for his services. Ruiz was named Grand Pilot of the Southern Ocean, Pedro de Candia was named Chief of Artillery, and all of the Men of Gallo not hidalgos by birth received that social status by royal decree. They too were *caballeros*.

No man could question the generosity of the monarchs—but all those salaries and appointments were strictly on the cuff. The Land of the Four Sections still was to be conquered, and for the expenses of that conquest the crown and the council contributed not a singe maravedi. The partners were exempted temporarily from certain taxes, and the King's Fifth was reduced to a tenth *on metals obtained from mines.* The royal commission remained at the higher figure on all metals secured by the customary methods of loot. The entire expense of the expedition was placed upon Francisco Pizarro. He was given until January 26, 1530, to raise and equip a force of two hundred and fifty men—one hundred of them could be obtained in the colonies—and was compelled to set sail for Peru within six months of his return to Panamá. Such were the methods by which the government of Spain "stimulated the ambitious hopes of the adventurer by high-sounding titles and liberal promises of reward contingent upon his success, but took care to stake nothing itself on the issue of the enterprise. It was careful to reap the fruits of his toil but not to pay the cost of them." So summarizes Prescott.

It is anticipating the narrative very slightly to remark that the provisions of the *capitulacion* were far from satisfactory to the two partners who had remained in Panamá. That the crown had paid off in promises was only to be expected—neither Almagro nor Luque expected any substantial financial aid from the home government—but hate and distrust which ended only with death was born of those clauses which so definitely named Francisco Pizarro as both military and civil commander and which granted him sole administrative and patronal rights over the yet unconquered province. He

94

had sailed from Nombre de Dios as one of three; he returned with dictatorial powers vested in him alone.

Much has been written of that apparent treachery of Francisco's toward the men with whom he had sworn so solemnly to share equally. His defenders and admirers have taken the word of his cousin, Pedro Pizarro, who sailed for Peru as Francisco's page and afterward wrote an historical account of the Conquest, that the crown and the council had refused to divide the authority by naming Pizarro as Governor and Almagro as *Adelantado*. His relative, says Pedro, had either to take all or receive nothing; he had either to accept all the high posts for himself or permit the entire project to fail. Others have pointed out that the shrewd Luque had distrusted Pizarro from the beginning and had urged that another ambassador be sent.

There may be some truth in Pedro's contention that the government had seen the disastrous results of division or duplication of authority in the colonies and did not wish a repetition of those rivalries in Peru. Pizarro may have urged that his friend and partner Almagro be named *Adelantado*— certainly he obtained for Luque the bishopric which he wanted but which he did not live to enjoy. There is no record, however, that the old soldier protested either long or loudly when he was granted supreme command; and it is significant—it must be significant!—that immediately upon the signing of that *capitulacion* he left Toledo and journeyed with all speed to Trujillo in Estremadura where he had been born and that he there surrounded himself with the only men he felt that he could trust, his brothers. On that twenty-sixth day of July in the year 1529 the story of the conquest of Peru ceases to tell of one Pizarro, but tells instead of four. Four who bore the name of Pizarro and yet another half brother, a son of Francisca Morales, who called himself Francisco Martín de Alcántara.

Francisco Pizarro must have known that he had not lived up to the terms of the contract executed with his partners. Possibly that failure was unavoidable; it is equally possible that his treachery was quite deliberate. He and Almagro had come close to blows before and for far less important reasons. He must have known that the tough old one-eyed fighting man would not quietly accept a subordinate position and that it were well if he, before returning to Panamá, assemble a personal staff upon which he could rely. His visit to Trujillo and his enlistment of his brothers and kinsmen cannot be otherwise explained. Fraternal affection could have had nothing to do with it. The man had been absent in the colonies for twenty years, and it is highly improbable that there had been any communication between him and his brothers during that period. There is nothing to indicate that there was any recognition of the young Francisco Pizarro by his elder brother Hernando, the legitimate son of old Gonzalo, during the years of their boyhood. Juan was but a youth when Francisco set out for the Indies, the younger Gonzalo was a baby in arms.

There was purpose in Francisco Pizarro's visit to Trujillo, and that purpose was not to embrace the brothers, half brothers, and cousins he had not seen for so many years, or to flaunt the red cross of a Knight of Santiago before those citizens who might remember a miserable little swineherd. That he sought men to enlist for the expedition of conquest is obvious, but he sought also aides whose allegiance would be undivided. He found them among his brothers, and the history of the Conquest is that of their loyalty. It is not enough to say that those Pizarros were poor, proud, and avaricious, hence leaped eagerly at any opportunity which seemed to promise sudden wealth. The years of their lives had seen many recruiting drives for service in the Indies, yet all had resisted those easy promises of loot in the new lands of the Tierra Firma. Poor they may have been, but not so poor as to give up what little they had in Trujillo until Francisco returned and told them the tale of Darien and of Gallo and the Land of the Four Sections.

He promised them vast rewards, of that there can be no doubt. He told them that the loot of a golden empire was theirs for the taking, and he also told them that he, their brother, would have the distribution of *repartimientos* without number and of encomiendas larger than the whole province of Estremadura. They enlisted with him—the half brothers Hernando, Juan, and Gonzalo; another half brother, Francisco Martín de Alcántara; and the cousin Pedro Pizarro. The last was probably a second cousin, too young to be enrolled as a man-at-arms. He enlisted as Francisco's page boy.

Hernando Cortez, conqueror of Mexico, then cooling his heels at court, was of considerable aid in obtaining recruits for the expedition and may have supplied the capital for the purchase of necessary supplies, which were loaded upon two ships at the port of San Lucar de Barrameda. The *capitulacion*, however, stipulated that one hundred and fifty men be recruited in Spain. Only one hundred and twenty-five had been signed up by January 26, 1530, when the six months' period of grace expired. Francisco then proved himself an apt pupil of the wily Pedrarias. He sailed with one ship and a portion of the men. Hernando was left behind to explain to the king's officers that the required number had been enrolled and that all who were not on his rolls had embarked with Don Francisco. That trickery concluded, Hernando sailed and met his brother at Gomera in the Canaries, and the two vessels made the transatlantic passage together.

Twelve full months after that sailing from San Lucar the expedition for the conquest of Peru departed from Panamá. It was a year devoted for the most part to violent quarreling between Francisco Pizarro—Governor, *Adelantado*, Lord High Constable, etc.—and Diego Almagro, who believed that some of those titles were rightfully his. Luque and Espinosa, who also had a stake in the enterprise, finally patched up an approximation of peace. Francisco passed the title of *adelantado* on to his partner and petitioned the government to confirm that transfer. More, he pledged that Almagro would eventually have a provincial governorship for himself and that none of the Pizarro brothers would receive titles or offices until Almagro was provided for. In short, any private plans for a Pizarro-dominated state were definitely quashed; stout Almagro, who had already given his eye for the sake of conquest, was to be paid for his sacrifices—and as an added safeguard the three re-executed the former contract and pledged anew an equal division of the spoils.

On December 27, the Day of St. John the Evangelist, the banners of the expedition were consecrated in the Cathedral of Panamá, and all members of the force partook of the sacrament. A few days later, early in January of 1531, the little flotilla of three ships weighed anchor. One hundred and eighty men, twenty-seven horses, and a few pieces of artillery set out to conquer an empire.

98

Chapter Five

TTAHUA-NTIN-SUYU, the Land of the Four Sections, the Empire of the Incas, has been called the most rational governmental machine ever set up by man, a statement which is sufficient justification for a divergence from the story of the lives of the brothers Pizarro. The bones of three of those brothers lie to this day in Peruvian soil; the four rose to fame as the ancient empire crumbled in a cloud of golden dust; they died as the last vestiges of Incaic domination collapsed; the story of the land is their story.

There is no place here for any mention of the Andean and coastal cultures which preceded the rise of the Quechua-speaking peoples whom we know as Incas. There were such cultures, possibly originating with migrants from Central America long before the rise of the Mayan culture. Those first settlers in western South America had advanced at least a stride beyond the primitive stage of the nomadic hunter, and during the first half-century of the Christian era they developed the cultures which we now identify as Tiahuanaco I, Chimu, and Nazca. A fourth culture, identified by the archaeologist as Tiahuanaco II, eclipsed them, only to decline in its turn as the millennium drew to a close. It left behind it, in the valleys and tablelands of the eastern Andes, the elements upon which the Incas were to erect their political hegemony.

In those uplands, wherever there was water to irrigate the soil or sufficient ground for cultivation, lived a peaceful agricultural people. They had domesticated the llama and alpaca; they grew maize where the altitude was not too great, and they cultivated the potato, the potatolike *oca*, the cereal *quínua*, and other food crops. Wood was very scarce and in some sections nonexistent, so they built of stone: thatch-roofed hovels with walls of irregular stones laid none too expertly in clay or mud. The social unit was the *ayllu*, a small group of households living in the same locality and loosely united for agriculture and for protection against those neighbors with less fertile fields. Intertribal quarrels were not rare, but there was no organized warfare.

Some six or seven of those *ayllus* lived in the Cuzco Valley, an area on the western slope of the eastern cordillera, well watered by several small streams of the Urubamba drainage. The site, even then, was old, and the heights north of the valley were protected by a fortress of huge stones erected by a people whom those living there had forgotten.

During the eleventh century the Cuzco Valley was invaded and subjugated by a foreign *ayllu* led—so legend tells us—by one Manco Capac. The conquerors came from Tampu-Tocco, the Inn of the Windows, which may or may not have been the present Ollantaytambo, forty miles north of Cuzco. Tambu-Tocco is as legendary as Eden, Manco Capac little less mythical than Adam or Noah. What matters is that in that invading *ayllu* was the seed of greatness, the ability to conquer and organize and advance to fresh conquests and

100

new organizations, and that from the line of the culture-hero Manco Capac there sprang a dynasty without parallel in the world's history. Sinchi Roca, son of Manco Capac, became war chief—the title of Inca was yet unknown—of the remote mountain valley about 1105 A.D. In 1529, four and one quarter centuries later, his lineal descendant Huáscar succeeded to the throne of an empire which extended from Ecuador to Chile and included all of the present Peru and Bolivia, considerable territory now in the Argentine Republic, and some marginal lands now within the boundaries of Brazil. It was an empire of some 380,000 square miles, as large as all the Atlantic seaboard states from Maine to Florida. No nation in sixteenth-century Europe even approached the Land of the Four Sections in size or in potential strength; none approached it in wealth or in the number of trained soldiers it could put in the field, yet it was conquered by a few hundred desperate adventurers quite unaided by any native allies such as those thousands whom Cortez had found waiting only a leader to rebel against their Aztec overlords in Mexico.

Had that conquest been delayed a few centuries, when social and political economies had become sciences, a far more rational view would have been taken of an exceedingly rational governmental scheme. As it was, many phases of Inca life were quite beyond the comprehension of the Conquistadores. Nor can one blame them, for there in Peru, from 1100 to 1500 A.D., there was developed an applied socialism in which one may find many of the basic doctrines of Marx, the Hegelian philosophies, some elements of communism and collectivism, plus a simon-pure dictatorship—and it worked!

101

The individual peasant was a hard-worked but not over-worked man. He may have worked harder than his descend-ant in Peru and Bolivia today, but with a far greater sense of security. Then, as now, the Indian was at the base of the pyramid, but he was neither exploited nor oppressed. The Incas saw the need for social security and old-age "pensions" with far clearer eyes than today's political altruists. The years from twenty-five to fifty were recognized as those of a man's prime during which he was expected to render full service to his community and the empire either by agricul-tural labor or by some equivalent service as a soldier or worker. After fifty a man was done with toil; he could sit in the sun.

There was no money in that empire; there was not even an approximation of coinage, a standardized medium for barter, or any standard of value. Since there was no money, there was no wealth. A minor official might advance to a higher post, but such promotion bore with it no increase in salary. Every official, military or civil, every priest from the Villac Umu—High Priest of the Sun—to the most humble cleric, served only for the love of that service. Therein may be seen the freedom of the state from any form of ecclesiastical inter-ference. The priesthood exercised no temporal powers nor, so far as can be seen, were such powers ever coveted. They found enough to do in attending to strictly religious matters, the maintenance of the temples and shrines and the manage-ment of the many ceremonies through which Inti, the Sun, was adored. There is no place here for analysis of the compli-cated religious structure; it was a worship of the sun and to a lesser degree the moon behind which—and sometimes far behind—was a monotheistic reverence for Viracocha, the Creator-God, who had survived in the land from the days of the little-known people of Tiahuanaco in Bolivia.

There was no money, nor was there any private ownership of land. The arable fields and those which could be made arable belonged to the *ayllus,* the household groups. Each head of a household was assigned holdings proportionate to the size of his family and his ability to cultivate the acreage given him. Other lands in the neighborhood were assigned to the Inca and to the Sun—to state and to church—and tilled by the people along with their own. The chroniclers are vague as to the proportions, but it is clear that the requirements of the *ayllu* were met with before other assignments were made. Only in land and in the sense of the necessity of the land was there any approach to our modern conception of value. All the lands of the empire were redistributed every year, but in that redistribution the individual worker seems always to have received the same fields. The Sapa Inca or an individual high in the Incaic caste could give state lands to some favored commoner, but such tenure was only for the life of the individual. Man is few of years, but the land and the nation are permanent.

There was no money, no private ownership of land, hence no commerce. Each *ayllu* was a completely self-contained and self-sustaining unit. There was barter, of course, but the markets were local, the merchants were the householders, and there were no foreign imports or luxuries. Where there was no money there was no standardized medium of barter or rate of exchange. Potatoes for corn or *chicha* beer or pottery; the quantities determined by buyer and seller without

103

interference. One may see such markets operating today in Cuzco and La Paz and other cities and towns of the Andean highlands.

There was no money, no private ownership of land, no general commerce, hence no middlemen, speculators, or commercial monopolies, nor any personal property beyond one's clothing and bedding and tools. The agriculturist owned his tools, his wife her loom; the soldier owned his weapons. An individual might own a few llamas, but the herds and their increase were frequently community property. There was no hoarding since there was nothing to hoard, hence no jealousies. Theft existed and was punished severely, but there was little that was worth stealing. Gold and silver were abundant, but were the property of the state and possessed no intrinsic or commerical value. They were used only for decorating the shrines and temples of the Sun and the palaces and persons of the Sapa Inca and his court. As with gold and silver, so with rare feathers to be used in textiles, such luxuries as fish from the sea or vegetables from the coastal regions, and the exquisite wool of the vicuña.

Since there was no money or any monetary equivalent, it follows that there were no banks, no mortgages, no loan sharks or time payments, and no stock markets or gambling upon the success or failure of crops yet unsown. Should crops fail, all suffered, but there could be no accompanying panic caused by monetary inflation or deflation. As a matter of fact, the possibility of crop failures was shrewdly anticipated by the ruling caste. No small portion of the products of the church and state fields was stored away in granaries to be redistributed to the people of any district afflicted by flood or drought or other disaster.

There were taxes, of course, if one wishes to interpret as taxation the direct tribute made by the individual household to the church and the state. That tribute was apportioned very justly according to the productive capacity of the community, and it was payable in work, either in the fields or in building the shrines, temples, palaces, and other structures which were everywhere in the land. The Incas were builders upon a scale grander than that of any other prehistoric people of this hemisphere. They were builders on such a scale that their conquerors explained such huge construction works as the fortress of Sacsahuamán, on the heights above Cuzco, very simply as being the handiwork of the devil—an explanation which may have been entirely adequate for the devout of the sixteenth century but is rather unsatisfactory archaeology. The Conquistadores tried zealously to destroy the Incaic structures but admitted failure very early in the game. An unbelievable number of walls in Cuzco stand today as they were in pre-conquest days, and the Inca Pachacutec himself has walked between the dark barriers on either side of Hatunrumiyoc Street.

It may be a slight exaggeration to say that Pachacutec—"possibly the greatest man ever to spring from a native race in America"—walked. On occasions of state and on his journeyings from one section of his empire to another, he and his empress rode in palanquins borne on the shoulders of men. Only the head of the state was so honored, however. Ancient Peru had its aristocracy, but it knew no "man on horseback," no group which rode while the less fortunate walked. The Sapa Inca was little warmer beneath vicuña wool than was the humble farmer in a poncho made from the coarser fleece of the llama. The Sinchi Rosa Palace was little more comfortable during the Andean winter than the huts of the *ayllu cuna*. The thatched roof of one leaked or burned as readily as that of the other; neither possessed fireplaces or chimneys; and the lice of Cuzco probably leaped as readily from peasant to Inca as they leap today from Quechua Indian to upper-class Peruvian or to the gringo visitor.

The language of those Quechuas, and there are some three million of them in Peru today, is identical with that spoken by the Incaic peoples from which they are descended. It is possible that the members of the Inca caste spoke among themselves a dialect differing slightly from the speech of the commoners, and the inference has been drawn that this "court language" was the tongue spoken at mythical Tambu-Tocca, whence the culture-hero Manco Capac came to conquer Cuzco Valley, and was carefully preserved as evidence of caste superiority. That may have been, but for ordinary purposes the ruling caste thought run-of-the-mine Quechua quite satisfactory, sufficiently so that one of the first steps after the military conquest of any area was the introduction there of the Andean speech. That last is no small point among the many of Incaic shrewdness. National traditions vanish quickly as the language in which they are preserved dies.

The political, religious, and economic aspects of pre-historic Peru are vital to any study of the Conquest, and little can be lost by this pause to examine them—especially in this year of grace 1942 when machines of later development are running with such questionable efficiency.

The germ of greatness was in the *ayllu* or the small group of *ayllus* which entered the Cuzco Valley and either conquered the original inhabitants or dispossessed them and took over the area. Greatness and all that goes to make national supremacy: the germ of dynasty, of political and social organization, and a religion which was capable of expansion and which, expanding, could absorb. Even at the height of their imperial power the Incaic rulers never forgot that their empire found its roots in the household and in the individual. With the empire at its greatest there were only eight officials of political authority between the most humble farmer—the *camaya-cuna,* head of a household—in the most remote province and the divine person of the Sapa Inca in Cuzco.

The Land of the Four Sections, that empire was called, and those sections were named, quite simply, the North, the South, the East, and the West. Over each was an official—of the Incaic caste, of course—who might be called a viceroy. Beneath him was a varying number of governors, each responsible for a *quamán* or province, which consisted of approximately forty thousand households. At the foot of the ladder was the individual, the head of the household, with a "chief," supervisor, deputy, or whatever one may wish to call him over each ten household groups, another over each fifty, each hundred, and each five hundred and thousand. Then came the "chiefs of ten thousand," four in each *quamán.* There were no contacts between officials of equal rank, hence no questionable or conflicting authority. The chain led far more directly from the peasant to the Sapa Inca than from the American citizen to the nation's chief executive. There were rough equivalents of township, borough, city, county, or state government, but no legislatures, no political parties or elections. There were judges, yes, but no such elaborate judicial system as democratic government has developed. Since there was no written language there could have been no governmental red tape.

107

There were other officials, of course, but none which interfered with that direct line. There were tribute collectors and "keepers of the *quipu*," the last being those responsible for figuring the accounts and the amount of tribute due church and state from each locality. The *quipu*, as the reader probably knows, was a varying number of knotted cords used both as a mnemonic recorder and as a calculating device comparable to the abacus. It has been said—usually in fiction—that to those initiated in its mysteries the *quipu* was equivalent to a written record and that all of Incaic history and lore was preserved thereby. The statement is quite untrue and has little support even in the misinformation so frequently set down as fact by the chroniclers.

There were laws, naturally, and the penalties for breaking them were severe. Theft was punished by public flogging for the first offense, by flogging and torture for the second, and by death for the third. The death penalty was also exacted for the killing of any female llama, alpaca, or guanaco or for killing a vicuña of either sex. The last-named animals were crown property, and only members of the Incaic caste might wear garments woven from their soft fur. The rape of an *accla-cuna*, a Chosen Woman, picturesquely called Virgin of the Sun, also was rewarded by death if the rapist was a commoner. Such pastimes were reserved for the Sapa Inca and his immediate court.

There were various methods of inflicting the death penalty. It might be—and usually was—swift and comparatively painless strangulation, it might be a lingering agony under torments somewhat less ghastly than those introduced to the land by the Conquistadores, or it might be hanging by the

108

feet—a method somewhat slower than by the neck but swifter than would be imagined.

To revert for a moment to the punishment for theft: if the individual stole because of hunger or personal misery the penalty was inflicted upon the official whose business it was to see that no such forgotten men existed in the community.

The prisons were usually reserved for traitors or conspirators against the Inca, and if the chroniclers' descriptions of those institutions are to be relied upon they were the ultimate in horror. The offender was thrust naked into labyrinthine passages, their floors strewn with sharp flints, where vipers, scorpions, and other venomous creatures had been released. The unfortunate who escaped the poisoned fangs and stings might expect to fall victim to the ferocious pumas, bears, and tigers (jaguars) which also had the freedom of the gloomy tunnels. How many of the beasts of prey were killed by the adders and scorpions is not stated. It is probably true, however, that near Cuzco was a prison where offenders who were members of the Incaic caste were immured for life. Royalty has never been eager to make public display of its scandals.

On the whole, one is less impressed by the barbarity of the punishments inflicted than by the great number of crimes which were entirely absent from the penal code under the empire. Since there was neither money nor commerce, there were no such crimes as embezzlement, forgery, breach of contract, or a host of others which exist under civil law.

The state church of pre-Conquest Peru is of comparatively little significance to this narrative. It was, as has been said, a sun worship that was intensified rather than complicated by the veneration accorded the Sun's wife-sister *Mama Quilla*,

109

the Moon. The stars were the children of that celestial pair and respected as such. The thunder and the lightning, the rainbow, meteors, and comets also had place in the pantheon; nor was there any home that did not have its *conopas,* its lares and penates, the little kindly gods of the hearth and the threshold. It is more than possible that the sun worship of the Quechua-speaking highlanders grew from the earlier, more primitive animism the existence of which would be evidenced by the survival of the household deities.

More than that primitive animism was preserved in the worship of the Sun, however. Several of the surviving origin legends state that the conquering *ayllu* under Manco Capac came to the Cuzco Valley from the south, from the region of Lake Titicaca and the high plateaus of Bolivia where grew that culture, far older than the Incaic, which is called Tiahuanaco from the great city which once stood some fifteen or twenty miles east of the extreme southern tip of the lake. Tiahuanaco was no "empire" in the sense of the imperial proportions and organization of the Incaic dominions, but its sway extended throughout the Titicaca drainage, to Cuzco and Ollantaytambo in the north and to the coastal regions of Peru. Over all that area men bowed to the god of Tiahuanaco—the Creator-God, who was Viracocha in the highlands and Pachacamac on the coast. He had other names —Con was one of them—but all that matters is that he was a deity who within a few centuries might have developed into an abstract God, Creator and All-Father. Tiahuanaco, so far as we can tell, died of slow decay; there is no indication, ethnic or archaeological, that it was a victim of conquest. But Viracocha lived and was remembered, and his worship was borne to the Cuzco area by the legendary Manco Capac

110

and preserved throughout Incaic times behind the convenient screen of the more popular, more easily comprehended veneration of Inti, the Sun. Pachacamac, on the coast, degenerated to a rather sordid and filthy image worship; but in the clean, cold air of the highlands the cult of Viracocha retained a rich and pure philosophy until the end of the empire.

From the very beginning of the Incaic period, Viracocha was the god of the classes; worship of him and instruction in his philosophies were strictly reserved for members of the Incan caste. The masses had Inti, the Sun, and the lesser deities. They had the temples and shrines which were built throughout the land. The elaborate festivals and ceremonies were developed for them—but the rulers who participated in those festivals and ceremonies knew that the sun and the moon and all else in nature were but aspects of Viracocha, who was supreme over the universe. The Sapa Inca, especially when the eyes of his people were upon him, bowed respectfully to the Sun or its image in the temple; in his private adoration of Viracocha he prayed humbly to God.

It is greatly to be regretted that so little, so pathetically little, is known of the worship of Viracocha by the imperial caste in Peru. The Conquistadores and the priests who came with them saw Viracocha only as the grotesque anthropomorphic bas-relief carved upon the famous monolithic doorway in ruined Tiahuanaco. Viracocha worship and Sun veneration were but heathen idolatry to be overthrown and demolished and replaced by the Cross. Were our knowledge of that private spiritual philosophy of the Incan rulers more adequate, the task of analyzing the growth of the empire would be much simpler.

111

Viracocha, the Creator, was a father-god far more kindly than the God of the Conquistadores. The Incas conquered, but as soon as their conquests were completed they proceeded swiftly to reconcile the subjugated peoples by kindness and by tolerance—a policy which imperialists and dictators of all time might well emulate. The high Andes never looked down upon such wholesale blood orgies as were practiced in Mexico and in Yucatan. Human sacrifices were not unknown in ancient Peru, but they were made very rarely. A Chosen Woman, consecrated to the Sun, might be sacrificed to that divinity and sometimes was. Far more often, however, lifelong preservation of her virginity was all that the benignant deity asked. For such humanities the hidden Viracocha worship was undoubtedly responsible.

Let it be said here that the Houses of the Chosen Women did shelter those who were truly Virgins of the Sun. The houses were established everywhere throughout the empire with the largest, naturally, in Cuzco, and primarily were a source of supply of concubines for the Inca and members of the Inca caste. There was no disgrace in such service. Others were given in marriage by the Inca to courtiers or officials whom he wished to honor by such personal attentions. The ruler of a conquered province, brought to Cuzco as a hostage, was frequently given a wife from among the *accla-cuna*.

From the beginning the Incas were conquerors. There were ten in the line from the culture-hero Manco Capac, and their reigns covered a period of four and one-quarter centuries—from about 1105 A.D. to 1529. Ten emperors, and there was none of them that did not add something to the empire, who did not leave the Land of the Four Sections greater than he had found it. The roll of those emperors may

112

be briefly called that we may follow the growth of the empire and set the stage for the landing of Pizarro and his brothers.

1: SINCHI ROCA, THE WAR-CHIEF ROCA. [*circa* 1105-1140]. According to legend the son of Manco Capac. He conquered the Urubamba Valley from Cuzco south to Vilcañota [La Raya] and consolidated that long strip of territory. In his reign, the first of which we have record, the foundations of Incaic pomp and ceremony were laid.

2: LLOQUE YUPANQUI. [1140-1195] His accession established the dynasty. He extended the empire to the south, entering the territory of the Colla peoples and bringing all of the western shore of Lake Titicaca under Incaic domination.

3: MAYTA CAPAC. [1195-1230] First of the empire builders. Conquered the eastern Collao, including the ruined city of Tiahuanaco where he and his engineers learned the architecture which resulted in the massive structures reared in Cuzco. He then added to the empire all territory west and southwest of Titicaca to the Maritime Cordillera and the coastal slope.

4: CAPAC YUPANQUI. [1230-1250] Strengthened the empire's hold over the transcordillera region and extended the domain to tidewater. Was first to become a ruler rather than a military leader and delegated much of the campaigning to his generals. Took the field himself in conquering more of the territory included in the present Bolivia. Was first of the rulers to practice the transfer of large numbers of conquered peoples to areas that were thoroughly "Inca-ized," and replacing them with those who could be depended upon to establish Incaic cultures in the new territories. The empire at the time of his death included about 120,000 square miles. By this time, too, the Incas had established the dynastic custom of thoroughly training the heir to the throne in the arts of war and of government.

5: INCA ROCA [1250-1315] He, too, extended the conquests to the south and moved the boundaries of the empire eastward from Cuzco to beyond the Eastern Cordillera. He brought war to the Chancas, whose territory blocked Inca expansion to the west and northwest and achieved a tenuous hold upon their lands. Under Roca the systematic enlargement and beautification of Cuzco began.

6: YAHUAR HUACCAC. [1315-1347] The only weakling among the Incan rulers, and the only one who was forced to abdicate. He was supplanted by his son Hatun Tupac when he would do nothing to block the advance of a Chanca force toward Cuzco. Under his reign, however, there was a small expansion of territory in the extreme south.

7: VIRACOCHA INCA [1347-1400] Born Hatun Tupac and as crown prince had a vision in which the Creator-God appeared to him and warned him of the Chanca attack. He deposed his father, organized the defense, and whipped the Chancas in a great battle. He pushed the imperial domain beyond the Chanca territory and added Tucma—modern Tucamán—in what is now the Argentine. Though he added comparatively little to the empire, which included 150,000 square miles at his death, he greatly strengthened the internal organization.

8: PACHACUTEC. [1400-1448] "A very great man, possibly the greatest that ever sprang from a native race in America." So writes the scholarly Means of the Inca under whom the Land of the Four Sections attained the apogee of its glory. He extended the conquests in every direction and increased the territorial area of the empire to 260,000 square miles yet preserved political unity throughout the vast domain and greatly strengthened the internal organization. The famous fortress city of Machu Picchu, on the Urubamba north of Cuzco, was built during his reign.

9: TUPAC YUPANQUI. [1448-1482] Established at least a nominal jurisdiction over the jungle tribes of the Madre de Dios and Beni River basins, bringing war to them by means of an immense flotilla of canoes. Extended the empire south as far as the Maule River in Chile and north to the frontiers of the Kingdom of Quitu, the present Ecuador whose capital, Quito, preserves the ancient name. The actual subjugation of the kingdom was accomplished by the armies under the leadership of the twenty-year-old Crown Prince Titu Cusi Hualpa. It is perhaps interesting to note that the marriage of Tupac Yupanqui to his sister, Mama Ocllo, is the first union of that nature in the dynasty which seems to be definitely proven. Many of the early chroniclers—oh, so easily shocked by heathen customs!—have asserted that such incestuous marriages were the rule among the Incaic emperors.

115

Shortly before his death Tupac Yupanqui abdicated voluntarily because of ill health and relinquished the "crown"—the *llautu,* a thick, particolored fillet of vicuña wool which was wrapped several times about the head—to Titu Cusi Hualpa, who reigned as:

10: HUAYNA CAPAC [1482-1529] Truly, the last Sapa Inca, the last Lord Inca of the Land of the Four Sections, which under him reached its greatest territorial extent, an area approximately that of all the Atlantic seaboard states. Centralized rule could not be maintained over so vast a domain even with the aid of the remarkable system of communications by means of runners who traveled over the even more remarkable roads which radiated from Cuzco to the most distant provinces. With Huayna Capac the empire had already entered upon the decline which comes inevitably to over-expanded organizations; a decline which was not permitted to continue its normal course but which ended, abruptly and terribly, in the Conquest.

He is a romantic figure, this Huayna Capac, last of the Incas and the only one whose heart has been bared to us. As legal wives he had two of his sisters, or more probably half sisters, putting aside the first when she proved sterile and taking a younger, Mama Rahua Ocllo, who bore him the legitimate heir to the throne, Tupac Cusi Hualpa, whom history was to know as Huáscar. That royal chore being chored, Huayna Capac was free to turn to the woman he loved, to Paccha Duchicela, who was the daughter of the King of Quitu. After the conquest of her homeland she had been brought to Cuzco and placed in the great House

116

of the Chosen Women which stood between the Huaca Pata, the Holy Square, and Coricancha, the Temple of the Sun. Huayna Capac found her there and mated with her. That in itself was not unusual. There were some twelve or fifteen hundred Chosen Women in the Cuzco house, and all save those few who had been formally consecrated to the Sun and dedicated to life-long virginity were available to the Sapa Inca. Throughout his life Huayna Capac maintained a harem which can be regarded only with awe and described only as enormous. He mated with many maidens from distant provinces, with daughters of conquered chieftains, but it is certain that he loved his princess from the northern lands and equally certain that he transferred that love to the son she bore him; the son Atahualpa, who also was to be called the last Inca.

Paccha Duchicela died there in Cuzco, and after her death Huayna Capac—and by this we may judge the depth of his passion—turned his back upon the city which had been the capital of the empire for four centuries and took his son Atahualpa—the "cherished bastard" as he has been sneeringly called—back to the lands over which his maternal ancestors had ruled. The legitimate heir, Huáscar, was left in Cuzco in charge of the priests, statesmen, and generals who were to educate him and prepare him for the day when he should wear the particolored *llautu*.

Huayna Capac may have seen that the huge empire was tottering by reason of its own topheaviness, hence should be broken up into smaller states more easily

117

governed. He may have wished only to assure the future of Atahualpa, who had, through his mother, a legitimate claim to the crown of Quitu. The latter is the more probable, for Huayna Capac did that of which none of his predecessors had even dreamed: he proposed that a conquered province should be restored to its former status. Quitu, he said, should again become an independent kingdom and be given to Atahualpa; all the rest of the empire should pass to the legitimate Huáscar. If there were terms other than that fiat of the Sapa Inca, we have not learned of them, but the crown prince journeyed from Cuzco to Quitu and pledged obedience to the decree.

Power politics, perhaps, that partition which was determined upon in 1523 or 1524, but there is more to be told of the passion of Huayna Capac and his love for the northern Andes where Paccha Duchicela had been born. He lived for several more years, long enough to hear rumors of strange men with white skins who had landed on the northern coasts. The empire was at peace, and the Sapa Inca never returned to Cuzco. He divided his time between his palaces and harems in Tumipampa and those in the capital, Quitu. He died, and his body was borne to Cuzco and there wrapped in cerements and placed with those of his ancestors. But the heart was first taken from that body and interred in the Quitu he loved so well.

Huayna Capac died about 1526, and within little more than a year the land was torn asunder by civil war. There is no

118

place here for more than the briefest mention of that fratricidal struggle, on the causes and the conduct of which no two of the authorities are in complete agreement. Huáscar may have been gentle and easy-going, lulled into false security by the peace which had blessed the empire for a dozen years or more. He may have proved an unpopular ruler, iconoclastic in his disregard of ancient traditions and equally ancient privilege, and thereby have created enemies and potential rebels among his own courtiers. It was Atahualpa, however, who refused to be contented with the crown of Quitu and whose ambition—doubtless encouraged by the anti-Huáscar faction in Cuzco—led him to recruit a force of some thirty thousand warriors and march to the southward. A thousand miles in an air line, more than half as far again over the mountainous terrain, lay between Quitu and the Incan capital. One must choose between violently contradictory accounts of that march and of the campaign of which it was a part. Atahualpa may have encountered virtually no opposition until he was at the very gates of Cuzco. He may have engaged in mighty battles while he was still within his own frontiers and have been forced to fight his way over every league of the long march.

All that really matters—and on this there is agreement—is that the invaders eventually reached the Plain of Xaquixahuana, the present Zúrite, less than twenty miles from Cuzco, where their force met an army about its own size, all the troops which the easy-going or ill-advised Huáscar seems to have been able to muster. The battle that followed resulted in an overwhelming victory for the Quiteños. Huáscar was taken prisoner, and his generals and principal officers were either killed in the fighting or summarily slain after the rout.

The imperial *llautu* was stripped from the emperor's head and wound about the brow of his half brother, the "cherished bastard," who marched into Cuzco in triumph and there proclaimed himself Sapa Inca of the Land of the Four Sections.

That usurpation may have been marked by the execution of some who were loyal to Huáscar and the idea of legitimate dynastic succession. There is nothing credible, however, in the lurid account of Garcilaso de la Vega which tells of the wholesale and treacherous slaughter of every man, woman, and child of the Incan caste who could be found, in order that no legitimate claimant to the *llautu* might appear to contest the usurpation. Were that even remotely true, it is scarcely likely that Huáscar would have been spared—as he was spared—and imprisoned in the fortress of Jauja, and there treated with the kindness and courtesy due his blood and the exalted rank from which he had fallen. It seems far more evident that the usurpation of Atahualpa was accepted with amazing placidity by noble, priest, and commoner throughout the vast empire. The accusations of diabolical atrocities, says Prescott, are "not to be admitted on the evidence of an Indian partisan, the sworn foe of his house, and repeated by Castilian chroniclers who may seek by blazoning the enormities of Atahualpa to find some apology for the cruelty of their countrymen towards him."

What ceremonies, one wonders, attended the first formal appearance of the Sapa Inca Atahualpa before his people? Was the black llama, the perfect beast, coal black from nose to tail, sacrificed as at the great Feast of the Sun at the time of the summer solstice? Did the Villac Umu, the High Pontiff, rip open the struggling animal's side and tear out

120

entire the still-pulsating heart, the lungs still expanded by the last breath, and read from the steaming viscera the omens promised by the Sun to the new ruler? Did the Villac Umu —the "Soothsayer Who Speaks"—dare read those portents aright and tell Atahualpa that the white strangers of whom he had heard would come again to the shores of his empire and that within two years of their coming he would die miserably and the Land of the Four Sections become a conquered province?

Chapter Six

OF ALL THE CAMPAIGNS in the conquest of the New World, only in that of Cortez in Mexico is it possible to trace, almost from the beginning, a definite plan. Cortez—religious zealot, ambitious imperialist, and military commander unsurpassed—learned, not only of the power and wealth of the rulers of Tenochtitlan, but of the hatred with which the caciques of the neighboring states regarded their conquerors. He demonstrated Spanish strength by the weight of Spanish swords; but he promptly reconciled the chieftains thus conquered, and when he approached the Aztec capital his little force of some four hundred men-at-arms was supported by six thousand Indian allies.

No such long-distance view characterized the approach of Francisco Pizarro to the shores of Peru. Indeed, when he left Panamá early in January of 1531 his only objective seems to have been the looting of the rich coastal city of Tumbez where he had been received so hospitably on his previous visit. That accomplished, he would establish a settlement similar to that of Darien, a bridgehead from which fresh troops could extend the conquest. Diego Almagro, as usual, was left in Panamá to recruit those reinforcements from

122

among the new arrivals from Spain and the veterans of the Central American conquests.

Francisco Pizarro was not, nor would he ever be, a truly brilliant military leader. Few men had survived suffering and privation as terrible as those he had experienced in Darien, at the Port of Famine, and on the Isle of Gallo—yet within a fortnight of his sailing from Panamá he deliberately repeated the error which had caused only disaster in the past. When head winds and ocean currents threatened to prevent the little squadron from rounding the cape of Santa Elena, he ordered the captains to drop anchor in San Mateo Bay where he disembarked the fighting men. He would advance along the coast to Tumbez, he said, while the ships stood off from the shore and endeavored to round the point.

That march may have served to toughen soldiers who for nearly a year had idled in the wine shops and bordellos of Panamá—both less numerous in 1531 than in this year of grace and enlightenment—while their leaders bickered. Floundering through the coastal jungles, swimming the many short rivers which plunged from the mountains to the sea either toughened men or killed them. There was one pleasant interruption when they reached a village where— after slaughtering the inhabitants—they replenished their exhausted food supplies and found a considerable store of gold and silver ornaments and of emeralds, a gem which the chroniclers assure us was very abundant in that region. The veins in which the bright beryl is found may still exist in the coastal mountains of Ecuador, but the Indians of the region have guarded their secret well for more than four centuries. Only on the map will one find *esmeraldas* in Ecuador today, in the name of a river and of a squalid little hamlet near its mouth.

Still, we are told that one of the emeralds taken by Pizarro was as large as a pigeon's egg and that the soldiers collected many others nearly as fine. Stout fellows, those men-at-arms, and devout religionists all. To doubt the word of a priest was akin to heresy, and they believed the Dominican friar de Pedraza when he told them that the true emerald would not shatter even when struck with a hammer. They tested the gems they had taken and tossed them aside as false when they broke. Pedro Pizarro must have noticed that the good father carefully picked up the fragments, and he must have heard that the friar sold them for an excellent price in Panamá; otherwise he would not have mentioned the incident in his account of the discovery and conquest of Peru.

From that village of Coaque, Pizarro sent his three ships back to Panamá with the usual order to return with more men and more supplies. He also forwarded, as a stimulus to recruiting, twenty thousand castillanos in gold. The sight of the gold induced many to enroll under Pizarro's banner, and several detachments of reinforcements joined the expedition before it turned the point of Santa Elena and reached—the natives ferried them from the mainland in canoes—the Island of Puná in the Gulf of Guayaquil. Here, Pizarro decided, he would wait for his ships before advancing upon Tumbez.

There was little friendship between the islanders of Puná and their neighbors at Tumbez on the mainland, although a truce seems to have been called some time before Pizarro and his men reached the island, else a number of the men of Tumbez would not have paddled their *balsas* across the bay to renew their friendship with the Spaniards who had visited them a few years before. The white men were told nothing of conditions in the mainland city nor of the men who had remained there when the previous expedition set sail for Panamá, but the Indian interpreters Pizarro had obtained there speedily informed their masters that the islanders were planning a treacherous attack. Pizarro believed the story and made prisoners of the plotting caciques before they could act. It matters little whether the men were guilty or whether the story of the conspiracy was invented by the wily Felipillo. Pizarro considered the proof sufficient to warrant his turning the captives over to the men of Tumbez, who promptly butchered them.

There followed a sharp skirmish with the islanders. Several Spaniards were killed, Hernando Pizarro received a spear-thrust in the leg, and the defeated natives retreated to the jungles and maintained a guerrilla warfare with the whites as long as they remained on the island. That battle was the last in which the invaders were to engage for some months. Pizarro had learned in Darien that the chances for successful colonization were infinitely greater if friendly relations were established with the natives. He prepared to move across the bay to Tumbez with the intention of renewing his cordial relations with the people there. The advance was greatly facilitated by the arrival of two ships from Panamá, bearing the welcome addition of a hundred volunteers and a number of horses. The recruits were commanded by a young *caballero* whom Pizarro had met before and whom—it is reasonable to believe—his brothers may have known in their native Estremadura where he had been born. His name was Hernando de Soto; he had come to Darien in 1519, was a veteran of the fighting in Veragua, and had returned from the northern provinces shortly after the brothers had sailed from Panamá. He was to achieve considerable fame in Peru and—more important—a fortune of some two hundred thousand ducats which enabled him to marry a daughter of Pedrarias Davila and establish himself in a style befitting a *caballero*. The niche he occupies in history, however, is one to which he is not entitled: Hernando de Soto was not the discoverer of the Mississippi River.

The Spaniards found Tumbez in ruins. The great Temple of the Sun still stood, as did the fortress and a few of the more substantial houses, but of the remainder of the city scarcely one stone stood upon another. The magnificent golden decorations of the Temple and the adjoining House of the Chosen Women had vanished. So, incidentally, had Alonso de Molina and his unidentified companion or companions who had remained there. Neither the sacking of the city nor the disappearance of the Spaniards was ever satisfactorily explained. That Molina and his companions had been killed for attempting to despoil a Virgin of the Sun is quite understandable, but it is difficult to believe that so strong a city would have fallen before the attack of the islanders of Puná. That, however, was the story told Pizarro by the former *curaca*[1], or governor, of the place, who was captured in some skirmishing which attended the landing from the ships and the approach to the city. As to the fate of Alonso Molina and the other Spaniard, the governor said first that the men had died of disease, then that they had

---

[1] The man was called a *curaca*, or hereditary chieftain, by Pedro Pizarro. He was probably of much higher rank in the Incaic political setup. A *curaca* was merely the headman of a small village or of several *ayllus*.

been killed in the fighting which resulted in the destruction of the city, and finally that they had been slain for their outrageous acts. One of the Indians gave the leader a note which one of the doomed men had left for any of his countrymen who might come to Tumbez. "Know, whoever may chance to set foot in this land," Molina or his companion had written, "that it contains more gold and silver than there is iron in Biscay."

The situation at Tumbez came as a terrific blow to Francisco Pizarro and the shrewd Hernando, who was his second in command and most trusted adviser. The two had counted on the gold from that rich city to pay their debts in Panamá, to stimulate recruiting there, and to prove to the soldiers under their command that the "land of gold" was indeed a reality. Now, the ruined city could not even be considered as a site for a settlement—not with Puná and its savage inhabitants just across the bay—and the soldiers who had counted on looting the temple declared freely that Pizarro had merely invented that tale of wealth and that the Molina note, too, was a hoax.

Francisco Pizarro, the man, is never seen to better advantage than in such situations. In matters political and as an administrator, he was frequently vacillating and indecisive, but when the problem was entirely one of leadership and of a firm hand he proved himself a commander of extraordinary ability. He remained at Tumbez only long enough to gain all possible details of the civil war which had resulted in the overthrow of Huáscar and the accession of Atahualpa to the throne of the empire, then marched south some eighty miles to the Chira Valley where—in late May or early June of 1532—he attached the name of his patron saint to that of a Peruvian village and founded San Miguel de Tangarará, first attempt at permanent European settlement within the Land of the Four Sections. San Miguel de Piura, established in 1587 a few leagues farther south, is a direct descendant of that original settlement where the ruins of the not unpretentious structures erected by Pizarro may still be traced.

Several of the chroniclers have commented on the rigid discipline which Pizarro enforced on his men during that short march, and others have deduced therefrom the inauguration of a conciliatory policy toward the Indians encountered. The half-truth is dangerous. There was no wanton slaughtering of the peaceful agriculturalists, who received the strangers most hospitably, but when lands were needed for settlement and when local caciques must be taught to bow to the *regidor* and other civil authorities set in office, those lands were taken and that obedience enforced by the sword. A number of local headmen were killed as examples to their followers, who might object to being allotted, family by family, to the new officials—for the heinous system of the *repartimiento* was immediately installed. Busy soldiers— even if they are kept busy only in superintending the labor of Indian slaves—have little time to complain or to plan rebellion, and the two Pizarros saw to it that the men under their command had few idle moments. Too, some store of golden ornaments had been taken at Tumbez and in the robbing of the caciques of the Chira Valley, and these were publicly melted down. No better example of Francisco's hold over his men, or of Hernando's glib persuasion, can be found than in the circumstance that the soldiers relinquished their claims and turned their shares over to the two brothers: a loan which would be repaid them, it was promised, from the first major loot taken. The funds thus obtained were sent back to Panamá with the ships and applied upon the leaders' debts.

The major loot was closer than any of them imagined. While San Miguel de Tangarará was building, Hernando de Soto and the small force of cavalry was employed in exploring the upper Chira Valley and the western slope of the mountains. Here he learned—and promptly informed the Pizarros—that the Inca himself, the great Atahualpa, was now at a mountain city only ten or twelve days' journey from San Miguel. His army was with him, the same army which had won the fight at Xaquixahuana, but there was little information of the size of that force, and nowhere in the history of the conquest of the New World can one find an instance of the Conquistadores' being daunted by numbers alone. Man to man or a hundred to one; it was all the same. Pizarro left a garrison of some fifty men, the most of them sick or otherwise unfitted for active service, to hold the settlement of San Miguel and on September 24, 1532, turned his face toward the mountains. His force amounted in all to 177 men of which 67 were mounted. In the entire company there were but three arquebusiers—hence but three mobile firearms!—and fewer than twenty crossbow-men. Some horsemen may have carried maces at their saddlebows, pikes were borne by possibly a third of the foot soldiers, but the weapon which all bore and upon which the Spaniard placed his greatest trust was the sword. One hundred and seventy-seven men with three clumsy, inaccurate firearms to conquer an empire! Forget the motives of that conquest: the lust for gold, the sordid hatred of the priests for the heathen, the petty politics and scheming jealousies among the leaders—

is there anywhere in all of history an example of more sublime courage?

It has been said that the expedition ascended the Chira Valley from San Miguel, then followed along the western foot of the cordillera for nearly a hundred miles to the Rio de la Leche, by the valley of which the party achieved the painful climb to the highlands. It is far more probable that the barrier of the Andes was surmounted more directly by following the Chira and its principal southern fork. Only by such a route could the invaders have reached Huancapampa, which is nearly seventy miles north of the headwaters of the Rio de la Leche. Too, we read that Pizarro and his followers found shelter in the *tambos*—properly *tampus*—or inns which were spaced regularly along the great road. This road followed the mountains and their interior valleys; it was not laid in the western foothills.

By whatever course, it was a long and perilous journey, and before it was well started Pizarro took those steps necessary to eliminate malcontents or potential trouble makers. He repeated the challenge to manhood which he had first made on the Isle of Gallo. No one, he told his men, was wanted on the expedition who had the slightest doubt of its eventual success. San Miguel was poorly garrisoned, and he, the commander, would be glad to see the force there strengthened. Those who wished to turn back could do so now without disgrace. As for himself and his brothers, their purpose was to continue the adventure to the end with those —whether few or many—who chose to accompany them.

Nine men quit, five horsemen and four from the ranks of the infantry, and thus did Francisco Pizarro strengthen his hold over those who remained. If they weakened now, if

130

they complained of hardship or of toil, there was none to say that the opportunity to withdraw had not been given him. It is easy to imagine that the two elder brothers smiled grimly as the nine men left the camp and that there was a keener note in the trumpets' summonses, a sharper command in the captains' orders as the ranks were formed the next day for the march to Zaran, to Cajas in the hills, and then on to Guancabamba (today's Huancapampa), which lay on the great road which the Incas had flung over plain and desert and mountain from Quitu to the capital of Cuzco. Farther south on that road was the mountain city of Cajamarca, whither the Inca had come to enjoy the warm waters of the mineral springs for which the place was famous.

Throughout the march the Spanish leaders were in communication, both direct and indirect, with Atahualpa. Hernando de Soto, ordered to scout the town of Cajas, returned from that place with an Incan noble who presented Pizarro with various gifts and in the name of his master Atahualpa invited the Spaniards to visit the Inca at his mountain retreat. The emperor was extremely curious and sublimely confident. There were a thousand places along the road where the little force of whites could have been trapped and annihilated, but that course never entered the imperial mind. Atahualpa wanted to see the white-skinned strangers in the flesh; he wanted to hear their tales of another king beyond the seas who claimed that all the Land of the Four Sections was his. It never occurred to Atahualpa or his generals that this little handful of men could even dream of conquering an empire which counted its soldiers in the hundreds of thousands. Nor, let it be said, is there the slightest evidence that Pizarro, at this time, entertained any thought of a mili-

131

tary victory. With every league of his advance into the high-lands, he gained additional knowledge of the strength and the resources of the Inca. He saw the six-foot road, sometimes paved for many leagues with stone slabs, and the suspension bridges by which that highway crossed the mad mountain torrents and the deep ravines. He learned that the road led to Cuzco, the capital, and that others like it radiated from that navel of the empire—Cuzco, in Quechua, means "navel" —to all sections of the land. This Inca was no petty cacique such as those with whom he had fought in Darien; he was a king of a mighty land, a land far larger than Spain itself, and it would be victory enough if Francisco Pizarro could win that ruler's friendship, could obtain permission to maintain his settlement at San Miguel, and trade hawks' bells and mirrors and bright glass beads for the gold which was held valueless in this land of Peru. So thinking, Pizarro accepted the invitation to visit the Inca, he sent presents by the ambassador who had called on him, and he continued his march to the south. And then . . . and then, when within a few days' march of Cajamarca, he was informed that he had been cleverly victimized. He and his small force were to be permitted to reach the valley in which Cajamarca stood and would then be surrounded by the army of the Inca and slaughtered.

The most ardent defender of the Pizarros cannot find even a shred of evidence to indicate that the Incan leaders had made such a plan. The story was wrung from a prisoner taken by Hernando Pizarro in some mountain village, who first refused to answer the questions put to him. Under torture —how severe it was we are not told—he found his tongue and blurted out the tale of Incan treachery. Atahualpa and his army, he said, were encamped in the mountains surrounding Cajamarca and would swoop down upon the little force of white men as soon as it entered the valley.

The task of the historian and biographer would be simplified if there survived a record of the council of war which took place that night or the next day in the commander's quarters. The two Pizarros were present, of course, and Hernando de Soto, another veteran fighter, must have been heard; nor is it difficult to imagine that the scheming Dominican, Friar Vicente de Valverde, chief of the altogether reprehensible crew of ecclesiastics who accompanied the expedition, raised his voice to assure the more practical-minded strategists that God and Saint James would fight for them should fighting be necessary. There was but one decision possible for that council: to advance might be to walk into a trap which the wily Inca had set for them, but to retreat would be fatal. They had already penetrated so deeply into the mountains that it would be impossible for them to win their way back to the sea unmolested. They must advance and take what might come. It is possible that at that first council or those which followed it was suggested that Pizarro emulate Cortez in Mexico and by some bold stroke capture Atahualpa as Cortez had captured Montezuma and held him as a hostage for the good conduct of his subjects. It is possible, although there is no hint of such premeditation in the words with which Oviedo tells us Pizarro encouraged his troops.

"Go forward as Spaniards should," he said, "and do not fear either the great number of the savages or the smallness of our Christian force. For God helps and protects His own in their greatest need, and He will destroy the heathen and humble their pride and bring them to a knowledge of our holy Catholic faith."

And, the historian continues, all shouted for him to lead on as he thought best and they would follow with a right good will and do their duty in the service of God and the king.

Francisco Pizarro took command of the advance, forty horsemen under Soto and sixty of the infantry; his brother Hernando led the smaller force which followed with the meager baggage and the artillery—if that term can be applied to the two small cannon called *falconetes* which, with three arquebuses, were the only firearms the little army possessed. The chroniclers have given us a lurid account of the difficulties encountered in crossing the last ridge of mountains to the open valley where Cajamarca stands upon the Eriznejas River, more than nine thousand feet above the sea. Anyone who has visited Cajamarca is justified in assuming that the Conquistadores either had no local guides, did not trust the guides which they may have had, or were deliberately misled by the Indians, who may have wished to delay the strangers' entrance to the city. There have been no changes in the Andes since 1532, and there are several passes in the ranges west of the city which offer comparatively easy access to the valley. The delaying action seems the most probable, since we are told that Pizarro was visited in his camp by ambassadors from the Inca, who conveyed the ruler's wish to provide suitable accommodations for his visitors in the city. The envoy brought a gift of several llamas to the Spanish commander and offered him *chicha* to drink. The Europeans had probably tasted the maize beer of the Andean highlands many times, but it is doubtful if the beverage had ever before been offered them in a golden cup.

The Pizarros and their followers entered Cajamarca on November 15, 1532. They found the town, then housing considerably more than its present population of about six thousand, completely deserted. Moreover, the mountain slopes to the south, overlooking the city, were covered with the tents and pavilions of the mightiest army which any of those fighting men had yet beheld in the New World. The suspicion that they were indeed walking into a trap flared up anew, nor can we blame them therefor.

It seems odd that a city of eight or ten thousand would be evacuated in order to make room for less than two hundred men and some sixty horses, which was the explanation given by the Inca's ambassador, but nowhere is there any indication that the Inca and his generals had actually planned the ambuscade which the Spaniards feared. The only explanation which seems to fit the circumstances is that Atahualpa wished to dazzle the strangers with the triumphal entry which he afterward made and to impress them with the power of a ruler so mighty that his mere word could empty a city.

Cajamarca was an important place and had been under Incaic domination since the days of Tupac Yupanqui. Here the invaders saw for the first time the impressive masonry used by the Incas in all their public buildings. All who wrote of the entry into Cajamarca tell of the massive buildings which surrounded the irregular plaza, of the "fortress" at one end, and of the other "fortress" built on a hill commanding the town and surrounded by a spiral wall which made three circuits of the hill. The second building was probably a defensive structure; it is more probable that the first was a

135

palace used by the Inca on his occasional visits to the city. The plaza was surrounded by low buildings, also of stone, which the chroniclers describe as having been barracks for the Inca's soldiers. The Sun Temple was on the outskirts of the city and was far less sumptuously adorned with gold than similar structures in other cities.

The city was entered late in the afternoon at the height of a sharp, though brief, storm of mingled snow and sleet. Francisco Pizarro, after a hasty survey of the place, ordered Soto to take forty horsemen and visit the Inca's camp—ostensibly in friendship but actually to scout the Peruvian position and report upon the strength of the Inca's forces. Soto could scarcely have reached the edge of the city before the commander sent his brother, Hernando Pizarro, after him with twenty additional troopers. The action, in all probability, was taken to impress the Inca and his court with the sight of virtually all the cavalry in the little army of the invaders; Hernando's detachment could scarcely have been a reinforcement in the event of hostilities. The Peruvian camp was in plain sight, and Pizarro undoubtedly realized how heavily he was outnumbered. The elder Pizarro left a complete record of that interview in a letter which he sent to the Royal Audience of the Indies, and the communication reached Santo Domingo while the historian Oviedo was living there. Oviedo, as excellent a reporter as ever lived, recognized the news value of the letter immediately and quoted it in entirety in his *General History of the Indies*.

Hernando Pizarro overtook Soto, and the two envoys rode together to the Inca's villa about a Spanish league south of the city where a number of warm springs poured into a large stone pool which had been built for the exclusive use of the

136

royal visitors. Atahualpa was seated on a low stool, which later accounts magnified into a massive golden throne but which actually was of wood. Soto seems to have identified him immediately by the *borla*—the name given by the Spaniards to the fringed *llautu*—he wore, and the deference paid him by his courtiers. The two Spaniards approached the Inca respectfully, we are told, but their contempt for any Indian, king or commoner, is clearly shown by the fact that neither they nor their men dismounted, an incivility which later events indicate was not prompted by a desire to be ready to escape on a moment's notice.

The conversation which followed, if Hernando Pizarro's report thereof is trustworthy, revealed Spanish arrogance on the one hand, Indian imperturbability on the other. Atahualpa did not reply, nor did his face change expression when the interpreter Felipillo repeated in the Quechua tongue Soto's invitation that he visit the Spanish commander in the city. One of his courtiers broke the long silence by saying, simply, "It is well."

That did not satisfy the irascible Hernando Pizarro, who brusquely ordered Felipillo to repeat the invitation and request the emperor to answer "with his own mouth." Atahualpa's reply was that he was observing a fast (a statement which was probably untrue since at that time of the year there were no celebrations so important as to be observed by fasting) but that it would end on the morrow when he and his court would visit the Spanish commander. "He may occupy the buildings on the plaza, and no others, until I come," the Inca concluded, "when I will order what is to be done."

An odd command, if translated correctly and if quoted

with equal accuracy by those who reported that interview, especially when we recall that the white men had been informed that the entire city had been evacuated that they might choose whatever quarters they might desire. There is much that is odd, much that is difficult to reconcile, in the various accounts. One would have it that Hernando Pizarro replied with a snarling attack on the fighting ability of the Peruvians; another that Atahualpa forgot his fast and his imperial dignity and berated the white men for their various excesses on the coast and especially for having stolen in Tumbez certain textiles which belonged to him.

It is difficult to accept fully either of those incidents. Far more credible is the exhibition of horsemanship attributed to Hernando de Soto. Neither the Inca nor any of his courtiers had ever seen a horse, and their dark eyes must have quickened at the sight of the ranked troopers and the tossing heads and nervous stampings of their mounts. Soto recognized that curiosity, or was informed thereof, and obliged by putting his trained charger through its paces. One maneuver, Father Cabello declares, was a leap which cleared twenty feet—this with a man in armor on the beast's back! In conclusion, Soto clapped spurs to his charger and raced in full speed toward the throne, nor halted until he was so close to the emperor that Atahualpa was sprinkled with the foam from the animal's lips. The Inca—call him usurper if you will, but he was a king and of the blood of kings!—neither moved nor changed expression although several of his courtiers retreated precipitately. They paid for that ignoble timidity with their lives, according to Pedro Pizarro. Atahualpa ordered them slain as soon as the Spaniards had left the camp.

The parley concluded with the still-mounted Spaniards being served with "sparkling" *chicha* in huge golden goblets offered by "dark-eyed beauties" of the Inca's harem. The vessels undoubtedly were of gold, the dark-eyed maidens may even have been beautiful by European standards, but "sparkling" *chicha* is quite another matter. If "sparkling" be correct, the quality of the maize beer known anciently as *aca* has degenerated greatly in four centuries. All of the brew which this writer has seen and the little which he has reluctantly tasted can be compared only to American home brew of unhallowed memory. Vile stuff, nor is it less vile when one of squeamish appetite blots from his mind the knowledge that today's manufacturing methods are identical with those followed in the reign of Sinchi Roca. It is made by the women, who thoroughly masticate the corn and then spit the mass, or mess, into a vessel where it awaits fermentation.

Night must have fallen before the cavalry detachment returned to Cajamarca. The splendor of the Inca's court, the huge numbers and the excellent discipline of his soldiers had made a marked impression on the troopers, who had waited in ranks while their leaders parleyed with the emperor. The story they told their fellows in the stone barracks about the plaza was a gloomy one. This was an army they faced, not a handful of screeching tribesmen; and they were outnumbered not ten to one or even fifty to one, but by two hundred to one. "Did you see any gold," an infantryman may have asked, "the gold of which our commander has told such mighty tales?" "Gold! *Por las llagas de San Antonio,* there is more gold in that camp than there is in all Europe, but between each one of us and that gold there stand two

139

hundred fighting men. Kill ten of them, kill ten times ten, there will still be another hundred to beat you down with great clubs which have spiked heads of copper and silver and of gold!" Thus they must have talked, those soldiers, for in the accounts of that night of November 15, 1532, is one of the few instances in all the histories of Spanish conquest when Spanish chroniclers admit that Spaniards were afraid.

Here again we see Francisco Pizarro most favorably. When the outlook was darkest he entrusted nothing to his subordinates. He made the rounds in person, talking to the men of every mess, to the guard detail, and to the sentries, who stood where they could see the campfires of the Peruvian host twinkling against the dark background of the Andes "as thickly as the stars of heaven." Here was the end of the long trail which he had followed from its beginning in the Darien jungle more than twenty years before, and there could be no retreat. They were few in numbers, he told his men, but the hosts of heaven were with them. God and the saints who had fought for Spaniards before would not forsake them in this desperate hour. And then, doubtless, he reminded them of the golden loot and the women of the Inca's harem that would be the rewards of victory. A devout religionist, this Francisco Pizarro, but practical withal.

The priests attached to the expedition spent the entire night in prayer, but Pizarro—his soldiers heartened—summoned his officers in council of war. Did any of those officers urge a diplomatic and conciliatory approach to the mighty Lord of Cuzco? We do not know, but many plans must have been presented and discussed, for the deliberations continued until the stars were paling. All the evidence indicates that the desperate coup which was executed on the following day was planned at that night council.

140

Chapter Seven

WHEN ONE CONSIDERS the events of the following day, there is genuine pathos in the regal gesture with which Atahualpa and his advisers planned to impress their visitors. These white men had come from beyond the sea to behold a king, and a king they would see. All the display and ceremonial of the Incaic court attended the entry of Atahualpa, Sapa Inca of the Land of the Four Sections, into his city of Cajamarca. The weather was good. Snow from the brief, fierce storm of the day before dusted the mountains and lay in the deep ravines of the rolling summits, but the sun shone brilliantly through the scattered cloud-islands; those heavy, flat-bottomed clouds of the high Andes, so white above, so darkly purple below.

It was late afternoon when the Spaniards heard the booming drums and the shrill treble of the *antara cuna,* the panpipes, from the camp at the hot springs and saw the slow, stately march begin. First the slaves, sweeping clean the path before the Inca, and then company after picked company of soldiers armed with javelins, with bows, with slings, and with great spike-headed war clubs. The soldiers sang as they marched, and their battle chants or hymns of praise seemed to Spanish ears the shrieking of demons from hell's deepest pit. One can only guess at the strength of Atahualpa's escort. Two thousand, possibly twenty-five hundred, as a conservative figure which does not consider the unarmed thousands, the residents of Cajamarca and members of the imperial retinue who followed at a respectful distance that they might gaze upon the person of the sovereign and see the mysterious strangers of whom so many tales had been told.

Last in the procession was the royal litter carried on the shoulders of trained bearers and surrounded by a bodyguard of Cañaris, fighting men from the mountain tribes of southern Ecuador who had protected the imperial person since the days of Tupac Yupanqui. Their uniforms were azure, we read, and other uniforms in that dazzling parade were pure white and of checkered white and red. Even that colorful display was dimmed by the gorgeous apparel of Atahualpa and the courtiers who surrounded his litter. Feathered cloaks, exquisitely wrought of the multicolored plumage of tropical birds, swept the ground. Other feathers rose from the headdresses, wide golden bracelets gleamed on brown arms, and three-inch discs of the precious metal hung in the distended ear lobes of the Incan nobles. Atahualpa's litter was covered with golden plates to the value, we are told, of 25,000 ducats. The Inca's finery outshone that of his most brilliantly arrayed courtier, and his throat was encircled with a necklace of huge emeralds.

There was a brief delay when the procession halted on the outskirts of the city and Atahualpa sent to Pizarro the unwelcome message that he would camp there and delay his formal entrance until the next morning. The Spaniards had been under arms since early in the day. None knew better than their commander the severe tension of those long hours of waiting; none was more aware of the break in morale which might follow a postponement of the clash for which they were now prepared. The ambassador was sent back with another message, bitterly true. All was ready in Cajamarca for the Inca's reception, and Francisco Pizarro counted upon dining that night with the emperor. Atahualpa changed his mind once more. Again the drums and pan-pipes and the trumpets of baked clay and resonant shells sounded the advance. Six thousand Indians—Spanish count of troops and spectators—marched into the plaza, then a most irregular quadrilateral no two sides of which were equal or parallel. Finally came the Inca, borne high upon the necks of slaves, and soldiers and citizens prostrated themselves before the person of the Son of the Sun.

That was all. The central area of the plaza remained empty save for the long shadows cast across it by the sun, which was low in the western sky. No one advanced across that space to bow before the emperor. All the magnificence, the display, and the ceremony had been wasted. So long did the silence continue that Atahualpa himself was compelled to break it by inquiring, rather querulously: "Where, then, are the strangers?"

The most skillful stage director could not have arranged a more studied anticlimax. The figure of one man emerged from the gloomy portal of one of the low stone buildings. It was that of the Dominican friar, Vicente Valverde. His tonsured head was thrust above the folds of his soiled and faded robe like the bald pate of an Andean condor—nor were his cold eyes less cruel than those of the bird of prey. He was no envoy bearing gifts from the King of Spain to

143

a fellow-emperor; his right hand clutched a breviary, his left held aloft a crucifix that the pagan Inca might look upon the tortured body of mankind's Redeemer. A sordid fanatic, that Fray Vicente, and one for whom even his contemporaries have nothing to say in praise. He has been called, among other things, a ruffianly ecclesiastic, and no description could be more appropriate. He marched alone across the plaza until he stood within an arm's length of the Inca's litter and the Inca's person; then was joined by the vindictive interpreter, Felipillo.

The priest delivered a long, politico-theological harangue. Even if Atahualpa had understood the Spanish speech, it would have been largely incomprehensible. Translated into Quechua it must have been ridiculous indeed. How can one express, in a tongue which has no equivalents for the terms, the abstract conception of God and the Trinity? There was one God and there were three Gods, Felipillo is quoted as saying, and three and one were four. The speech must have been a long one, for Valverde seems to have covered religion from Eden to Calvary before digressing into politics by way of Saint Peter and the theory of apostolic succession. He told the Inca of the bull of Alexander VI by which that pontiff, in 1493, had conferred upon the Spanish sovereigns all lands in the New World beyond a line drawn from pole to pole a hundred leagues west of the Azores—an act which automatically brought Peru and its people under the Spanish crown. The friar spoke of paganism and its consequences and, in conclusion, held the crucifix before Atahualpa's eyes and earnestly beseeched him to embrace the one true and Christian faith and thereby acknowledge himself a vassal of Charles I.

144

All of which Felipillo was supposed to render into colloquial Quechua. It is doubtful if Atahualpa gathered from the translation more than that some foreigner called a pope had given the Land of the Four Sections to another madman and that he, the Sapa Inca, was being ordered to forswear Inti, the Sun, and pay homage to a pale image on a stick. Naturally, he was furious, but he controlled his rage until Valverde had finished. Felipillo then had the task of rendering into Spanish the Inca's contempt for the Spaniards, their pope, their king, and their God, who, he said, "had been put to death while my God still lives!"—and in testimony of that truth he pointed to the setting sun. By what authority, the Inca continued, did the friar make these demands upon him? Valverde laid his breviary in Atahualpa's hand. A book could have meant nothing to the Inca, who had never seen anything remotely resembling the odd object. He glanced at it negligently, then tossed it on the ground at the feet of the priest or, as other accounts have it, threw the holy writing to the pavement and shouted furiously that the invaders would be compelled to pay for all the wrongs they had committed in Peru.

One guess is as good as another as to why the long-winded religious discourse was permitted to precede the attack which the Spaniards launched, as swiftly and as unexpectedly as a thunderbolt, upon the massed Indians. The Inca's irreverent handling of the breviary could have had nothing to do with the matter, for certainly that attack had been planned long before the head of the royal procession approached the plaza. The two *falconetes* had been double-shotted and laid, the three arquebusiers placed where their fire would prove most effective, and the cavalry and infantry were in position in the shelter of the long buildings which opened on the plaza.

Valverde, we read, retrieved his breviary from the dust and scuttled to the doorway where Pizarro waited. The friar may have spoken the words attributed to him—that courtesy and diplomacy were futile with a dog so full of pride. "Attack! I absolve you!" It is scarcely probable that Francisco Pizarro waited for a priest to give the command or to tell him that the moment was at hand.

He leaped from the doorway and gave the signal—a white scarf waved above his head—for which the troopers waited. The gunners pressed their glowing matches to the touch-holes of the *falconetes*, and the three arquebusiers pulled the triggers of their pieces. The black powder roared, the walls of the buildings tossed the echoes back and forth, and the balls and bits of scrap metal with which the firearms were loaded tore into and through the close-packed ranks of Indians. Then, while the echoes still rumbled and the white clouds of stinking smoke billowed across the plaza, the horsemen and the men-at-arms charged, and the echoes rose again to the shout of the old battle cry of Spain: "Santiago! Santiago!"

The charge, too, was planned. Each detachment which launched itself from the various doorways had a common objective, to hack a path straight to the imperial litter and to seize the Inca. The great majority of the Indians were unarmed, and one must regard skeptically the tale that they deliberately threw themselves upon the Spanish swords to protect the person of their beloved ruler. The attack was not launched until sunset, and it was pressed to a victorious conclusion in the brief space of mountain twilight. A few

146

of the Inca's immediate bodyguard rallied sufficiently to offer some slight resistance; aside from that the engagement was a rout in which the Indians trampled one another and broke down walls in their insane terror to escape from the plaza and from the terrible swords which there rose and fell, were thrust and withdrawn to thrust once more. There in Cajamarca's plaza a mighty empire collapsed in the blind panic with which the Indian races ever received the first shocking contact with firearms, with horses, and with soldiers who attacked and attacked and attacked because they could not retreat.

Atahualpa's litter bearers tossed their burden from their shoulders, and the ruler of Peru was tumbled head over heels to the ground. Miguel de Estete snatched the imperial *llautu*, other hands clutched at the Inca's necklace of emeralds and his gold-bedecked robes. Francisco Pizarro thrust his own men back, shouting that the man who injured the emperor would pay for the act with his life. In the scrimmage about the litter the Spanish commander received a trivial scratch on his hand—the only wound suffered by any of the attackers in the engagement. The number of Indians slain—there was no count of the wounded—is given by the most conservative narrator as two thousand. It is inconsequential whether that or the maximum figure of ten thousand is correct; it is enough that the empire founded by Manco Capac fell within the space of perhaps half an hour of furious slaughter. The news that Atahualpa had been captured spread to the troops who were camped outside the city, and they fled precipitately lest they too be slain by the mysterious strangers who commanded the thunder and the lightning. So complete was the victory that the Spaniards themselves would scarcely

147

believe that it was due to their own courage and the fury of their attack. The powers of heaven must have aided in so complete a victory, and within a few years it was solemnly recorded that Saint James, on whom they called —clad in white armor and mounted on a white charger— had ridden the sky above Cajamarca and struck down the infidels. The saint was accompanied by the Virgin and the Holy Child—doubtless as spectators only.

Atahualpa was treated with kindness. None realized better than his captors that the Inca's person represented their sole hold over the thousands who still acknowledged him as their lord. After the battle he dined—one wonders with what appetite—with the Pizarros and their principal officers and then was shown to an inner room which had been prepared for him. At dawn the following morning a detachment of thirty horsemen under Hernando de Soto was sent to loot the camp at the hot springs and to inform all who might remain there that no harm would befall their leader so long as no attempt was made to rescue him. Many of the Inca's personal retinue, including a number of his concubines, entered willingly into captivity that they might continue to serve their master. The booty from the camp —gold and silver, feather-cloth and jewels, and the incomparable textiles of Peru—filled many rooms of the barracks from floor to ceiling. Every soldier, officer or man, slept under soft robes of vicuña wool and had at his command more slaves, male and female, than he knew what to do with. Thousands of the Inca's soldiers, veterans of many battles, were in the vicinity of Cajamarca, yet not one of the Peruvian generals seems to have entertained the thought of a smashing raid which, though it might bring death to Atahualpa, would eliminate utterly the handful of white men. Fear, superstitious awe, the sanctity of the Inca's person—all these were factors in preventing any counter-attacks, but it is inescapable that history records no surrender as easily won and as complete as that of the followers of Atahualpa.

The Inca himself discovered in short order that the Spaniards were but men, and remarkably sordid and avaricious men at that. They told him strange stories of a king far beyond the seas and quite incomprehensible accounts of the God who had led them to victory and whose Son was represented in the tortured figure which the long-robed priest bore. That was their talk, yet their every action showed that they wanted only the useless metals, gold and silver, which were so abundant in this land. Atahualpa learned that there was no fragment of gold so small that these men would not seize it; they had stripped his camp of gold, had taken the golden plates of his litter, had robbed the slain nobles, and had ripped the golden discs from the ears of the living. If it was gold they wanted, he would give them more than they had ever dreamed of; he would give them enough gold to buy freedom for an imprisoned king.

Go to Cajamarca today, and you will be shown the house still known as La Casa del Inca. Your guide will lead you to the room which was Atahualpa's cell and where he stood —early in December of 1532—with Francisco Pizarro and his brothers. Hernando de Soto must have been there, too, along with Diego de Mora, Francisco and Diego de Chaves, and the grim-faced friars of whom Valverde was head. It is a large room. Francisco Pizarro's secretary, Jerez, says that it was twenty-two feet long, seventeen in width; Hernando Pizarro's famous letter adds thirteen feet to that length. The chamber you will be shown today is close to the dimensions first given, eight average paces in length, five long ones in width. A line is drawn on the wall several inches above the greatest reach of your fingertips if you are a man of average height. You will be told that the Inca Atahualpa—who must have been standing on a chair at the time—drew the original of that line and told Francisco Pizarro that he would contract to fill the entire room with gold to that point as the price of his freedom. A king's ransom, indeed! Thirty-two hundred cubic feet of gold. It would not be solidly packed, of course. The Inca had seen his goblets and other vessels melted down into ingots, and he stipulated that the articles included in the ransom must remain in their original form until the payment was complete. If we assume that only a third of the space was actually occupied by the metal, a thousand cubic feet of gold is still staggering to contemplate. And as though that were not enough to satisfy his captors, Atahualpa offered to fill a smaller adjoining room—that, too, is shown to the visitor—twice over with silver.

The offer was accepted. Two months, the Inca said, would be required to collect the precious metal from the temples and palaces of Cuzco and the other cities of the land and to transport it to Cajamarca. That time limit was agreed to, and the terms were set down in a contract drawn up by the *veedor* or another royal officer and signed—by proxies, naturally—on behalf of the Inca and Francisco

Pizarro. That contract has vanished. Not even a copy of it exists, nor does it seem that the original was ever seen by any of those who in later years were to write the story of the conquest and of the Inca's ransom. We know that Atahualpa pledged the delivery of those millions, but we do not know whether Pizarro promised as solemnly that his captive would be freed when the huge sum was paid. Probably he did, binding himself by God and by Christ our Lord and all the other solemn oaths of his day—and afterward repudiated his pledged word in an act more treacherous and cruel than any in the history of a conquest which abounds with treachery and cruelty.

But of that, later. Atahualpa must have believed that he could buy his liberty, for he sent messengers to Cuzco and the other cities of his realm with his order to bring to Cajamarca all gold upon which his governors could put their hands. One of those couriers bore another imperial order which was delivered to the commander of the fortress at Jauja where Huáscar, the legitimate heir of Huayna Capac, had been confined after his defeat at Xaquixahuana. Atahualpa, quite rightfully, did not trust the half brother from whom he had stolen the throne. He suspected that Huáscar would judge the time ripe for a *coup d'état* which would oust the Atahualpa faction from control in Cuzco and replace the *llautu* on his own brow. There is some evidence, admittedly none too strong, that Huáscar was scheming to that end, but it is very plain that his party had not gained sufficient strength to obtain its leader's release from the remote fortress, many miles northwest of the capital. Atahualpa's orders were clear and were promptly executed, as was the unfortunate Huáscar. He was drowned in the Jauja or Angayacú River, which flowed past the prison. On that point all the chroniclers agree.

The first installments upon the ransom arrived without delay. Before the year 1533 dawned, the soldiers in Cajamarca had become accustomed to the sight of long trains of placid llamas or of porters even more heavily laden with gold and silver. Some may have recalled the note left behind by Alonso Molina or one of his companions when they had died at Tumbez: in truth, there was more gold in this land of Peru than there was iron in Biscay—as Pizarro and his men were now learning. For some five centuries the product of all the Andean placers—for gold was quite without intrinsic worth in a land where there was neither money nor any standard of value—had been the property of the Inca and had been used for the ornamentation of his temples and palaces. Let it be said now that there was no actual mining for gold in ancient Peru. Gold was found —and is still to be found—in many of the streams on both slopes of the interior cordilleras,[1] and it was trapped by means of artificial riffles built of stone across the stream beds. The deep shafts shown to the visitor today are all the remains of workings which were developed during the colonial period and abandoned when the veins were exhausted or when the abolition of slave labor rendered mining unprofitable. Had the conquest been delayed for another century subsurface mining might have been developed, for

[1] No gold came from the western slope of the Maritime Cordillera. Of the many short rivers reaching the Pacific only one, the Chuquicara, is gold-bearing.

the Incaic metallurgists had learned to extract both silver and copper from exposed veins by the smelting process. The necessary blast was furnished by the gales of the high Andes, and the crude furnaces are still called *guayras,* the Quechua word for wind.

It is staggering even to think of the amount of gold—the actual metal already fabricated into various ceremonial, decorative, and useful articles—which existed in pre-Conquest Peru. The ransom paid for Atahualpa amounted to millions of dollars, yet it could have been but a very small percentage of the precious metal in the land. Not all the temples were stripped to purchase the Inca's freedom, nor was all the gold collected for the ransom actually delivered to the avaricious conquerors of Cajamarca. The histories of the first decade of the Conquest abound with accounts of temples looted and of caches discovered. Similar discoveries were made throughout all the colonial period and are being made to this day. There are few Peruvians who cannot tell you of some humble *cholo* or *mestizo* who rose suddenly to wealth through his unearthing of some long-buried treasure. None can be more skeptical of legend—especially the legends of lost mines and of buried loot—than this writer, yet he must acknowledge that there is sound foundation for many of the tales which are current in Peru today. There is more than fancy in the legend of the Peje Grande and the Peje Chico. One of those "fish" represented the undelivered portion of Atahualpa's ransom and was sunk in an Andean lake rather than permit it to be seized by the Spaniards who had murdered the Inca. The lake usually named is Titicaca, which is a very long way

153

from Cuzco and much farther from Cajamarca, whither the ransom was bound. Titicaca, let it be said, is a very large and a very deep lake.

There is factual foundation for the legend of Platerriayoc, the lost fortress which stands somewhere on the Urubamba below Machu Picchu. It was built after the Conquest, you will be told, as a refuge for the Incaic "government in exile" and as a hiding place for all the remaining treasure, which was stored there against the day when the Spaniards should be driven into the sea and the worship of Inti restored. Legend? The magnificent fortress-city of Machu Picchu was legend until 1912 when the expedition under Hiram Bingham stripped away the earth and the jungle which had hidden for centuries its temples and terraces.

Legendary, too, is the Golden Chain. The archæologist will tell you that it was not a chain but a long and heavy rope of braided black wool. That one made at the command of Huayna Capac and used in celebrating the birth of his heir, the ill-fated Huáscar, whose name, in Quechua, means "rope," was also of the black wool which tradition demanded but was lavishly decorated throughout its great length with plates and strands of gold. The more conservative archæological version is probably correct, but long before there were archæologists men wrote that the chain of Huayna Capac was of solid gold, that it was 699 feet in length, and that two hundred men could scarcely lift it from the ground. After the puppet-Inca, Manco, lost his last battle with the invaders and retreated down the Urubamba to Vilcapampa the priests of the Sun realized that the ancient dynasty and the ancient faith were alike doomed. They sank the golden chain of Huayna Capac in a deep mountain lake—

154

invariably the lake nearest to that place where today's traveler hears the story. In Peru today there is no town so humble, so forgetful of the land's glorious past, that one cannot hear legends such as those mentioned; there are few towns where one will not be shown lakes or valleys or deserts or the ruins of ancient structures where wealth incalculable awaits the fortunate searcher. The historians of the Conquest and of the colonial era knew whereof they spoke when they wrote that the vast sum paid for Atahualpa's ransom was but a small tithe upon the existent wealth of the Incan empire.

That ransom arrived in Cajamarca quite steadily, yet all too slowly to satisfy the men-at-arms, who were already spending in anticipation their share of the loot. The first shipments consisted of massive plates, some weighing as much as fifty or seventy-five pounds and designed for purposes now unknown. The smallest treasure convoy reported brought gold in the amount of thirty thousand *pesos de oro,* a sum for the tenth of which any one of those complaining soldiers would have cut his mother's throat or denied his God. Still they whined that the chamber could not possibly be filled within the two months' limit set by Atahualpa, and rumors circulated through the garrison that the captured Inca was playing for time while planning an uprising of his people and the annihilation of all white men in the realm. That gossip was borne to Atahualpa, who promptly disclaimed all the charges and suggested that Pizarro send his own representatives to Cuzco to superintend the collection of the ransom at its principal source and see for themselves the nature of the terrain over which the convoys had to travel. The Inca's relations with his captors seem invariably to have been aboveboard and honest—the direct opposite of the treatment which he was to receive. The cruelty and the treachery was reserved for a later day; while the money was rolling in, the Inca was considered a royal prisoner and was given many of the privileges of his rank. A number of his courtiers shared his captivity and maintained in the prison a semblance of the pomp of Cuzco. He had his women and his priests, although he also had to endure the proselytizing of Friar Valverde—called by Means a "sacerdotal chatterbox."

The rumors of Incaic treachery continued, and the expedition which presently set out from Cajamarca may have been planned to give employment to some of the more vocal of the gossip mongers. Hernando Pizarro led the party, and his goal was Pachacamac, a coastal city which included, so the Spaniards believed, an enormous temple where the votive offerings of centuries had accumulated. The expedition was Hernando's first independent command in the New World, and he proved himself as able a leader as ever wore rapier. Pachacamac was some five hundred miles from Cajamarca, and the long and tortuous trail thither crossed some of the most formidable ranges of the Peruvian Andes. Hernando had with him some fifty or sixty men, twenty of whom were mounted, and before setting out with his little force he did something which seems to have occurred to no other leader in the history of conquest with the exception of that greatest of the conquerors, Cortez. He actually delayed his start until he had learned something of the country which lay before him, of the rivers and mountains which must be crossed, of the cities through which he would pass, and of the distance to

Pachacamac. More, he obtained guides who had themselves been over the route and were competent to lead him up the Marañon Valley and across the cordillera beneath the twenty-two-thousand-foot peak of Mount Huascaran and on through Huaraz and Huaylas to Parmunca where—now on the shores of the Pacific—the Spaniards stared in amazement at the remains of a seven-walled citadel which once had guarded the southern frontiers of the Chimu kingdom, conquered by Inca Pachacutec. From there they followed the coast to Pachacamac, which they found to be a large and thriving city but whose inhabitants offered no opposition to the invaders.

The Spaniards hurried to the temple, but instead of a gold-walled shrine they found only a muddy niche where stood a blood-smeared idol which stunk of many sacrifices. Of the treasure there remained only a few emeralds and the torn fragments of the golden plates which had hung about the fane. The priests of Pachacamac had learned of the capture of Atahualpa and of the white man's lust for the yellow metal. They had stripped the temple of its treasures and had hastily buried them—four hundred man-loads, it is said. Either the cache was not well hidden, or one of those who had been employed in the burying was persuaded to reveal the hiding place, for Rodrigo Orgoñez and several of his companions uncovered in the temple grounds a hoard amounting to some seventy thousand *pesos de oro*. That figure was raised to ninety thousand by various smaller sums extorted from the townspeople, but the undying legends of Peru assert that the bulk of the treasure of Pachacamac still lies beneath the sands of the arid coastal desert south of Lima.

157

Hernando Pizarro demolished the wooden idol and elevated the Christian cross in its place, then marched away with the gold he had taken. Various explanations have been given for his decision to return to Cajamarca over another route, but all indicate that he learned while on the coast that Chalchuchima, one of Atahualpa's generals, was holding the mountain city of Jauja, almost directly east of Pachacamac. That general was probably the individual directly responsible for the drowning of Huáscar; he may have been slow in collecting and dispatching that portion of the ransom which was to come from the Jauja area. Hernando may have desired to investigate those matters, but it is equally possible that the selection of the new route was dictated by the circumstance that an Incan road led directly from Pachacamac to the interior and offered an easier crossing of the Maritime Cordillera than the perilous trails over which the expedition had reached the coast.

At any rate, he marched his handful of men to Jauja and there by smooth words persuaded the general to accompany him to Cajamarca, which, Hernando argued, must now be regarded as the seat of government. Chalchuchima must have considered the argument reasonable, for he relinquished the command at Jauja—Hernando says there were thirty-five thousand men in the city and its environs —and made the long march to the north with the little force of invaders. Pedro Pizarro has described the general's humble approach to his captured sovereign. Chalchuchima was barefoot, as custom demanded, and he bore on his shoulders the burden which, however light, symbolized that in the presence of the Inca the greatest noble in the land was but a slave. The general wept, says Pedro, and

158

he knelt before Atahualpa and declared that his lord would never have been captured had Chalchuchima and his legions been at Cajamarca on the fatal day. Poor devil! Within a few months he was to see Atahualpa, Son of the Sun, die in Cajamarca's plaza; before the year was out he too was to die, miserably, at the hands of those Spaniards whose specious words he had believed. He is but one of many pathetic figures in the bloody history of conquest, that Chalchuchima who was guilty only of loyalty and whose name is quite forgotten in the land; one of many who died that we might perceive the true natures of those men who rode to conquest in the name of God and of Saint James and of the Man of Nazareth whose image they so distorted.

A digression, that, but inescapable because Chalchuchima enters history when he prepared to accompany Hernando Pizarro from Jauja to Cajamarca. Their way led up the Jauja River to its source in Lake Junin, anciently Chinchacocha, which lies more than twelve thousand feet above the sea; thence around the Nudo de Pasco, one of the "knots" of the Andes which divides the drainage of the Ucayali from that of the Marañon and where, later, would be developed the Cerro de Pasco mines, which would produce more than four hundred million dollars in silver. The marchers halted at Huánuco, on the highest headwaters of the Marañon, and it may have been there that the cavalry horses were reshod with silver taken from the eighty loads of treasure which represented the loot of Pachacamac and the ransom-tribute from Jauja.

A memorable march, that of Hernando Pizarro and his little band, although it is dismissed very briefly by virtually

159

all of those who have written of the Conquest. When one considers the difficulties overcome, however, it is an exploit far more remarkable than Cortez' advance from Vera Cruz to Mexico or the march of Coronado into New Mexico and southern Kansas. It can be appreciated only by one who has struggled for breath in the thin air of the Andean passes, who has known the misery of the *soruche,* the "mountain sickness," which is the penalty for even slight exertion, and who has seen—if only from the comfortable cabin of a Panagra airplane—the clefts of the *quebradas* which Hernando and his men crossed on the flimsy suspension bridges flung across those deep ravines by the Inca road builders. There is much that is despicable in the character of the eldest of the Brothers of Doom, but the leadership he displayed on that perilous journey was splendid indeed.

He had left Cajamarca on January 5, 1533; he re-entered the city on April 25. Much had occurred during his absence. Although the two months' time limit set by Atahualpa had long since expired, virtually all of the vast sum pledged by the Inca had at last been received. Two hundred loads of gold had been forwarded by the envoys sent to Cuzco, and those coarse fellows had returned from the Incan capital with great tales of the magnificent palaces which stood about the Holy Square and of their own amorous exploits among the Virgins—in a manner of speaking—of the Sun. A mighty meteor had cloven the night skies above Cajamarca, greatly to the distress of the royal prisoner. Such a phenomenon, he asserted, had presaged the death of his father, Huayna Capac, and this one augured him no good. Nor was that all the news given to Hernando Pizarro. Her-

160

nando de Soto, with his cavalry, had explored much of the surrounding country but had met with no opposition from the Indians of the mountain villages. And—a final item— Diego Almagro was now in Cajamarca! He had arrived with some two hundred recruits in February and had declared his intention of assuming his rightful position as co-leader of the Conquest.

Chapter Eight

DIEGO ALMAGRO must have been the subject of many anxious conferences between the two brothers. It is certain that the presence of his partner was far from welcome to the dour Francisco although he and Almagro—for the benefit of the gallery—publicly embraced one another and reaffirmed their mutual devotion. The entire history of the strange partnership shows that Francisco Pizarro, whatever his intentions may have been, did not enjoy actual association with the man he had made *adelantado*. Always, up to that February of 1533, it had been Pizarro who held the active command, Almagro who acted as recruiting officer, chief of the service of supply, and commander of the base at Panamá. To date, the one-eyed fighter had been satisfied with that division of authority. The two had quarreled bitterly when Pizarro returned from Spain with the famous *capitulacion* which raised him almost to viceregal status; but those differences had been patched up, and Almagro continued in the capacity in which he had served the former expeditions.

That state of affairs changed abruptly when the junior partner reached the settlement of San Miguel de Tangarará late in December of 1532. He had sailed from Panamá a month before with three vessels, guided by the veteran pilot Ruiz. Aboard were about a hundred and fifty footmen, including twenty arquebusiers with their weapons, and fifty cavalrymen. Some were veterans of the fighting in Nicaragua, trained soldiers and men who—if not hidalgos —were at least of better class than the footmen which Almagro had dragged from the jails, bordellos, and wine shops of Panamá. The news of the triumph which had at last rewarded Pizarro had not yet reached Panamá, so Almagro had been compelled to accept any man who could be bribed or made drunk enough to enlist in an enterprise which so far had known only misery and failure. Much of the cruelty and treachery of the next few months has been blamed upon those rowdies who followed Diego Almagro, and they seemed to have merited some portion of that censure. When commanders are at daggers' points with one another, discipline and order and common decency vanish from the ranks.

Almagro learned at San Miguel that his partner had been successful beyond their wildest dreams. Pizarro was master of the land, the Inca was his prisoner, and more gold than had ever been seen in all the Indies—ay, or in Mexico!— was being paid as ransom.

There may have been those—Hernando Pizarro on the one side, Antonio Perez on the other—who deliberately encouraged suspicion between the two partners; but the fire of hate requires little fanning, and Almagro had hated and distrusted Francisco Pizarro for years. The scheming of Perez, who served as Almagro's secretary, brought him little profit, for his chief hanged him there in San Miguel before setting out for the highlands. A forthright individual, old one-eyed Diego, and as tough a fighting man—with one exception—as shall appear in these pages.

Almagro rode to Cajamarca where Pizarro made show of welcoming him most cordially to a land where there was gold and glory enough for all, proving the first thereof by showing him the steadily mounting pile of treasure. By that time—mid-February—nearly half of the promised amount must have been received, and the sight was enough to gladden the heart of any man. Almagro's more active suspicions subsided, and he settled down in the position to which his rank entitled him and to the easy routine of garrison duty. The ill feeling flared up anew with the return of Hernando Pizarro from Pachacamac. Hernando had been the *diabolus ex machina* during the long months of wrangling in Panamá before ever this final Peruvian adventure was launched. Now, full of pride, he returned to Cajamarca to find Almagro there at the head of a force slightly larger than that of the original conquerors. There were several sharp clashes between the arrogant and irascible Hernando and Almagro, quarrels which were settled with some difficulty by Francisco, who at one point compelled his elder brother to make public apology to the one-eyed fighter.

The ransom was declared paid in full on May 3. The bulk—for as yet all the gold was in its various fabricated forms—seems to have fallen slightly short of the line marked upon the wall of the chamber, but the Spanish commanders declared the contract fulfilled. The soldiers were becoming impatient and were demanding the division which had been promised so long ago on the isle of Puná.

For more than a month, the chroniclers assert, Indian metal-workers were employed day and night in breaking up the exquisitely wrought pieces and in melting the fragments down into ingots of standard weight. A few of the finest articles were spared. They were allotted to the Royal Fifth and sent in their original form to Charles I, whose aesthetic appreciation has not been recorded. The tall golden vases, the ears of corn, and the delicate flowers so beautifully fashioned from the precious metal were dutifully admired at the Spanish court, then consigned to the melting pot. Hernando Pizarro was named to convey that Royal Fifth to Spain and to give Charles a direct report upon the Conquest. The appointment was a diplomatic *coup* by Francisco Pizarro. Though neither courtier nor hidalgo, Hernando was well qualified for the mission, and certainly the fame of the conquering Pizarros would not suffer when the eldest of the brothers talked before the throne. Francisco gained a loyal ambassador and removed a potential troublemaker. Alone, he felt, he could handle Diego Almagro, and the events which followed demonstrated that ability.

Even after the king's 20 per cent had been set aside, the treasure which remained was the greatest ever accumulated. It totaled 1,326,539 pesos in gold alone—a sum that is staggering when one considers that it was to be divided among so few. Scarcely four hundred men, including the garrison at San Miguel, Ruiz and his sailors, and Luque and Espinosa in Panamá, were entitled to any share in that loot. To how much would it amount today? There is virtually no standard by which it could be reduced to dollars and cents. Prescott, writing in 1847, estimated it at $15,-

500,000, and subsequent authorities and pseudo-authorities have reduced that figure to a beggarly $2,650,000 and inflated it to the princely total of $50,000,000. Means, foremost of modern scholars, has discussed all those sums and the methods by which the figures were obtained, but wisely refrains from making any approximations of his own. There is some doubt, too, as to whether the total of 1,326,539 *pesos de oro* included the Royal Fifth or represented the value of the loot after deduction of the crown's share. Regardless of how the Spanish texts are construed, even the most conservative of the amounts cited must be expanded considerably if expressed by the dollar of 1942. At the very least there was the equivalent of some $3,000,000 to be divided among four hundred men.

There were sharp differences of opinion as to how the various shares should be apportioned. The men-at-arms who reached Cajamarca with Almagro declared loudly that they should share equally with the members of the original expedition. Pizarro's troopers retorted that it was they who had done the fighting, who had captured Atahualpa, and who had determined the ransom terms—mere garrison duty in the already subjugated city could not be considered as service of equal value.

The hot dispute was settled without bloodshed and with a complete victory for the Pizarro faction. Their leader received 57,222 *pesos de oro*, 2,350 *marcos* in silver, and an additional gratuity of the gold from the Inca's chair— probably the litter on which Atahualpa was borne to the disastrous encounter in the plaza—which was valued at another 25,000 pesos. Brother Hernando was rewarded almost as richly—31,080 pesos in gold, 2,350 silver marks.

The dashing cavalry leader, Hernando de Soto, was given 17,740 pesos, 724 *marcos,* and the troopers under him received an average of 8,880 pesos, 362 *marcos,* per man. The younger Pizarros drew shares far larger than the negative record of their services would indicate they deserved. To Juan Pizarro: 11,100 gold pesos, 407 silver marks; to young Gonzalo, 9,909 pesos, 384 marks; and to the other half brother, Martín de Alcántara, 3,300 pesos and 315 marks.

The infantrymen were paid less generously than their mounted fellows. Some twenty men received exactly half of the cavalry allotment; the remainder, numbering between eighty and ninety, were given 25 per cent less. The richer reward to the horsemen is easily explained. The majority of those troopers were hidalgos. They were gentlemen adventurers, sons of somebody, who owned the horses they rode and the swords they wielded. The Spaniard has never had a high regard for that democracy which considers all men equal.

The *Acta de Reparticion del Rescate*—the original document attested by the royal notary from which Prescott obtained the particulars of the division as given above—does not state how much was awarded to Diego Almagro. Under the terms of the original partnership he and the vicar Luque were to share equally with Francisco Pizarro, and that compact must have been adhered to, for there is no record of Almagro's having made any complaint and his hold over his men was sufficiently strong that he compelled them to be content with the division of a beggarly 20,000 pesos— 100 pesos for each man. They were promised a full share in any future loot, and that seems to have satisfied them.

There were other awards. Twenty-two hundred pesos

167

were given to the church of St. Francis in Cajamarca, first edifice of Christian worship in Peru, and some 15,000 pesos were sent to the men of the San Miguel garrison. Ruiz probably drew a generous share, although his name is not mentioned in the articles of division. Oviedo, that 17th-century Winchell, states that Hernando Pizarro's share was purposefully made far larger than he deserved so that the unpopular brother thereby might be persuaded to remain permanently in Spain. It is more probable that the large sum paid Hernando included a considerable portion of the treasure which he had obtained at Pachacamac.

There may have been a later and unrecorded division. One contemporary chronicle, none too reliable, observes that a considerable portion of the ransom was held in the vaults, greatly to the dissatisfaction of those who knew of its presence; and this unadvertised reserve may have been drawn upon to pay the younger Pizarros, unmentioned in the original articles, and to increase to 100,000 pesos the amount allotted to Almagro's followers.

What did the soldiers do with their wealth in a land where money and values were quite unknown? They did what soldiers have done since the days of Alexander— they gambled. The dice were rattling in the leathern cups before ever the division was completed, and by the next dawn many of them had lost the last maravedi of their suddenly acquired fortunes. Of the entire company only twenty-five men declared that they now could live out their lives in comfort in Spain. Twenty-five men out of four hundred packed their kits and made ready to accompany Hernando Pizarro to Panamá, to Nombre de Dios, and thence on the long journey to their native land.

The spoil was divided early in June, and Hernando Pizarro set out from Cajamarca almost immediately. A long train of porters and of llamas was required to bear the bulky treasure making up the King's Fifth and the additional half-million pesos belonging to the returning adventurers. The point is not brought out in any of the chronicles, but if that sum represented the booty of only the twenty-five who left Cajamarca with Hernando, each man's share averaged twenty thousand golden pesos—more than the allotment granted to Soto. It would certainly indicate that the twenty-five included many of the more fortunate gamblers.

The story of the Pizarros abounds with errors of judgment and of action, but no decision resulted more disastrously than that which sent Hernando to Spain. Francisco may have wished to be represented at court by an able ambassador upon whom he could rely. After the lean years, the fat. He had scored a magnificent and bloodless victory and was delivering to his king the richest treasure ever produced by the New World. His ambition may have led him to vision his appointment as viceroy as the only reward commensurate with his services to the crown. On the other hand, he may have wished only to rid himself temporarily of the elder brother whose every meeting with Diego Almagro resulted in a quarrel. Francisco knew that the Conquest was far from complete and that disaster was inevitable should the Spanish ranks be split by partisan hatreds and jealousies. All is speculation, for the illiterate governor left no memoirs and the few glances we obtain of his dark, suspicious heart are from the words of men who knew him. Whatever his motive, in making Hernando his envoy he deprived himself of the one man who might have advised him intelligently and whose counsel he might have trusted. In all his adventurous life he had complete confidence in no man save his half brothers.

The situation in the conquered city was a sorry one. It is impossible to view dispassionately the events of that dark week in August of 1532, but its events cannot be understood without careful consideration of numerous factors and of the characters of the individuals involved. Francisco Pizarro, as Governor and Captain-General by royal decree, held supreme political and military command. He lacked the strength and the spiritual courage to assert that command and to compel obedience from Diego Almagro and his impatient soldiers. Too, there was the question of partnership and of the oath which they had affirmed and reaffirmed in Panamá. Both of the old soldiers were then nearly sixty years old. They distrusted one another, but they had little confidence in the royal officers or the younger knights who accompanied the expedition. Neither man possessed the exalted religious fervor of Cortez, so they could not and did not turn to the church for advice. The church was represented by the Dominican friar, Vicente Valverde—a true disciple of that other Dominican, Tomás de Torquemada. The wisdom of any counsel which Valverde might have given will be seen.

Among the younger officers was Hernando de Soto, and his advice, had it been taken, would have changed history and have spared Spain the blackest stain that can be found on her record of conquest in the New World. Soto's counsel was not invited. He was an hidalgo, a gentleman by birth and not by the whimsical decree of an avaricious monarch.

Neither Pizarro nor Almagro were comfortable in the presence of true *caballeros*. Those two were only a few years removed from the ranks, a few years from the station when they had stood to one side and removed their hats when approached by men like Soto—twenty years their junior—or Riquelme, the royal treasurer. Now positions were reversed, and the gentlemen of coat-armor uncovered before the one-time common soldiers, but no royal decree could remove class consciousness or grant an hidalgo's sense of honor to an Estremaduran swineherd.

The troops in Cajamarca seem by all accounts to have been out of hand. They had known no fighting save the bloody slaughter in the city plaza when Atahualpa had been captured. Less than half of the four hundred now in the town had participated in that engagement. They had suffered no losses, nor had they experienced the tightening of discipline which comes only to those fighting men who have looked upon their own dead. A rich share in the Inca's ransom had gone to the men in the ranks, but they wanted more, and their greed was shared by the reinforcements led by Almagro, who had been less generously rewarded. They raised the cry of "On to Cuzco!"—the capital where so much gold yet remained—and they repeated and added to all the wild rumors which said that the Peruvians were planning to attack Cajamarca, rescue their Inca, and seize the gold which remained in the town. One tale, springing from nowhere, told that a huge army had been recruited in Quito, Atahualpa's homeland, and that it would be reinforced by no less than thirty thousand Caribs, the cannibals whom the Spaniards feared somewhat more actively than they did the demons of the pit. There can be

171

no question that it was the fear of retaliatory attacks which nourished the conviction that to release Atahualpa would be disastrous. True, the ransom had been paid, but expediency demanded that the conquerors continue to hold the emperor. Then came the clamor that the Inca be executed.

It is impossible to say with whom that idea originated. Those records which endeavor to place the blame and the shame lay the onus collectively upon some two hundred men—Almagro and his followers and the royal officers who were in Cajamarca. Valverde, too, is blamed. Blackguard, so far as this writer has been able to discover, is the only printable epithet which has not been applied to the wily Dominican for his role in the swift succession of events. Valverde's hatred for Atahualpa can be explained only by the fact that the Inca preferred Viracocha and the Sun to that terrible, jealous God of vengeance in whom the Dominican believed most sincerely and of whom he preached incessantly.

The belief that Spanish safety could be assured only by Atahualpa's death did not originate with Francisco Pizarro. The governor undertook rather reluctantly the investigation of the rumored revolt, and he accepted, temporarily at least, the assurances of the Inca and his generals that the reports were groundless. In those investigations, however, Pizarro was forced to rely upon Felipillo, the coastal Indian, to interpret the words of the emperor and his nobles, and that young devil distorted Atahualpa's frank words into a tissue of lies of his own designing. He, too, hated the dignified prisoner. He had dared to make advances toward one of the women who shared her lord's captivity, and Atahualpa had demanded that Felipillo and

172

all his kindred be slain. The punishment, which was no more than the low-born Felipillo deserved by the Incaic code, was not inflicted. The guttersnipe may not have been so much as censured for his amorous ambitions; but from then on he cherished an implacable hatred toward the Inca, and it was his efforts, more than those of any other one individual, which brought Atahualpa to his fate.

Hernando de Soto and a few other honorable cavaliers pled vainly for more considered action. Their protests were ignored, and Soto—perhaps the loudest in Atahualpa's defense—was sent rather hastily to reconnoiter the country around Guamachuco where the hostile forces were said to be mobilizing.

Atahualpa, ruler of the Land of the Four Sections, was then brought to trial. He was charged with usurpation of the throne of his half-brother Huáscar and with having ordered the slaying of the deposed emperor. Those charges, though it is difficult to see how they were any business of the Spaniards who sat in judgment, might be considered just indictments, but they were bolstered by others which varied only in their degree of asininity when one considers the circumstances under which they were made and that virtually all of them were based upon Spanish—and Catholic—concepts of morality. He was accused of having used the national income for his own purposes, with having been polygamous, with having contracted an incestuous marriage, with being an idolator, and, lastly, with having plotted the overthrow of his captors. Those absurd charges were formally made in what Oviedo, a few years later, was to characterize as a "badly contrived and worse written document, devised by a factious and unprincipled priest,

173

a clumsy notary without conscience, and others of like stamp, all of whom were concerned in this villainy." [2]

It was Valverde, that factious and unprincipled priest, who acted as prosecutor in the hasty trial which determined the fate of the last native American emperor. The judges were the two leaders, not yet active rivals, Pizarro and Almagro. The witnesses summoned were Indian, the only interpreter the vindictive Felipillo.

A small minority fought for Atahualpa and pointed out the only path which was compatible with honor. Soto was absent, but his ideals were stoutly upheld by the brothers Chaves, by Francisco de Fuentes, Blas de Atienzo, Hernando de Haro, and many others. They called to the judges' attention the fact that Atahualpa was a sovereign and hence could be judged only by his peers. Since his land had been taken by Spain, only King Charles was competent to pass upon the Inca's guilt or innocence. The point was one well calculated to appeal to men who were sticklers in matters of precedence and authority. The upholders of justice, however, were greatly outnumbered by those who shouted for the Inca's death. Valverde was determined that Atahualpa should die, as was Felipillo, who distorted the evidence as it pleased him. Interpretation of the charge of idolatry into the Quechua tongue was an utter impossibility, yet it was achieved somehow by Felipillo and endorsed most heartily by Fray Vicente, who signed the judgment. Atahualpa was found guilty—of how many of

[2] Prescott's rather free translation. The unnamed priest was Valverde, of course; the notary was probably that Pedro Sancho who drew up the ransom agreement.

of the charges we are not told—and he was sentenced to death by burning at the stake.

Here, again, the hand of the malevolent Valverde is apparent. Atahualpa's idolatry, his sturdy refusal to accept the Christian faith were crimes far more heinous in the priest's eyes than polygamy, incest, or treachery. The Inca's fate was that reserved only for offenders against church law, for pagans, idolaters, and unrepentant heretics. The entire machinery of the Holy Inquisition is evident in the trial and death of the last Inca.

That very night, the night of August 29, 1533, was set for the execution. A stake was erected in the plaza, and Peruvian slaves set to the task of gathering wood and piling the faggots. The good Fray Vicente prayed zealously with Atahualpa, telling him of the powers of the Cross, of the beauties of Christianity, and of Christ's mercy to all who repented their sins and accepted Him. So did the familiars of the Confraternity of San Pedro Martir pray with those who marched in yellow *sanbenito* and *coroza* to the Cathedral Square in Toledo to participate in the ceremony so impiously called an Act of Faith; so did they labor with the unrepentant until driven back by the flames which rose about the stakes at La Dehesa where the unfortunates abandoned to the secular arm were burned. It was never too late to repent and thereby receive the merciful boon of strangulation instead of the agony of the flames. A blackguard Valverde may have been, yet his fanaticism was only that of his times. There was none who watched Atahualpa marching toward the stake who did not believe that the miserable man could escape an eternity of hell-fire by embracing the cross which the lean-faced priest held before him.

The Inca had his moment of weakness during the few hours of life which remained to him. Once, we read, he bitterly reproached Pizarro for inflicting such cruelty upon one from whom he had received so much, and he offered a ransom twice as large as that already paid if he were given his life. It was refused, although Pedro Pizarro goes on to say that he saw his kinsman weep as he left Atahualpa to Valverde. From that moment, the same chronicler continues, the Inca resigned himself to his fate.

A ghastly, shameful business from beginning to end, that trial and execution of Atahualpa. It is made no less shameful by the circumstance that the Inca was not burned alive. The time was two hours after sunset. Torches flamed about the plaza, and by flickering light the enslaved people saw their ruler brought from his prison. The Indians must have watched in stoical silence, for the wailing of Atahualpa's wives, we read, rose above all other sounds. The chains were passed about his body, the faggots were in place—and then some words of Felipillo's pierced the doomed man's consciousness. There was, then, an escape! Not from death, that was too much to ask, but at least from agony. He raised his voice and—through the interpreter—asked Francisco Pizarro if what he heard was true. The answer was yes. He could repudiate the pagan gods he worshiped and accept baptism at the hands of Fray Valverde. Then he would be strangled.

The Inca accepted. The act of repudiation and the rite of baptism must have been quickly accomplished. Atahualpa, twelfth Inca in line of descent from Manco Capac, was baptized in the name of the Father, the Son, and the Holy Ghost and given the name of Francisco de Atahualpa

—a bit of irony which may have been deliberate on the part of the grim friar since Francisco Pizarro would scarcely have requested that honor.

The Inca made two requests of those who were about to murder him. First, that he be buried in Quito, the land he had ruled and loved; second, that Pizarro pledge himself to protect the children who would be left fatherless. He was then strangled by means of the stick and twisted cord called the *garrote*. It is more merciful than fire. "Thus by the death of a vile malefactor," writes Prescott, "perished the last of the Incas."[3]

His body was buried first in the new church of Saint Francis in Cajamarca—Fray Valverde sang the requiem mass and was assisted by that Fray Marcos de Niza who a few years later was to seek far to the north, in the present New Mexico, for the Seven Cities of Cibola. Loyal followers removed the body and bore it to a secret grave in the land we now call Ecuador. History is silent as to how well Pizarro kept his promise to care for the dead Inca's children, but he took as his mistress a half sister of the man he had brought to death. This daughter of Huayna Capac was known as the Doña Inez Huaylas Ñusta, and she bore the conqueror a son, Gonzalo, who died in childhood, and a daughter, Francisca, who afterward became the wife of her uncle, Hernando Pizarro.

A word must close this dark chapter. Retributive justice may exist in this far from perfect world. Fray Valverde be-

[3] Prescott and several others have said that Atahualpa was baptized as Juan "in honor of John the Baptist on whose day the event took place." Later researches have revealed that he was given the name Francisco. It is scarcely necessary to mention that June 24, not August 29, is celebrated as St. John's Day.

came Bishop Valverde of Cuzco, and he remained in Peru until 1541 when he set out for Panamá. The ship touched at Puná in the Gulf of Guayaquil, and Valverde and all his companions were captured by the Indians there and hacked rather slowly into small pieces. Felipillo's just reward was not so long delayed. He accompanied Diego Almagro when that doughty leader marched to the south with the laudable intention of conquering Chile. There Felipillo told his last lie and perverted testimony for the last time. Almagro ordered him hanged, then quartered.

Chapter Nine

A SHABBY HERO, this Francisco Pizarro, conqueror of Peru. Physical courage was his in full measure, but his character shows little of decency or honor or the spiritual strength that is close kin to those two. When rebuked by Hernando de Soto, who expressed his opinion of the murder of Atahualpa in the old ranker's own speech, the governor attempted weakly to shift the blame and the responsibility to Almagro, Valverde, and the others. These retorted with the accusation that Pizarro had been first to propose that Atahualpa be executed, that he had speeded the hasty trial and had been first of the two judges to vote for death. Soto made little effort to sift the truth out from charge and countercharge. What would it serve? Atahualpa was dead, and neither proof of innocence nor evidence of grave injustice can restore the dead to life. The annalists of the time are almost without exception apologists for Francisco Pizarro, who could certainly have halted that trial at any time had he truly desired that Atahualpa should live. The governor had received his primary education in politics from Pedrarias Davila, and policy dictated that Peru have a ruler who could be called Inca. Atahualpa might have served if he had been willing to become a puppet king, vassal of Charles of Spain and subservient in all things to Francisco Pizarro, Governor-General. We do not know if the son of Huayna Capac was offered the opportunity to buy his life and his crown with his honor. We do not know if he refused. He was killed, and Pizarro promptly declared an obscure youth named Toparca, a younger brother of the murdered man, to be Inca of Peru. The *llautu* was placed on his head in a hastily contrived ceremony which followed in some measure the solemn pomp of the Incaic custom, and he was hailed as emperor by those of his subjects who were in Cajamarca.

That done, and with some degree of unity restored in their own ranks, the conquerors marched out of Cajamarca and turned their faces to the south toward Cuzco: Cuzco the imperial capital, Cuzco the golden, Cuzco from which only a tithe of the gold had been stripped for Atahualpa's ransom. The route was that followed by Hernando Pizarro from Jauja, but long before the Spaniards reached that town they learned that the path to the capital would not be an easy one. The highlanders were not ready to accept the unknown Quiteño, Toparca, as their liege. Bridges were cut and villages burned, and rumor told of a huge army which was being massed by an Incan noble and general who bore the amazing name of Quizquiz. The governor halted in Jauja where Toparca occupied the palace built for the periodic visits of the emperor. Friar Valverde stripped the Sun Temple of all symbols of Inti-worship and converted the pagan fane to a Christian church where he, Friar Marcos de Niza, and the other priests sang masses regularly throughout the period of Spanish occupation.

Hernando de Soto was given his usual scouting assignment. At the head of sixty horsemen, he was sent to examine the country toward Cuzco, still nearly three hundred miles away. The advance was a series of skirmishes with the now aroused Peruvians, but Soto pressed forward until he reached Vilcaconga, a location which I have been unable to identify with accuracy but which was in the region of the present Vilcambamba or Quillabamba, some sixty miles northwest of Cuzco. There the peaks of the Eastern Cordillera rise steeply and grandly above the tortuous valleys of the Apurimac and Urubamba rivers, and there Soto and his little force marched into an ambush. Less indomitable fighters would have been annihilated by the sheer weight of the Indian army which swept down the steep hillsides, but the Spaniards rallied again and again to the battle cry of "Santiago!" and when night fell had established a reasonably secure position on level ground where the cavalry might maneuver.

Reinforcements were close at hand, although Soto and his weary troopers did not know it. Far more able than the majority of his contemporaries, Soto had maintained contact with the main force at Jauja and had kept Pizarro advised of the mounting tide of opposition. The governor sent Diego Almagro forward with a supporting party, which, marching swiftly on Soto's trail, joined him during the night—a bit of good fortune which is most discreditable to the Peruvian scouts but is another example of the sheer luck which marked so many Spanish exploits.

The Peruvians withdrew at dawn—a retreat explained most inadequately by their dismay when they found that their enemies had doubled in number during the hours of darkness. Soto and Almagro marched unopposed to a better position and sent a report of the engagement to Pizarro, who prepared to advance upon Cuzco with the balance of the army.

There was work to be done first, the bloody work which the conquerors called justice. Chalchuchima, the Incan general, was still with the invaders although nominally a free man. He was accused of having plotted with Quizquiz to overthrow the Spanish domination and with having fomented the uprising which had blocked Soto's progress. Chalchuchima denied the charges, but he was chained hand and foot and told that he would be burned alive as soon as Pizarro's command joined the advance detachments. He could save his life, said his captors, only if every insurgent patriot laid down his arms and swore fealty to Spain. The horrid sentence was executed—after a travesty of a trial—on the plain of Xaquixaguana (Zúrite) where Atahualpa's Quiteños had defeated the armies of Huáscar. Fray Valverde accompanied Chalchuchima to the stake. "He seems always to have been present at this dreary moment, anxious . . . to work the conversion of the victim. He painted in gloomy colors the dreadful doom of the unbeliever to whom the waters of baptism could alone secure the ineffable glories of paradise. It does not appear that he promised any commutation of punishment in this world." [1] The chieftain was of sterner fiber than his lord Atahualpa. He refused baptism and the boon of strangulation and died in the flames with the name of Pachacamac—the Creator-God of the coastal peoples—on his lips.

The puppet-prince Toparca had died—apparently of

[1] Prescott, from Herrera.

natural causes—at Jauja, which may explain why Pizarro delayed his triumphal entry into Cuzco and remained at Zúrite to negotiate with Manco, a younger brother of Huáscar, whose claim to the throne was as legitimate as any other's. Manco, regardless of his subsequent actions, was quite willing in November of 1533 to co-operate with the white strangers who had taken his country. Pizarro received him joyfully, although his satisfaction may have been masked by the chilly dignity suitable to a governor. Manco was a scion of the old line, the Bourbons of Peru rather than the upstart Napoleons from Quito, and there in the Zúrite camp the conqueror promised him the *llautu* of the Sapa Inca. The young aspirant and his courtiers were given places of honor in the procession which on November 15, 1533, marched into the Huaca Pata, the Holy Square, of Cuzco.

The historian and the archaeologist would forgive all the cruelty and rapine and lust and greed of the Conquistadores if one of them—only one—had left a truly accurate description, with maps and sketches, of that city as it was on that day. Cuzco was more than a capital; it was as holy as Rome is holy to the devout Catholic or as Mecca is holy to every Moslem from Morocco to Burma. The man approaching Cuzco stepped aside for him who was coming from the Holy City; the latter had acquired holiness merely by his visit. For more than four hundred years each Inca had added to the beauties of Cuzco. Their engineers and architects had looked upon the huge monolithic construction of the Tiahuanaco peoples—where single stones weighing as much as fifty metric tons were incorporated in the walls—and from it had developed the most remarkable prehistoric masonry to be found anywhere in the world. They built palaces and schools, temples and "convents," aqueducts and bridge-piers, in regular courses of cut stones laid with mathematical precision and fitted so closely that to this day one cannot thrust a knife blade between the dressed ashlars. It was severely plain and magnificent in its austerity, that Incaic masonry. To carve stone, other than for strictly utilitarian purposes, seems never to have occurred to those who raised the tapering walls of the Temple of the Sun in Cuzco or the houses of the upper ward in Pisac, that gem of the eastern Andes. One can travel the length and breadth of Peru and find nothing which even approximates the deeply carved stelae of Mayan lands or the Mexican pyramids, but the traveler will remember the austere walls of Cuzco when Chichen Itza and Teotihuacán are forgotten. Over the space of four centuries the Incas were building, and for a period equally long the walls they raised have resisted the deliberate vandalism of the Conquest, the reconstruction of the colonial period, and later attempts to obtain ready-cut building stones. There is scarcely a building, public or private, in Cuzco today whose walls do not include at least a few courses of undisturbed Incaic masonry; the lower walls of the larger structures are almost wholly Incaic. The cathedral was once the palace of the Inca Viracocha; the Church of the Jesuits (La Compañia) was the palace of Huayna Capac. The great *accla-hausi*, the House of the Chosen Women, is now indeed a convent, the home of the nuns of Santa Catalina, nor does legend record that their orisons are ever interrupted by the laughing voices of long-dead women who there served another god. The Dominican monastery was the mighty Temple of the Sun, given to Juan Pizarro when the loot of Cuzco was shared. The very stones in the walls which now look down upon the altar and the Cross, which echo to the *Te Deum Laudamus*, have been spattered with the blood of black llamas sacrificially slain and have heard the voice of the Villac Umu chanting hymns to Inti and to Viracocha.

The Incas were conquered. The male line was exterminated remorselessly by Pizarro and the governors who followed him; their women were taken as mistresses. The Incan peoples, the Quechuas of the Peruvian highlands, are today a crushed nation living in filthy hovels and toiling for those who exploit them and whose fear is that some day another Manco Capac will rise among the mountain *ayllus*. But Cuzco lives, a monument as great as Rome to a civilization and culture that was inferior only in letters to that which rose on the Tiber. Cuzco and its surroundings are not "The Wonderland of Peru." The title—and it has been used —is contemptible. Cuzco is Athens without obsequious Greek guides and personally conducted tourists; it is Rome without Italian beggars or nobles who are too proud to work except at cheating the gullible visitor; it is Cairo without Arab filth and Levantine panderers and the snobbery of Shepheard's; it is Chichen and Angkor made accessible. Cuzco is Cuzco, magnificent, indestructible.

Pizarro's first order, given while the troops still stood in ranks in the Holy Square, was that the inhabitants of the city and their dwellings should not be disturbed. There is nothing in the chronicles to indicate that the order forbade looting, as it has been interpreted. On the contrary, Cuzco and its temples and palaces were frankly given over to the soldiers for pillage. There is no description of the orgy of greed which followed and which continued for many weeks. The order sparing private dwellings was disregarded from the beginning, and the most humble home was sacked as enthusiastically as the Sun Temple. Graves were opened and robbed, and the wrapped cadavers of long-dead Incas were despoiled.[2]

Much gold remained in Cuzco. Some was in the form of large plates, the purpose of which is difficult to determine from the meager descriptions. Another precious object was a thick disk, entirely of gold, which the Conquistadores and many others have believed was the symbolized Sun which hung above the high altar in the temple. Archaeology, however, has demonstrated that the famous object was the lid of a beer can, nothing more! It was the cover of one of the enormous stone containers into which the *chicha* offered to the Sun was poured. That it was utilitarian rather than sacramental detracted not at all from its intrinsic worth. In the division of the loot it was awarded to Don Mancio Sierra de Leguizano, who lost it in one wild night of gambling.

A number of rich caches of hidden treasure were uncovered. Golden effigies of four llamas and several "statues" of women in both gold and silver, all life-size, were found in a cave near the city. Women's dresses made up entirely of gold beads were among the loot. Ten strips of solid silver were found hidden in a hut where a Spanish party had stopped to eat. Each was twenty feet long, one foot in width, and in thickness measured *tres dedos*—very slightly

---

[2] The Incas Huayna Capac, Viracocha, and Tupac Yupanqui, and the bodies of the wives of the two latter, are now buried in the courtyard of San Andrés Hospital in Lima.

more than two inches. Later writers have increased the number of those strips or planks to 150, but Pedro Pizarro, who should know, says there were ten and that they had been manufactured to ornament the home of an Incan noble.

Accounts vary as to the amount of the loot. Four hundred and eighty men, counting the garrison of Jauja, shared in its division, and Pedro Pizarro says that each horseman received 6,000 gold pesos and each foot soldier half that sum —an accounting which would place the soldiers' share alone at nearly 1,750,000 pesos. The notary Pedro Sancho, Pizarro's secretary, certified to less than half that sum—580,200 gold pesos and 215,000 *marcos* of silver, which was accepted by the governor and the royal treasurer. There is considerable collateral evidence that Charles I did not get all that was coming to him from the loot of Cuzco. The annals give no precise information of the awards made to Pizarro, Almagro, and the other leaders, nor was the King's Fifth considered when the royal palaces, the temples, and the homes of the Incan nobles were distributed among the conquerors. The yet uncrowned Manco must have realized his vassalage when he saw the white men taking possession of the buildings which his forebears had erected, when he saw the horses stabled in and around the palace of Huayna Capac—given to Hernando de Soto, the cavalry commander —and when he was told of the wholesale raping of the Chosen Women, who, regardless of their virginal status, were truly revered by all of the Incan caste. To the Spaniards the *acclas* were booty, and they were treated as such.

The complete surrender of the Peruvian people is impossible to understand. The race which had created a mighty empire by military prowess, whose generals had led armies

187

of a hundred thousand trained warriors; that race produced no man capable of organizing a revolt and sweeping into the sea the tiny force which had ravaged the land. As that *año triste* of 1533 drew to a close there were scarcely six hundred Spaniards in all of Peru, and they stood absolutely alone. They had won over no large forces of Indian allies such as followed Cortez to Tenochtitlan, and a single smashing attack must inevitably have annihilated them, yet that attack was never made. Through those months the white men took up their arms only once, to crush Quizquiz, Atahualpa's general, whose guerrilla tactics interfered with the pleasant tasks of pillage. Almagro took over that job, trounced Quizquiz in a brief battle near Jauja, and sent him and his soldiers in hasty flight to Quito where the general was killed by his own troops.

Not until March 24, 1534, were the eager looters of Cuzco able to turn from plunder and rapine to more formal duties. On that day the ancient capital was declared to be a Spanish city. Municipal officers were appointed—Juan and Gonzalo Pizarro were named among the eight *regidores*—and allotments of land and of Indians were made to those who had already been granted houses. A full report was sent to Spain, one item being the request that Fray Vicente de Valverde be appointed Bishop of Cuzco. That ecclesiastical promotion was promptly made by Paulus III. The pontiff appreciated the devoted labors of the friar *in partibus infidelibus*. A site for a cathedral had already been set aside. It included the Viracocha Palace, occupied by the present cathedral building. Fray Vicente's other labors in the faith included a visit to Quenco, near the fortress of Sacsahuaman, where he battered into a shapeless mass of stone one of the few

188

examples of Incaic sculpture—a huge boulder which achae-
ologists think may once have been hewn into the form of a
puma. The friar did his work well, for only the most active
imagination can see any resemblance to a puma or anything
else in the peaked rock which stands detached from the
tunneled cliffs at Quenco.

Next on the agenda was the formal coronation of Manco
as Sapa Inca. The ceremony was an ironic travesty of the
ancient pomp and ritual. The wrapped cadavers of the
young prince's ancestors, "with such ornaments as remained
to them," were solemnly paraded about the Holy Square.
The nobles, stripped of their former magnificence, humbled
themselves before their liege. All rival claimants of the
llautu had been "liquidated" under the terms of a private
arrangement between Manco and Diego Almagro. Largesse
was distributed to the common people, and vast quantities
of maize beer were consumed.

There the resemblance to ancient ritual ends. There were
no prayers to Viracocha the Creator, nor did the new ruler
prostrate himself before the Sun in the Coricancha Temple.
Fray Vicente took care that no such blasphemies marred
the day. He conducted a Christian mass, and Manco and his
nobles then pledged allegiance to Spain and to His Catholic
Majesty Charles I and to the Governor and Captain-General,
Don Francisco Pizarro, who—as soon as the protracted ceremonies were over and the last drunken soldier had recovered
from his tippling—set about further steps necessary in
organizing the thoroughly subjugated province.

Only passing mention can be given here to what may be
termed the Alvarado incident. News of the rich loot of Peru
had reached Panamá and been carried to Don Pedro de

189

Alvarado, one of Cortez's principal lieutenants, who had hewn a bloody victory for Spanish arms in Guatemala. The cavalier promptly organized his own expedition of conquest on the South American mainland. At about the time of the Cuzco ceremonies Alvarado landed some five hundred men at Caraquez (Ecuador) and marched directly across the mountains toward Quitu, the capital of the ancient kingdom, which in these pages has been given its present name of Quito. It was a reckless undertaking, and more than a hundred of Alvarado's men perished in the snows of the high cordillera. Their leader had achieved nothing by the adventure, for one of Pizarro's officers, Sebastián Benalcazar, had reached Quito some months before by following the great north road of the Incas from his post at San Miguel. He met and defeated the Quiteño general, Ruminavi, and entered the city in triumph. Benalcazar has been accused of making that invasion on his own initiative and to his own greater glory, but Pedro Pizarro states definitely that the governor had directed the advance in order to prevent the occupation of the region by a rival conqueror. Quito, as Francisco Pizarro knew, was well to the north of the territory assigned to him by the royal *capitulacion*. Moreover, as soon as he learned of Alvarado's landing, Pizarro sent his partner Almagro to the north. By the time Alvarado had emerged from the mountains and had reached the interior plateau in the vicinity of Riobamba, Almagro was there waiting for him. There was some skirmishing between advance units of the various forces but no real fighting. Diplomacy carried the day—August 6, 1534—and a lawyer named Calderón drew up the agreement under which Pedro de

Alvarado was to abandon his dreams of conquest in return for 100,000 gold pesos, cash in hand. His men were offered the opportunity to enlist under Pizarro's banner, and all but a handful of them accepted. Alvarado, now a welcome guest, was escorted to Pachacamac and spent the closing months of the year with the governor in that city. His reward must have been paid him there since no such amount of gold was available in Quito.

There is a curious discrepancy in the accounts of that payment. The majority of the chroniclers and the historians who came after them assert that Pedro de Alvarado got his money and returned to Guatemala, his honor unsullied. That is confirmed by Bernal Diaz del Castillo, historian of the Cortez expedition, who states that Alvarado came back from Peru "a very rich man." Yet Cortez himself, in his letters, says bluntly that the *Adelantado* of Guatemala was victimized by the unscrupulous Pizarro and Almagro. Only a small number of the gold and silver ingots he received were actually of the precious metals. The great majority were of lead, plated with silver and gold.

If he was duped, however, Don Pedro never admitted it. He swallowed the bitter pill like a *caballero,* doubtless remarking that it was no more than one might expect from such low-born *pelados.* One of the most vivid personalities in the entire history of the Indies is this tall, red-bearded and red-haired man whom the Indians of Guatemala called Tonatiuh, the Sun, and whose conquests were marked by a sheer lust for murder on a wholesale scale. He lived for seven years after his Peruvian adventure, dying in Guadalajara, Mexico, in 1541 from injuries received when his horse fell with him in charging rebel Indians in Jalisco. He is buried in the cathedral in Guatemala City, but the exact location of the grave is unknown.

To continue the digression momentarily, Alvarado's widow, Beatriz de la Cueva de Alvarado, is the only woman, to date, ever to head a government in the western hemisphere. She was *Gobernadora* of Guatemala for two short days, September 9 and 10, 1541, dying on the night of the second in an earthquake and flood which swept the capital. In Guatemalan history she is *Beatriz la sin Ventura*—Beatrice the Unlucky.

Chapter Ten

THE BLOOD WHICH DRIPPED from Francisco Pizarro's scratched hand on Cajamarca's plaza was the last he was to shed for Spain and Spanish conquest. Never again was he to raise his voice in the "Santiago!" and—spear point of the furious attack—hurl himself upon the foe. The reckless, swashbuckling old man-at-arms leaves the stage; the politician enters. Politician, not statesman, not diplomat, and a politician whose errors of judgment and of action far outnumber his achievements. No one will ever know whether or not the sword was sheathed on the advice of the older, more literate, and vastly more experienced Hernando. It may have been, for the swift transition from captain-general to governor was accomplished during the few months of Atahualpa's captivity. It is equally possible that Almagro's presence dictated the step. Almagro was a fighting man, let him do the fighting. The latter reasoning would account for the dispatch of the junior partner to Quito and his subsequent expedition to Chile. While Almagro, a potential rival, was engaged in military affairs, the brothers Pizarro could intrench themselves firmly in political control of the land.

Cuzco, high in the interior Andes and nearly four hundred

193

miles from the sea, was quite unsuitable for the capital of a Spanish province. Francisco Pizarro named his brother Juan as military governor of the Incan city, gave him ninety men as a garrison force, and made his way by leisurely marches to Jauja and thence to Pachacamac, the coastal city subjugated by brother Hernando more than a year earlier. The puppet-Inca Manco accompanied the expedition, showing himself to his subjects, receiving their homage, and demonstrating at every halting place that he was wholly subservient to the white conqueror.

Several sites of Spanish settlement were considered for the capital. Jauja was one, but it too was inland. Another was Trujillo, founded by Diego Almagro on December 6, 1534, in the course of his return journey from Quito. It was a short distance from the ruins of Chan-chan, once the capital of the Chimu nation. Almagro named it for Trujillo in Estremadura where the Pizarros were born. Pachacamac, too, was considered for a time, but three commissioners appointed by Pizarro reported in favor of the Rimac Valley, a few miles to the north and nearer to the harbor which was to become the port of Callao. There, in January of 1535, was located the site of the future capital, which Francisco Pizarro named La Ciudad des los Reyes—the City of the Kings.

The stately title fell into disuse almost immediately. Rimac became Lima through some twist of the Spanish tongue or through nostalgic longing for the *limas*, the lime trees of the homeland, and Lima it remained. Pizarro laid out the city and designated the limits of the Plaza de Armas about which the cathedral, the governor's palace, and other buildings were erected.

For a time there was peace in the land. Francisco was

194

secure in Lima, Juan and the younger brother Gonzalo were content as *regidores* in Cuzco. A satisfactory adjustment had been made of the Alvarado incident, and the Spanish strength had been greatly increased by the addition of Alvarado's troopers. More important, among those volunteers were many hidalgos, men of gentle birth, well educated by the standards of the time, qualified to command, and superior in every way to the riffraff of Panamá who had followed Pizarro and Almagro to victory.

Almagro presented something of a problem to the now politically minded Pizarro. He was finally appointed military governor of Cuzco and sent to the inland city where Juan Pizarro, obedient to instructions, stepped down gracefully for him. Juan was confident that he would soon regain that important post, for Almagro had been told to organize an expedition for the conquest of Chile and either to assume the command himself or to choose a leader from among his captains. It was incredible that the old war dog would refuse such an opportunity for fame, and it was expected he would linger in Cuzco only long enough to muster and equip the party. That confidence received a rude blow when Almagro, on the day of his entrance into Cuzco, was overtaken by a messenger who is nameless in all of the chronicles. A friend of Almagro's, we are told, whom he had sent to Spain with Hernando Pizarro to observe and report upon all that took place at the court of Charles I. Now the nameless ambassador had returned to tell Almagro of success beyond his most roseate dreams. Hernando Pizarro had reached Spain on July 9, 1534, on the ship *Santa Maria del Campo* and had been received with all the honor due one who laid an enormous treasure in golden ingots at the feet of his sovereign.

The king-emperor had been grateful and had demonstrated that gratitude so swiftly that Hernando had been able to set out on his return voyage about October 1 of the same year. Less than three months had been required to assemble at San Lucar de Barrameda one of the most splendid fleets which had ever sailed for the Indies, to create Francisco Pizarro a marquis of Spain, to confirm him as Governor-General of New Castile, as Peru was to be known, and to establish that province as extending southward for 270 leagues from the island of Puná. Moreover, reward had at last come to Don Diego Almagro for his long years of service. The crown had created the province of New Toledo adjoining Pizarro's New Castile and extending from that province's southern boundary "in an eastwardly [sic] direction along the coast of the South Sea for two hundred leagues toward the Strait of Magellan." The one-eyed Almagro was named Governor, Captain-General, and *Adelantado* of the new province!

Though it may prove wearisome, it is necessary to examine that grant of territory and the weirdly inaccurate concept of South American geography upon which it was based. The king's largesse was directly responsible for the bitterest of the civil wars, for the death of Diego Almagro and his son, and for the assassination of Francisco Pizarro. There was in existence no map or any approximation of a map upon which Charles I or his advisers could rule off the partitions which they so blandly made. Not until 1555 was there to be any attempt to outline the South American continent by a European cartographer. All that was known was that on the island of Puná was an Indian village—spelled in half a dozen ways—which the Spaniards called Santiago. Chincha, in Peru, was declared to be 200 leagues south of that village (it is actually 840 miles), and the boundary of New Castile was set at seventy leagues south of Chincha. All beyond that was New Toledo. All the boundaries were on west to east lines; both provinces extended inland indefinitely. The dispute which presently arose was over the location of Cuzco, Incan capital and the fountainhead of Peruvian gold. Was it in New Castile, or did the royal decree place it within the confines of New Toledo? There was much to be said on both sides. If only the distance of 270 Spanish leagues was considered, both Cuzco and Lima were well within Almagro's new territory; but with Chincha established as the point from which the final seventy leagues were to be measured, New Toledo's northern frontier was close to the present boundary between Peru and Chile. Diego Almagro enthusiastically adopted the first thesis and marched into Cuzco as a ruler in his own right.

Almagro's swaggering independence and Pizarro's policy of cautious appeasement can be explained only on the assumption that neither party knew, as yet, of the additional grant of seventy leagues of territory to New Castile. Almagro was confident; the governor feared that the confidence was justified and tried to straddle the point at issue. He sent couriers to Cuzco directing his brothers to resume their authority in that city. Another message, addressed to Almagro, reminded that pugnacious individual of the impropriety of assuming a position to which he had not been formally appointed by the crown. Wait, Pizarro urged, until my brother Hernando arrives from Panamá with the royal warrant—and in the meantime why not set out upon the Chilean expedition which you have planned?

Such double-barreled diplomacy was foredoomed to failure. Not only Almagro but many of his officers had tasted political power in Cuzco. They had seized dwellings, dispossessed the former occupants, and engaged themselves diligently in a search for any gold which might conceivably have been overlooked by their predecéssors. Juan and Gonzalo were equally determined, and an armed clash between the two factions was imminent when the governor arrived in the city.

Peace was effected by a repetition of the ceremony in which the two leaders had first pledged their partnership in the Peruvian enterprise. Fray Bartolomé de Segovia performed mass; Almagro and Pizarro partook of the sacrament and swore by the Host that neither would address letters or petitions to Spain without the knowledge of the other, that neither would move against the other in Peru, and that they would—as before—share equally in the expense and the profit of future adventures; "and may that one who violates this compact be damned eternally." The date was June 12, 1535.

The Chilean expedition was the most pretentious of the many which set out from Cuzco during the summer of 1535. Although the arrival of fresh contingents of troops is mentioned only rarely in the chronicles of the period, large numbers must have arrived from Panamá where Hernando Pizarro still lingered. Among the newcomers were veterans of the Mexican and Central American conquests, experienced fighters and campaigners, who were hungry for gold and ready for any exploit. Almagro dipped deeply into his private purse for enlistment bonuses and obtained the largest number of those veterans, assembling a force which totaled some 550 Spaniards and several thousand Indians described ingenuously as allies. Even "auxiliaries," as they have also been called, is a rather exaggerated term to apply to the burden bearers and slaves who died by hundreds in the course of the march which during the next two years took Almagro as far south as the present Santiago.

Other expeditions were little smaller than that which set out for Chile. Three hundred men accompanied Alonso de Alvarado to Chachapoyas, north and east of Cajamarca. Garcilaso de la Vega, father of the historian, had 250 men under his command on an expedition to the present Ecuador; as many more marched with Juan Poncel to conquer the mountain tribesmen north of Huancabamba on the road to Quito; and still another 150 were sent as reinforcements for Benalcazar in Quito itself. Thus was Cuzco stripped of its fighting men; thus were conditions made favorable for the first and the last major revolt of the Incaic people against their conquerors.

The puppet-Inca Manco had many reasons for his mounting discontent, all of them excellent. Many promises had been made to him, and he had been encouraged to believe that the ancient glories of the throne would be restored and that the *llautu* would regain its true significance as a symbol of sovereignty. Manco, doubtless, had shed few tears for Atahualpa, whom he must have regarded as a usurper and a murderer, and still fewer for the obscure Toparca of the same illegitimate line. His friendly alliance with Pizarro at Zúrite was prompted by the not wholly selfish motive of wishing the restoration of the legal dynasty in his own person. He waited for more than a year after his coronation, a year of sad disillusionment for one who had thought the bearded strangers were supernatural beings. Close association with

199

the Spaniards taught the unfortunate Manco that the white man had all the vices of the Indian, plus many of his own, and that he lacked the virtues of the austere, frugal highlanders. He saw Cuzco sacked, saw its palaces and temples distributed among the conquerors, saw the Incan nobles reduced to slavery, and—crowning impiety—saw the Chosen Women treated as common prostitutes and their convents turned into bordellos available to any soldier. The fate of women in a conquered land is never a pleasant one, and no man among the Conquistadores was able to understand the true significance of the Chosen Women and the reverence with which they were regarded.

The contempt which Manco must have felt was increased a hundredfold when Hernando Pizarro reached Cuzco. The eldest of the brothers arrived at the new capital of Lima in August of 1535 and there informed Francisco of the new honors which were his and told him that Cuzco was definitely within the boundaries of New Castile. The marquis—as he was henceforth called—made no attempt to notify Almagro, by that time embarked on his Chilean adventure. Instead, he appointed Hernando to be governor of Cuzco and sent him to consolidate the ancient capital and the mountain districts as integral portions of New Castile. Hernando's administrative ability is best indicated by the fact that within a few months the entire Indian population of Peru, under the leadership of Manco, had risen in bloody revolt against the conquerors.

Prescott has called Manco "crafty"—a literal translation of the term *taimado* indignantly applied to the Inca by Pedro Pizarro, who can scarcely be regarded as unprejudiced. In the eyes of his countrymen he was a patriot who fought the white men with their own weapons, with lies and broken promises and with barbaric cruelty. Full realization of his own position may have come to Manco when one of his women—usually described as a "favorite wife"—was dragged to the quarters occupied by a group of officers, stripped, and subjected to that treatment euphemistically known as debauching. Manco's angry protests were ignored, and the guilty men were not punished. Rape was a boyish prank, a natural expression of high spirits. Neither the church, the civil authorities, nor the military commanders recognized criminality in any outrages perpetrated upon infidels. The revolt was then unplanned, and Manco's attempt to escape from Cuzco and return to his people was discovered. Juan Pizarro pursued and captured the Inca, and he was brought back to Cuzco and kept under guard in his palace prison.

It was then that the puppet developed craftiness. A number of his nobles shared his quarters, and these men were permitted to pass in and out of the city without the strong "escort" of white soldiers which attended every movement of the Inca. Through these men he shrewdly planned the rebellion which was to burst into flame when he, the Sapa Inca, appeared to lead his people. He allayed Hernando Pizarro's suspicions by revealing several caches of gold, then told the governor of a far greater treasure. In a cave not far from the city, said Manco, there had been hidden a golden statue of Huayna Capac. He, Manco, could lead the way to that cave; but the appearance of a large force would alarm those who watched over the treasure, and they would take it to some other hiding place. Hernando snapped greedily at the bait and sent only two soldiers to accompany the Inca and to aid him in transporting the precious relic. It was thus that the crafty Manco, in February of 1536 and with the blessing of Hernando Pizarro, escaped from Cuzco and returned to his people.

A week passed before Hernando began to suspect that he had been duped. Then, angry, he sent brother Juan with sixty horsemen to round up the fugitive. That cavalier found first the two soldiers who had accompanied the Inca. Manco had not killed them but had preserved them as messengers to report to the white men that he now headed an army of thousands of fighters, who were united to drive the Spaniards out of the land. The incident which followed is a very minor one in the long saga of war which is the history of Spanish conquest, but there is no finer example of the indomitable courage of the men who rode behind the banners of Castile. Juan Pizarro did not return to Cuzco as a harbinger of insurrection. He advanced, with his sixty men, until he encountered the main body of the Indian host on the river Yucay, as a section of the upper Urubamba, circling the Cuzco Valley to the north and east, is still known. If the site is that pointed out as *el lugar de la battala,* near the village of Calca, a location less favorable for cavalry operations could not be imagined. The swift stream lay between Juan and his enemies, and all the terrain beyond was broken ground where the Indian archers and spearmen could maneuver far more advantageously than the armored horsemen.

"Santiago!"—and Juan Pizarro led the charge into the river. The Indians fell back as the first chargers reached the further shore. "Santiago!"—and the little troop hurled itself like a thunderbolt upon the massed Peruvians. The Indians, as always, broke before that smashing impact. It was not

202

cowardice, that disorganization and retreat before men whom they outnumbered a hundred to one, nor was it superstitious fear of the white men and of the horses they rode. It was the psychological inability of the American Indian from Chile' to Canada to understand a charge or to stand against it. The phenomenon has been proved on many rivers other than the Yucay, and the history of our own frontier would have been vastly different if our Crooks and Custers and Howards had adopted the tactics of Cortez and Alvarado and Pizarro and had learned never, under any circumstances, to assume a defensive position when in contact with an Indian enemy.

Juan Pizarro held the eastern bank of the Yucay for several days. He did not defend the position, he held it by a vigorous offensive and charged Manco's legions whenever they formed for attack. He refused, however, to follow the retreating Peruvians into the hills where an ambush could be prepared so easily. The Inca must have been with the opposing force, for Juan's maintenance of the position for so long a time could have been dictated only by the hope that one of his bold charges might result in Manco's recapture. Not all the revolutionaries were upon the Yucay, however. The rebellion was carefully planned and was nationwide in extent. Communication between Cuzco and the coast was cut off, Jauja and Trujillo were under siege, and another army was marching to surround the new city of Lima. The strongest force was in the mountains, intent upon the annihilation of every Spaniard within the holy city of Cuzco, and a courier reached Juan Pizarro with word that all the heights about the city were occupied by Manco's men. Juan promptly recrossed the Yucay and marched to rejoin his brothers Hernando and

Gonzalo. He was followed closely on that retreat, but his pursuers preferred the singing of chants of triumph to any attempt to cut off the cavalry detachment.

Two hundred thousand warriors, says Pedro Pizarro, surrounded Cuzco. That is a considerable number in any war, but even the conservative historian Means states that the Inca's forces probably amounted to half that number. Prescott paints a vivid picture of a forest of copper-tipped lances and waving battle-axes, of drab hillsides blooming into gay color as the chieftains in brilliant feather cloaks marshaled their battalions, and of the momentary dismay of Juan Pizarro's weary troopers when they beheld for the first time an army such as those which had followed Pachacutec and Tupac Yupanqui. It is a florid description but not overly exaggerated. The Peruvian tribesmen, like all Indians, loved gaudy colors, and the cloaks of the humblest were striped and slashed in rainbow hues. A huge force had rallied to Manco's call, but his leadership was far inferior to that of his predecessors. The army was not yet whipped up to fighting pitch, and the battalions fell back before Juan's handful of men and permitted the troopers to join their countrymen in the beleagured city. The assumption has been advanced that Manco wished to draw as many victims as possible into Cuzco in order that the city's meager food supplies might be consumed more speedily. If that be true, the Inca displayed neither sound tactics nor astute strategy.

Cuzco is not mentioned with Paris and Gibraltar among the great sieges of history, yet a book could be filled with the saga of fierce attack and counterattack, of savage retaliation upon captives, of hand-to-hand conflict, and of clear, bright courage which filled the days from February of 1536 to April of 1537. Throughout those fourteen months all of Peru was in a state of siege with the small Spanish garrisons penned within the occupied cities by huge forces of Indians determined upon regaining their ancient liberties. At Cuzco, less than two hundred Spaniards, aided to some extent by a thousand Indian "auxiliaries," held the city against an army of two hundred thousand Peruvians, if one wishes to accept the figures of Pedro Pizarro, who was there. He may have exaggerated the enemy strength, but there has been no amendment of his statement that less than two hundred Spaniards, horse and foot, held the city. Pedro was then twenty-two years old and had been promoted from the position of page to his cousin, Francisco. He was now a fighting man and, we may safely infer, a junior officer. The Pizarros would have placed none of their blood in the ranks.

Cuzco is surrounded by steep hills, which at many points rise precipitously from the dead ends of the narrow streets. To the north, immediately above the Santa Catalina convent, which once housed the Chosen Women, stands the fortress of Sacsahuamán, a triple-walled citadel, which has been called the most remarkable achievement of ancient man in America. Its walls were laid many years before the rise of the Incaic peoples, but it was enlarged under both Viracocha and Tupac Yupanqui and made the principal defense of the city. The small Spanish force which held it abandoned the position—or was recalled—as Manco's army approached. Hernando Pizarro was to regret that he had not held Sacsahuamán at all costs, for it was there that the bitterest of the fighting occurred during the months which followed. The Inca's forces promptly occupied the citadel and as the siege progressed shot fire-arrows and other missiles from its walls

205

to the thatched roofs of the houses beneath. The bow and arrow was the Indians' principal weapon, augmented by the ax, the javelin, and the spiked war club for contact fighting. They used the lasso, too, according to Herrera, a statement which Means corrects by describing what he calls the *ayllu,* three weights connected by long thongs, which were whirled about the head and thrown to entangle the feet of the horses. The Peruvians had lost all their awe of the Spanish chargers. Manco himself rode a captured horse and, we are told, managed it right dexterously.

Hernando Pizarro's headquarters were on the plaza, probably in the Suntur Palace where the Chapel of Triumph now stands adjoining the cathedral. The siege was a long pell-mell of street-to-street fighting, of fire and starvation and horror. Spanish courage was sublime; Spanish cruelty to those of the enemy taken alive was demoniacal. Captured Indians were hanged, they were burned alive, they were decapitated and quartered within view of their companions on the heights above the city. The Peruvians retaliated with like barbarity upon Spanish prisoners. The heads of eight Spaniards—*vecinos* who had been living on the lands granted them beyond the city limits—were tossed into the plaza by means of the catapults which were rigged to hurl red-hot stones and fire-balls upon the buildings.

Cuzco was burned several times, but in that timberless land only the thatched roofs offered fuel for the flames. The massive stone walls stood, but the fire which leaped from house to house threatened repeatedly to overwhelm the beleaguered garrison. The direct intervention of Saint James and the Virgin saved Hernando Pizarro and his men. A number of the troopers saw the Holy Mother in the sky and saw the flames halt and die down in obedience to her gesture. Saint James made himself visible, too, and in the same form in which he had appeared at Cajamarca. On a white charger, sword in hand, he rode beside Juan and Gonzalo Pizarro and the gallant Gabriel de Rojas—there was a man!—in the van of the attack even as the Great Twin Brethren "rode so well for Rome" at the Battle of Lake Regulus.

A miracle, of course, but one must be willing to accept the miraculous if there is to be any explanation of why the tiny force of battle-weary horsemen and foot soldiers was not overwhelmed by sheer weight of numbers. It was the miracle of Hispaniola and of Borinquen and Cuba and Mexico and Cajamarca. Perhaps Saint James did fight for the Spaniards, whose patron he was. God and the Saints were closer to their people in the sixteenth century than in these heretic years.

The key to Cuzco was the fortress of Sacsahuamán. So long as Manco held the citadel the Spanish plight was desperate. The southern walls, overlooking the city, could not be taken by direct assault, but there was some hope of winning the fortress if a position could be gained on the more open ground to the north. To this end, Hernando split his tiny company into three platoons commanded by his brother Gonzalo, by Gabriel de Rojas, and Hernan Ponce de Leon. These, attacking simultaneously, smashed the Peruvian lines some distance southeast of the fortress. Again a miracle. Hundreds—Pedro Pizarro says thousands—of the Indians were slain, yet of the attackers none was killed and only a few suffered wounds. The platoons returned to their base, and Manco established new lines considerably in the rear of his former position, which was precisely as Hernando Pizarro

207

wished. The way was now clear for a surprise assault upon the fortress, and Spanish warfare knew no other strategy than that of the attack.

The Indian has never been a night fighter, and the laxity of the besiegers is well demonstrated by the ease with which Juan Pizarro, at the head of all the men who could be spared, left Cuzco through the ravine of the Ccantoc River, which first follows a southerly course, then turns sharply to the west. He passed beyond the barrier hills and swung in a great circle which brought him—quite unobserved by the sleeping enemy—to within the first of the three walls which defended Sacsahuamán. The fight for the citadel started within that narrow interior court, from which the Indians were cleared by a direct cavalry charge. Sacsahuamán is a terraced fortress. After winning the first court, the attackers had to mount the second wall to the filled ground between it and the third. Juan had been wounded in the head by an arrow several days before and found the pressure of his steel helmet extremely painful. He rode bareheaded into the assault, confident that he could ward off the Indians' weapons with his *broquel*, the light shield strapped to his left arm. He was among the first to reach the terrace, where he was struck on the head by a large stone thrown from one of the towers. He was carried back to Cuzco where, two weeks later, he died "in great pain."

Thus died, gallantly, Juan Pizarro, first of the brothers to perish and by all indications the best of the lot. "Brave in body and in spirit,"[1] writes his cousin Pedro, "a gentle man, magnanimous and courteous." To which Zárate adds that he was "well beloved and respected by all." We know little of

[1] *Valiente y muy animoso.*

the man beyond those post-mortem eulogies, but if any of the Pizarros approached the true stature of a *caballero* it was that Juan whose bones lie among many others in the crypt of the Dominican monastery in Cuzco.

Chapter Eleven

JUAN PIZARRO WAS DEAD, and only the outer bastions of Sacsahuamán were taken. The fortress proper—the section within the third wall and the towers which commanded the entire area—was still held by the Inca's troops under the leadership of a chieftain named Cahuide. A gallant general that Incan noble must have been; a spectacular warrior whose boldness appealed greatly to the Spaniards, whose attacks he repeatedly threw back. He was easily distinguished by the captured suit of Spanish mail which he wore and by the huge club which was his favorite weapon for the hand-to-hand fighting about the ladders with which the attackers endeavored to scale the third wall. Hernando Pizarro gave explicit orders that Cahuide's life should be spared in the final assault, by which the Spaniards reached the terrace and the inner court at half a dozen points. Cahuide wanted none of the conqueror's mercy. Atahualpa and Chalchuchima had relied on the honor of the Pizarros, and their confidence had led them to the stake. Manco's general fought to the last, then flung himself headlong from the summit of one of the tall towers and died on the battlements he had defended so courageously.

Sacsahuamán was taken, and the besieged Spaniards breathed more easily. Starvation was an ever-present threat, but the menaces of fire and of constant harassing from the heights were removed. Too, the Indian legions had lost their first keen appetite for fighting. They, too, were hungry, and food could be obtained only if the crops were sown and the terraced fields cultivated. Manco had established his headquarters at Ollantaytambo, some sixty miles from Cuzco, and his army was strung out along the Urubamba Valley and was far more busily employed with agriculture than with fighting.

A sufficient force was maintained about Cuzco to keep the Spaniards busy, to make difficult their forays into the countryside for food, and to prevent any communication between them and the other garrisons of their countrymen. This last was demonstrated on September 8, 1536, when Hernando led a raiding party down the Chunchulmayo River. Lying in the trail were the bodies of five Spanish couriers who had been sent from Lima by Francisco Pizarro and who were almost within sight of Cuzco when they had been captured and beheaded. The mail pouches lay near the mutilated bodies, and Hernando learned then that Cuzco, Jauja, and Lima were also closely besieged.

Relief came, months later, from an unexpected source. Diego Almagro crossed the Vilcañota Pass and descended the Urubamba toward Cuzco. No thought of succoring his distressed countrymen prompted Don Diego's advance. His Chilean adventure had been a complete failure. Scores of Spaniards and hundreds of the Indian slaves had died in the eternal snows of the high Andes, others had perished in skirmishes with the tribesmen. Almagro had exacted fierce reprisals for the deaths of his followers, writing another bloody record of conquest in his advance from the Maule River to Coquimbo. Thirty caciques were burned alive before their tribesmen in reprisal for three Spanish deaths, and on another occasion ten Indians were impaled on stakes and left to die. Almagro had drawn heavily upon his own resources to outfit the expedition, and the loot of Chile was zero. The advance guard reached a point not far north of the present Santiago, and the troopers believed firmly that they were approaching the end of the world. They retreated to Almagro's camp at Coquimbo and clamored to return to Peru where there was gold and where the Indians were less hostile than these mountain tribesmen—and at this rather critical stage in the commander's fortunes Rodrigo de Orgoñez arrived with the royal warrant which certified the old fighter as *Adelantado* of New Toledo. That was enough for Diego Almagro. He was convinced that Cuzco was within his territory, and he turned to the north with no other thought than the ousting of the upstart Pizarros from the golden city.

The evidence is clear that Diego Almagro was considering only himself and, to a lesser degree, his son, who was now close to man's estate. He learned of Manco's revolt when he was in southern Peru, at or near that village at the foot of Mount Misti where Garcia Manuel de Carvajal and Juan de la Torre, Man of Gallo, were to establish the city of Arequipa. Almagro did not march his veteran fighters to Lima and the relief of the governor. Instead, he sent messengers to Manco, told the Inca of his quarrel with the Pizarros, and asked that a place be appointed for a conference which might be mutually satisfactory. No such request would have been made

212

unless supported by promises, and the only pledge which Almagro could have made would have been to support Manco in his revolt. That promise, or one tantamount thereto, must have been given, for the Peruvians offered no opposition to Almagro on his passage of the cordillera or during the long march to Urcos, scarcely twenty miles from Cuzco where Hernando Pizarro was fighting on starvation rations.

About one-half of Almagro's force remained at Urcos—the ancient Racche where one of the few temples to the Creator-God, Viracocha, had been reared—while the commander at the head of possibly two hundred men advanced some five miles to a spot picturesquely referred to by Prescott as "the vale of Yucay" and assumed by him to be at a considerable distance from Urcos. It is merely a spot where the steep hills—now as then terraced to their summits by the diligent highland agriculturists—recede from the river and leave an alluvial plain large enough for a campsite. It was there that Almagro met and talked with Manco, and it was there—if Pedro Pizarro's account is correct—that he either conferred with Hernando Pizarro or was spied upon by that commander.

There is much that is difficult to understand in the accounts. It does not seem possible that Manco would have so relaxed his siege of Cuzco as to permit Hernando to advance to the Urubamba and there make contact with his countrymen, yet it is quite certain that Almagro was permitted to send messengers to Cuzco while he continued his negotiations for some sort of alliance with the Inca. Those messengers brought no reassuring word to the beleaguered garrison and its commander. They bore a copy of Almagro's commission as *Adelantado* of New Toledo, they reasserted the old claims that Cuzco was within the boundaries of that province, and they demanded that the defenders of the city receive Don Diego as their lawful governor. That diplomatic sparring between those whom he believed to be mortal enemies was quite incomprehensible to Manco. He promptly formed the opinion—probably justified—that Almagro's expressed hostility toward the Pizarros was but a ruse to conceal some new plot of the white men upon his sovereignty, and he ended the negotiations with a sudden surprise attack upon Almagro's army.

Four hundred, possibly five hundred, men against fifteen thousand, and the smaller number won. It was the old story, once more repeated, of the inability of Indian troops to fight as a unit rather than as individuals. Manco's regiments were not only beaten back, they were overwhelmingly defeated, and the fleeing remnants were followed hotly by the hard-riding cavalrymen, whose red blades drew sweet revenge for the Chilean disaster. The cumbersome and inaccurate matchlocks played a part, but it was a minor one beside the smashing countercharge of the mounted and dismounted swordsmen. Manco withdrew to Vitcos, even further from Cuzco than his previous base at Ollantaytambo, and never again raised the banner of revolt. He promoted, or encouraged, occasional guerrilla raids against small bodies of Spanish troops, but none even approximated an organized rebellion. He had his women and a few courtiers who remained loyal to the pathetic remnant of the imperial court, and with them he was content. He was a nuisance, no more, to the provincial governors until 1544 when he was killed by some fugitives from the defeated Almagrista faction who had found refuge in his camp. The circumstances of his death will never be known, as the killers were themselves slain by Manco's followers.

The siege of Cuzco—and the entire revolt—ended with the Inca's flight. The Indians hid their weapons, killed the few horses they had captured, and returned to their villages and their fields. As the news spread, the forces threatening Lima, Jauja, and Trujillo also withdrew quietly to the mountains, and the Spaniards found themselves suddenly, if briefly, at peace.

A truce of sorts was patched up between Hernando Pizarro and Almagro. The latter agreed to stay out of Cuzco until competent navigators—there was none nearer than the coast—surveyed the distances and certified the boundaries between New Castile and New Toledo. Until such decision was given there was to be peace between the two factions, and Almagro was to remain quietly in the headquarters he had established at Urcos.

Whether Hernando Pizarro deliberately violated that truce is debatable. He was quite capable of such treachery, but it is equally possible that the activity of his men in repairing the ravages of the long siege was interpreted by Almagro as being an attempt to fortify Cuzco against him. The old soldier was also informed that several hundred men under Alonso de Alvarado were advancing from Lima to Cuzco. Almagro acted promptly. He marched into Cuzco on the night of April 8, 1537, and by morning was in complete control of the city. He tossed the Pizarros and a number of their officers into prison—an act of leniency which was not approved by Rodrigo de Orgoñez, his second in command. That cavalier, a veteran of the Italian wars, knew

215

the Pizarros. He advised that Hernando and Gonzalo be decapitated immediately and quoted the proverb, old even then, *"El muerto no morde"*—the dead do not bite. Almagro did not follow the counsel, which, judging solely from subsequent events, was most excellent. He spared the vindictive Hernando and the younger brother and sent messengers to Jauja where Alonso de Alvarado had been dawdling for some weeks on the excuse that the mountain town required his protection. Almagro must have been feeling a bit cocky when he dictated those letters, for he summarily ordered Alvarado to resume his march to Cuzco and there place himself under the command of the *Adelantado* of New Toledo. It happened that Alvarado was not taking orders that day from Diego Almagro. He arrested the ambassadors, put them in irons, and notified Francisco Pizarro of the action taken.

Thus started the first of the civil wars of Peru: a bitter, year-long factional quarrel marked by gallant and desperate fighting and by despicable treachery. Almagro must have been notified very promptly of the reception given his messengers in Jauja. It is quite possible the information was forwarded by Pedro de Lerma, one of Alvarado's officers, who was willing to sell out his leader. While Francisco Pizarro hesitated in Lima, Almagro acted. He marched toward Jauja and met Alvarado at the Abancay River, a small stream which enters the Apurimac from the west less than forty miles from Cuzco. There—with the help of Lerma and the "fifth columnists" that traitor had enlisted—he administered a crushing defeat to the loyalists. Alvarado was taken prisoner along with an unspecified number of his men, and the one-eyed victor returned triumphantly to Cuzco.

That battle took place on July 12, 1537, and Francisco

Pizarro had started to march from Lima to Cuzco. Ships had at last arrived from Panamá with the reinforcements he had requested to put down Manco's revolt. Among the four hundred men was a crack corps of two hundred and fifty under the personal command of Don Gaspar de Espinosa, he who had presided at the trial of Vasco Nuñez de Balboa in 1517, who had supplied Hernando de Luque with twenty thousand pesos to finance the 1526 expedition, and who now—since Luque was dead—ranked as a partner with Pizarro and Almagro. When word of the Manco revolt reached Panamá, Espinosa had decided to make a personal check upon his heavy investments and future prospects in the land of the Incas. An immensely wealthy man, and thorough in all things, he had enlisted and equipped the combined force of cavalry and infantry and had included a company of arquebusiers armed with the last word in projectile weapons. It is very possible that these new arms were wheel-locks. That improvement in ignition methods had replaced the older, less satisfactory matchlock in all sections of Europe by 1535 and had probably been introduced into the Indies. The weapons carried by Espinosa's men are not described in detail by the chroniclers, who were more impressed by the circumstance that the new guns fired chain shot—two heavy balls connected by a short length of chain —which was effective to a ghastly degree.

Pizarro could not have advanced much beyond the crest of the Maritime Cordillera near Mount Ticlio when he met the battered survivors of the Abancay battle and learned of Alvarado's defeat and Almagro's victory. He retreated hastily to Lima, strengthened the defenses of that city, and sent Espinosa to negotiate with the third partner at Cuzco. In that year of 1537 the Marquis Francisco Pizarro was at least sixty years old and had lost all taste for active campaigning. He was a politician now, a governor of a province, and a gentleman of coat-armor, and he acted politically.

Espinosa got exactly nowhere—and got there fast!—in his attempts to work out a solution which would assure peace in the land and satisfy the very touchy honor of the two leaders. He returned to Lima and informed the governor that his brothers were still prisoners and that Almagro had announced his intention of building his own coastal capital while retaining control of Cuzco.

The doughty *Adelantado* of New Toledo made good on that boast within the month. He left Gonzalo Pizarro in the Cuzco prison, took Hernando along as a hostage, and marched to the Chincha Valley, 150 miles south of Lima. There he plotted La Ciudad Real de Almagro, modestly conferring his own name rather than that of saint or king upon the city which would be the capital of New Toledo—the boundaries of which were still undetermined. He was there when he received the very unwelcome news that all the Cuzco prisoners, headed by Gonzalo Pizarro and Alonso de Alvarado, had escaped and joined the governor in Lima.

Almagro now had but one hostage of any value, and this undoubtedly influenced him in agreeing to reopen the negotiations and to accept the arbitration of one man, Fray Francisco de Bobadilla of the Order of Mercy. The friar had been identified with the Pizarro faction ever since his arrival in Peru, but Almagro believed that he would adjudicate the case impartially—an opinion which was not shared by Rodrigo de Orgoñez. Gonzalo's escape, that cavalier argued, was all the more reason for the immediate execution of the elder brother, Hernando. *El muerto no morde!*

The town of Mala, a tiny oasis where the Mala River cuts through the bluffs of the desolate coastal plain, was selected as a neutral meeting place for the two leaders. It was the Brenner Pass of 1537. The meeting ended almost as soon as it began. Gonzalo Pizarro, according to his cousin Pedro, had planned to cut off Almagro's retreat and capture the rebel chieftain and his party. The coup was foiled when one of the governor's officers refused to countenance such treachery. In Almagro's hearing this man sang or hummed a few bars from what Herrera says was an old song:

> *Tiempo es el caballero*
> *Tiempo es de andar de aquí*

which might be translated as "Now is the time for all good men to go to the aid of their party." Almagro took the broad hint and departed without the formality of a farewell. Safe in his headquarters at Chincha, he rejected the first proposals made by Fray Bobadilla but accepted a second set under which Cuzco would remain in his possession until a definite decision had been made by the crown. Hernando Pizarro was to be released under the pledge that he would leave the country within six weeks. The terms of that truce pleased none of Almagro's officers. His treasurer, Manuel de Espinar, exclaimed that Fray Bobadilla was no monk but, in very truth, a devil; Pedro de Lerma warned him that Pizarro would repudiate the treaty as soon as Hernando had been freed; and Rodrigo de Orgoñez "took his beard in his left hand and with his right made the sign of decapitation," and then addressed his own head, saying: "For the friendship of Don Diego de Almagro you have been cut off." Orgoñez had appraised Francisco Pizarro far more accurately than Almagro, who had known him for some twenty years.

The pledged word of the Pizarros was worthless. There is no vindictive hatred of the brothers in that statement, for the facts are incontestable. Gonzalo had escaped from Cuzco, and the negotiations with Almagro had as their object only the release of Hernando before the counsel of Orgoñez prevailed and the elder brother was given three hours to confess his sins and otherwise prepare himself for the ax which puts so conclusive a period upon all treachery. Almagro's own son—already known as El Joven, the Lad, to distinguish him from the father whose name he bore— escorted Hernando Pizarro to the governor's camp at Mala. The Lad was received most courteously, but the dust of his departure had scarcely settled before the Pizarros went into action. Francisco's statement to his followers, quoted in full by Herrera, is a sixteenth-century edition of the specious explanations of Hitler and von Ribbentrop. Hernando was formally released from all the solemn pledges he had made, and the active military command was given to him and to Gonzalo. The fighting men were told to take up their arms and to strike boldly "for the king and for Pizarro" until the last rebel went down in defeat. Further, Almagro himself was notified that the treaty, upon which the ink was scarcely dry, was now abrogated.

What followed can be briefly told. Almagro retreated to Cuzco. The old soldier was extremely ill from "a grievous malady, the result of early excesses," as Prescott tactfully renders the blunt *bubas* of the chronicles. Orgoñez, faithful unto death, told him that further attempts at negotiation would be futile, that his only hope lay in military action against the Pizarros. A decisive attack at that moment might have changed history, but Almagro held to the Cuzco area while the brothers leisurely organized and trained the army they had assembled. Nearly a year passed before the Pizarros crossed the ranges and approached Cuzco where Almagro waited. It was on April 26, 1538, that the two forces met at Las Salinas, the Saltpits, near the present village of San Sebastián, scarcely five miles southeast of Cuzco. The hillsides were crowded with the population of the city and with Indians from miles around, come to witness the strange sight of their white conquerors endeavoring to destroy one another. On the one side were between eight and nine hundred men led by Hernando and Gonzalo Pizarro; by Alonso de Alvarado, eager to revenge his defeat at Abancay; and by Pedro de Valdivia, whom history was to know as the conqueror of Chile. Almagro was borne to the field in a litter; active command of his six hundred men was taken by Rodrigo de Orgoñez, seconded by Enriquez de Guzman.

The battle was over in two hours, and the Almagristas were crushingly defeated. Orgoñez was dead: he surrendered and was then stabbed by a common soldier named Fuentes, who by that act assured his own immortality. A gallant soldier, Orgoñez, although he chose the wrong side. His head, stuck on a pike, was displayed in the Cuzco plaza for several days. Pedro de Lerma, whose treachery had encompassed Alvarado's defeat, was taken alive although bleeding from seventeen wounds. His death, too, gives us the name of another of the men-at-arms. He had once punished—by a flogging, perhaps—a soldier named Samaniego, who now

221

found opportunity for revenge and stabbed the wounded Lerma as he lay in bed. Almagro was made prisoner; his son, El Joven, was also captured and sent under strong guard to the governor, Francisco Pizarro, who had advanced from Lima to Jauja upon receiving word of the Salinas victory. Francisco received the captured Lad kindly, giving him the freedom of the camp and later sending him to Lima.

The true character of Hernando Pizarro is starkly revealed in his treatment of Diego Almagro. Their positions were now reversed: the former prisoner was now captor and conqueror. Hernando visited Almagro repeatedly in the Cora-cora Palace, built by the Inca Roca, where the old soldier was imprisoned. He inquired solicitously after Almagro's health, he assured him that his detention was merely a matter of form and that he would be freed as soon as the governor, his old friend and partner, arrived in Cuzco, and he sent the sick man such delicacies as could be obtained in the mountains. All the time he was marshaling charges, major, minor, and petty, against the *Adelantado* of New Toledo, and early in July Almagro was led from his prison and called upon to answer charges which covered no fewer than four thousand folio pages.

The trial was as much a mockery, the verdict as inevitable, as the proceedings against Atahualpa five years before. Indeed, we know far more of the legal travesty which sent the last Inca to death. None of the chroniclers has named those who sat in judgment upon Diego Almagro, and of the contents of the four thousand folio pages we are told only that the charges included making war against the king and the legal governor of New Castile, unlawfully seizing the city of Cuzco, and entering into a conspiracy with the puppet-Inca

222

Manco. He was condemned as a traitor and sentenced to die a traitor's death—public decapitation—upon the scaffold erected in the plaza of Cuzco.

It is quite possible that the entire proceedings were *in camera* and that the accused man was given no opportunity to reply to the long list of charges. Certainly he was not in court when sentence was pronounced, for that grim news came to him in his cell from the lips of an unidentified friar. Almagro refused to believe the cleric—additional proof that much of the evidence against him had been considered in secret session. It was confirmed by Hernando Pizarro himself, who took a sadistic delight in the condemned man's agony of mind and in refusing all his pleas for mercy or for permission to appeal the verdict to his old friend, the governor.

That appeal, if granted, would have been unavailing. The brothers had taken as their motto the words of Rodrigo de Orgoñez—a dead man does not bite. Pedro Pizarro, who in his memoirs strives ever to picture his distinguished cousin as an honorable cavalier, admits in an unguarded moment that Hernando sent a special courier to Jauja to report the trial and ask for instructions. The reply was brief. Deal with the matter, said Francisco, so that Almagro shall create no further revolts.

That was explicit enough for any man, and Hernando acted with no further delay. He ignored Almagro's warnings that the king would hear of the affair and that the royal wrath would fall upon the Pizarros. "Make your peace with God," said the eldest of the brothers, "and prepare yourself for death."

One boon was granted the man who had been created

Adelantado of New Toledo. Like Atahualpa, he was spared the ignominy of a public execution. Diego Almagro was strangled in his cell, and his lifeless body was then borne to the plaza where the usual mummeries were observed and the head was struck off. The blank-faced Quechuas of the highlands watched. None has told us what they thought of this new manifestation of the inexplicable customs of their conquerors.

Chapter Twelve

THE CHARACTER OF FRANCISCO PIZARRO changed again with the death of the man whose greatest error had been to trust him or his brothers. The politician had replaced the soldier after the fight at Cajamarca; now the politician was obscured by the figure of an arrogant grandee of Spain. The vacillation and indecision which had marked much of his career disappeared. He sought no more advice, and he ignored that which was offered. His last rival, the man he had always hated, was dead. Francisco felt that at last he was supreme in this land he had conquered, that none could or would question him, and almost overnight he assumed power that a viceroy would have hesitated to employ.

When one considers his deeds, no other interpretation of the man is possible. He entered Cuzco as a conqueror, and one of his first acts was to put into effect a policy of ruthless and relentless severity toward all the "Men of Chile," as Almagro's followers proudly called themselves, and all who had been sympathetic toward the Almagrista cause. It must be remembered that Diego Almagro had been created Governor and *Adelantado* of New Toledo by the crown. The appointment was quite as legal as that which named Pizarro to the same offices in New Castile and was in no way affected by the boundary dispute which arose between the two rivals. Determination of that boundary should have been left to competent and unprejudiced surveyors, of course, but that Almagro had fought for it did not constitute a revolt against his king or affect his property rights in the lands granted him.

Yet Pizarro's first decree was to erase, to all intents and purposes, the terms of the royal charter. He received Diego de Alvarado, brother of the conquerer of Guatemala, and listened to that cavalier's statement that Almagro had appointed him guardian of the Lad. As such, said Alvarado, his purpose was to withdraw to New Toledo and govern that region until young Almagro was confirmed as his father's successor. Pizarro would hear no more. He declared grandiloquently that the lands he governed had no boundaries but continued to Flanders! More, he confiscated the estates and possessions of all Almagristas and inaugurated a program of oppression directed against them and all others who had incurred his displeasure. Diego de Alvarado, rightly sensing that he could be of little service to the Lad in Peru, departed forthwith for Spain, there to plead the cause of Almagro's heir before the king. He was joined presently in Castile by Sebastián Benalcazar, who since 1534 had commanded the faraway garrison in Quito. In a series of bold advances, marked ever by fiendish cruelty to the conquered peoples, Benalcazar had extended Spanish conquest over much of the present Ecuador and northward into the watershed of the Magdalena. From those explorations came reports of "Canela," the Land of Cinnamon, abounding with gold and silver as well as spices, which lay to the east of the farthest mountains, but Benalcazar returned to Quito without crossing the Eastern Cordillera.

Rumor whispered to Francisco Pizarro that his lieutenant was planning to cut the ties which bound him to Lima and declare Quito a separate province. Perfidious himself, the governor was ever willing to credit others with similar perfidy. He sent officers to Quito with orders for Benalcazar to report immediately to Lima where it is more than possible he would have received the same treatment that had been accorded Diego Almagro. Forewarned, Benalcazar had already departed for Panamá and Spain where he was to prove an able second to Diego Alvarado.

Charles I had begun to suspect that his province of New Castile was not well ruled, but he was not one to act hastily against a governor to whom Spain owed the largest financial contribution received from the New World. He had heard before many of the stories told by Alvarado and Benalcazar. There was at court at this time a pestiferous and extremely vocal Dominican, Fray Bartolomé de las Casas, who pulled no punches in telling the king by just what methods the western world had been conquered. Casas talked facts, not hearsay. He had gone to the Indies with his father in 1498 and twelve years later had been admitted to holy orders, the first priest to be ordained in the new world. He had been in Hispaniola and in Cuba, in Mexico, Guatemala, and Nicaragua, and had witnessed the ruthless slaughter of thousands of natives and the enslavement of those who survived. One account of his life and work states that he visited Peru as well and spoke from first-hand knowledge of conditions there. That is questionable, very, but there is no doubt of the priest's personal opinion of Francisco Pizarro, whom he pictured as a rapacious and bloodthirsty demon. Charles listened to Casas and to his adviser and patron, Bishop Loyasa; he listened to Alvarado's plea for Almagro the Lad; he listened to Benalcazar's account of the territories his explorations had added to the royal domain and the suggestion that appointment as *Adelantado* of Quito might be a suitable reward for services rendered. Charles listened to them all, but he took no definite action. Any reorganization of colonial government was still hanging fire when Hernando Pizarro arrived at court and added his glib arguments to the chorus.

More than a year passed after the murder—for it was murder!—of Diego Almagro before Francisco Pizarro sent his own ambassador to Spain. The year had been a busy one, but Hernando had taken no particularly active part in the various campaigns, and there was no reason that he should not have set sail long before that day in June of 1539 when he left Lima. Military command had been turned over to the younger brother Gonzalo, whose role hitherto had been secondary to those of his elders but who from now on was to become more conspicuous as a conqueror. Gonzalo fought and whipped the tribes of the Collao and of the Charcas region—the Titicaca basin and southern Peru—and led several punitive expeditions against Inca Manco's guerrilla warriors, who were making impossible any settlement in the Urubamba and Apurimac valleys. Manco was not captured, and the raids on travelers and isolated camps continued, but the expeditions served as a finishing school for Gonzalo Pizarro, whose qualifications as a Conquistador worthy of the name he bore may be judged by the fact that captives in the Collao died in mass hangings; in the Charcas, where wood is more plentiful, they were burned; and at Urcos one of Manco's wives was stripped and paraded about the camp, then tied to a tree and after a savage flogging was shot to death with arrows. Gonzalo was rewarded for those loyal services with a large encomienda which included the enormously rich silver deposits of Potosí and with appointment to the command of Quito, vacated by Sebastián Benalcazar. The office carried with it instructions to explore and conquer the Land of Cinnamon, an assignment which pleased the adventurous Gonzalo no end but which effectively removed him from the stage of Peruvian history for the next couple of years.

Francisco, the governor, took for himself an immense tract in the mountains between Lima and Jauja. It was known as Los Atabillos and has been called a marquisate by several who have referred to Francisco as Marquis of Atabillos. Though vast enough for a duchy, it was nothing more than an encomienda. There is little to the credit of the autocratic governor during the three years which followed the execution of Almagro. The building of Lima continued, and several other cities were founded, of which Arequipa is the most noteworthy. Pedro de Valdivia was dispatched upon the expedition to Chile where he would find death in battle with the fierce Araucanans and win fame as the conqueror of the land which had been given to Diego Almagro. Reasonably regular communication was established between Lima and Panamá, with Trujillo and Isla Puná as ports of call for the vessels engaged. Such colonial developments and expansions were inevitable. As monuments to Francisco Pizarro they are small beside his cruel oppression of the Indians in all sections of the land and his relentless policy of vengeance toward all followers of Almagro who remained in Peru. Hernando, on the eve of his departure for Spain, had warned the governor that his contemptuous disregard of the Men of Chile might prove disastrous. Banish them to the mountains, said Hernando, and surround yourself with a trustworthy guard, for I will not be here to take care of you. Francisco merely laughed at that excellent advice and declared that every hair in the Almagristas' heads was a hostage for his personal safety. We will leave him, briefly, in that complacency.

Hernando returned to Spain in his former capacity as a bearer of rich gifts. Five years had passed since he had delivered the royal share of Atahualpa's ransom, and a large sum had accumulated during that period as a result of the usual methods of taxation and pillage, plus some abortive attempts at mining. As an expression of his own indebtedness to his liege, the governor added a generous gift for Charles himself and six large emeralds for the royal consort, Isabella.

A full year was required for the voyage. Hernando had been informed that he would be arrested if he landed at Panamá. No reason is given for that arrest, but some political machinations must have been afoot, for he was taken into custody on the gulf coast of Mexico after crossing the isthmus of Tehuantepec. He was taken to the capital where Viceroy Antonio de Mendoza ruled that the case, whatever it may have been, did not fall within his jurisdiction. Hernando proceeded to Vera Cruz, whither he had been bound, and sailed from there to Hispaniola. He reached Spain with his treasure intact about the middle of 1540.

His reception at court was a chilly one. The complete story of the manner in which Diego Almagro had been hustled to death had been told many times by Alvarado, by Alonso Enriquez de Guzman, and others. For a time it seemed almost possible that Hernando might pay for his crimes with his own head, but his principal accuser, Diego de Alvarado, died—so opportunely that poison was suspected. Charles looked at the gold, Isabella toyed with the emeralds, and the life of the arch-conspirator was spared. No formal charges were made against him, and he was not brought to trial. The king merely placed him under arrest and sent him to the Mota fortress, near Medina del Campo, where he remained for twenty years. He was given some freedom of movement, he retained his large fortune, and some years later was permitted to marry his niece, Francisca, daughter of Francisco Pizarro and his Peruvian mistress, Huayna Capac's daughter, whom the Spaniards called Doña Inez Huaylas Ñusta. For twenty years, however, he was given no opportunity to meddle in transatlantic affairs. He was an old man, a very old man, when Philip II granted him full liberty in 1560. He returned to his birthplace, Trujillo, and died there three years later, the only one of the brothers to die a natural death. He outlived all of his generation, but so far as his brothers in Peru were concerned Hernando died when the king's decree sent him to La Mota. They who had been four were now two, Francisco in Lima, Gonzalo deep in the jungles of eastern Ecuador.

The problems facing Charles of Spain were not solved with the incarceration of Hernando Pizarro. The king-emperor was a remarkable individual in an era which produced many such, but his colonial policy has been sharply criticized as one of indecision and of straddling, of injustice toward those who within half a century had made Spain a world power, and of the replacement of able men by incompetents. There is truth in those charges, but much that is unfair. Those who castigate Charles I for his treatment of Hernando Cortez are prone to overlook that the conqueror of Mexico did not enter court with clean hands; that he had challenged, fought, and defeated his own countrymen before marching against the legions of Montezuma. So far as Peru is concerned, it is difficult to see how Charles could have adopted a policy different from that which he now followed. Pizarro had conquered the land. He had made tremendous contributions to the royal treasury and had tapped a reservoir of gold which seemed inexhaustible. Peruvian gold was of more immediate value than the development of a colonial empire, and Francisco Pizarro had supplied that gold. Spanish policy in regard to overseas possessions was ever shortsighted, but Spain held her colonial empire, from the Rio Grande to the Straits of Magellan, over a much longer period than England retained control of her provinces on the Atlantic seaboard. The Conquistadores were ever restless, their eyes were ever fixed upon ultimate horizons, and as a natural corollary Spanish exploration was infinitely more extensive, Spanish consolidation and development far more comprehensive than similar activities in the possessions of the more static English, who, a century after Jamestown and Plymouth, were still confined to the narrow strip between the Alleghenies and the sea.

Charles of Spain, in the early autumn of 1540, appointed an envoy to proceed to Peru and make thorough investigation of conditions there. The man selected was the Licentiate Don Cristobal Vaca de Castro, "a member of the Royal

232

Audience of Valladolid . . . a learned judge, a man of integrity and wisdom, and, though not bred to arms, had such address and such knowledge of character as would enable him readily to turn the resources of others to his own account." Vaca was instructed to co-operate with Governor Pizarro in all things and to endeavor to formulate, harmoniously, an administrative policy for New Castile. The stories told by Alvarado and by Guzman may have enabled the king to form a very accurate opinion of the character of Hernando Pizarro, but neither they nor Fray Bartolomé de Las Casas were able to prejudice the monarch against Francisco. Still, Peru was a long way off, and many things might happen, so Vaca was given a warrant which appointed him Governor of New Castile in the event of Pizarro's death.

Vaca sailed from Seville late in 1540 but did not reach Nombre de Dios, the Caribbean port for Panamá, until February or March of the following year. He set out for Peru as promptly as possible, but the storms which had buffeted him on the Atlantic were nothing to those he encountered on the much shorter voyage from Panamá along the South American coast. He got no further than Buenaventura in the present Colombia where his pilot managed to bring the battered vessel to port some time in April. Vaca, his own health none the better for the suffering he had endured, proceeded slowly overland through the highlands of the Colombian interior. From Cali, on the Cauca River, he sent messengers to Quito advising the commander of that city of his plight and requesting that guides be sent him. At Popayán, still on the Cauca and several hundred miles from Quito, he was met by Don Lorenzo de Aldana, acting governor of Quito, who told him of the bloody events of June 26, 1541, in the capital of New Castile. His excellency the governor, said Don Lorenzo, was dead.

Two things impress one who reads of the last year in the life of Francisco Pizarro. The first is the man's arrogance, his supreme confidence in himself and his contempt for those whom he knew hated him as bitterly as men can hate their oppressors. The second is the solidarity of the Men of Chile and their loyalty to the young Almagro, the beloved Lad.

Many of the Almagristas had died at Salinas; others had left the country or had found refuge of sorts in Cuzco and the new settlements which were being established. A few had won amnesty by volunteering to accompany Valdivia to Chile, but a large number remained in Lima and there endured Pizarro's persecution. The governor disregarded the excellent advice given him by Hernando. He assembled no personal bodyguard, and when he sent Gonzalo to Quito he lost the services of one whose loyalty was unquestionable and who might have saved his life. Francisco was warned many times that the Men of Chile were plotting against him, yet he permitted them to remain in Lima and to maintain a headquarters on the plaza where the Lad lived with the leaders of his faction. There was nothing subtle in the Almagristas' plotting; their hatred of the governor and his cabinet was known to everyone, Spaniard or Indian, in Lima. Under cover of darkness the Lad's adherents decorated the gibbet —a permanent fixture of the Plaza de Armas—with three noosed ropes placarded with the names of Francisco Pizarro, his secretary Antonio Picado, and the *alcalde mayor*, Velasquez. The placards, they boasted, would be replaced by the individuals themselves as soon as the king's deputy, Vaca, arrived in the capital.

Then came the news that the squadron which had sailed from Panamá with the deputy had foundered beyond Cabo Pasado and that Vaca had been drowned. The Almagristas accepted that rumor as truth and were spurred to desperation. With Vaca dead several years would pass before another deputy could be appointed by the crown and reach Peru; by that time they would all have perished, either from starvation or on the scaffold. They decided to assassinate their oppressor and fixed the day, the hour, and the place for the deed. On Sunday, June 26, they would fall upon the governor as he left the cathedral after mass.

Pizarro was informed of the plot in all its detail, yet he remained fatuous. A priest who had received the story in the confessional hastened to the palace with the news, but Pizarro shrugged it aside with the remark that the cleric was seeking to curry favor and probably wanted a bishopric—a theory which may well have been true. He yielded at last to the pleas of Picado and of Francisco de Chavez and consented to refrain from attending the morning services on that Sunday, but he took no steps to investigate the priest's report or to arrest the Lad or the leaders of his faction.

Juan de Herrada—Rada in many of the chronicles—headed the conspiracy. A bold man and, certainly, a desperate one, for when he learned that the plot had been revealed to Pizarro he rallied his fellows and raided the palace itself. The Almagristas rushed from their headquarters and, shouting, "Long live the king! Death to the tyrant!" marched across the plaza. One man, Gomez Perez, turned aside a few paces to avoid some water which had overflowed from a drainage ditch. Herrada dismissed him from further participation in the desperate venture, telling him: "We go to bathe in human blood, and you refuse to put your feet in a puddle of water!"

The time was shortly after noon. Many of Pizarro's officers had heard that he was ill—the excuse advanced for his failure to attend mass—and had made courtesy calls at the palace. Some of those men are named in the chronicles. Martín de Alcántara, the governor's half brother, was there. So were Francisco de Chavez, the *Alcalde* Velasquez, the Bishop of Quito, and many others. The majority, Means observes, "were fully as unsavory as their opponents," an opinion perhaps justified by the circumstance that only three or four stood firm when a terrified servant rushed in and screamed that the Men of Chile had already forced the outer gate, had killed one man, and were on their way to murder the governor. The *Alcalde* Velasquez went out the second floor window in a photo-finish with his eminence the Bishop of Quito and a dozen gentlemen of coat-armor.

The old war dog Francisco Pizarro was of more stalwart heart. Men of Chile, forsooth! Let us see them stand before one who can call himself a Man of Darien and a Man of Gallo! He shouted to Francisco Chavez to bar the door while he and his brother, Alcántara, donned their armor. Chavez was killed before he could obey the order, and his body was thrown down the stairway. Alcántara leaped forward to hold the entrance. He was aided by "one or two cavaliers" and by two young pages, none of whom were thought of sufficient importance to be named by the chroniclers. They were all young men and no match for the desperate and experienced Men of Chile, but they killed two of the attackers before they were themselves cut down. Alcántara and the nameless pages were killed, but we are not told of the fate of the men who aided them—if, indeed, those men existed save in the imagination of Pedro Pizarro and other historians, who did not wish to admit that of the governor's friends only Francisco Chavez failed to think of his own hide first.

The old lion was left alone, nor was he able to adjust his breastplate without assistance.[1] He wrapped about his left arm the long black cloak embroidered with the Cross of Saint James and bared the rapier which had been sheathed since Cajamarca.

"Traitors!" he roared. "Have you come to kill me in my own home?"

He had not forgotten the tricks of swordplay, this old veteran who had fought his way from Yurbaco to Cuzco, this "bastard of Estremadura" who was now a marquis of Spain. He parried a stroke, lunged, and the bright blade was red halfway to the hilt as he returned to guard. Again! Another man fell and died on the floor at the governor's feet. The men of Chile drew back.

"Why are you so long about the matter?" Herrada shouted. "Death to the tyrant!"

A desperate man, Herrada, but not so brave as to cross swords with Francisco Pizarro. He seized a companion, one Narvaez, and thrust him upon the governor's blade. Narvaez

[1] The cuirass of the period protected only the front of the body and the shoulders and was secured by straps which buckled behind. The back, to judge from contemporary paintings, was unprotected. The thought of turning his back upon the foe seems never to have entered the mind of a Conquistador.

237

died, but before Pizarro could withdraw the sword Herrada's rapier bit through his throat. He sank to the floor, and the conspirators—all courageous now—ran him through and through.

"*Jesús!*" gasped the old warrior. He dipped his finger into his own blood, traced a cross upon the floor, and bent his head to kiss the sacred symbol as he received the death stroke.

Thus died Francisco Pizarro, Conqueror of Peru. Whatever his shortcomings in life, he was in death magnificent. He died, says Gomara, "with none to say 'God forgive you,'" yet he died as he probably would have wished: a soldier's death, face to the foe, with the ringing of steel upon steel as the last sound in his ears. That is not to perish like a wretched outcast, as one scholar has described the death of Francisco Pizarro.

With that victory, as they considered it, the Almagristas' ecstasy knew no bounds. They paraded the streets of Lima shouting of their triumph and calling upon all citizens to acknowledge the young Almagro, who by this bold stroke had become governor of New Castile! Some proposed that the dead marquis be decapitated and his head displayed in the plaza, but before this could be done the bodies were removed from the palace and secretly buried in the cathedral. The location of the governor's grave was known only to a few loyal followers, who supervised its opening a few years later when the remains were ceremoniously removed and reinterred. They now rest in the first chapel on the right as one enters the cathedral of Lima. The coffin is glass-topped, and for a small fee the sexton opens the barred gateway to the chapel and permits tourists and other sightseers to stare at the bones of the conqueror. The chapel is a dark alcove off the main portion of the cathedral, but the sexton carries a pocket flashlight to illumine a peepshow which reflects little credit upon either the Roman Catholic Church or the government authorities in Peru.

The character of Francisco Pizarro was not complex, although many pages have been written in the effort to portray him as a cryptic and mysterious figure. He has been called avaricious, ambitious, vacillating, and perfidious, as well as courageous and inflexible. He was all those things, yet none of the terms can be applied without qualification. He won a huge personal fortune, which he distributed swiftly and lavishly. He left no great wealth, and the enormous encomienda of Atabillos reverted to the crown. Ambition and inflexible determination may have spurred him after he began the series of expeditions which ended at the last in conquest, yet that ambition was dormant during the years of his prime in Darien, and until his association with Almagro and Luque he was content with the quiet life of an old soldier retired to a little *repartimiento* in Panamá.

His vacillation was political, never military. Hesitation in pronouncing a decision is natural to an illiterate man, who cannot wholly trust the better educated, the mentally more adroit individuals who surround him. And what has been called his perfidy is closely allied to that last. He loved no one, man or woman, hence for all his life was unloved. He sired children, yet his union with Inez Huaylas Ñusta, daughter of Huayna Capac, was a mating, no more.

The thought of marriage, even to legitimatize his children, never occurred to Francisco Pizarro.

His courage was physical, not spiritual. He was governor and captain general, yet at Cajamarca he lacked the moral fortitude to assert the authority of the dual office when he yielded to the pressure of Almagro and the perverted fanaticism of Fray Valverde and sent Atahualpa to an unjust death. In his relations with Almagro he violated again and again the solemn oath of friendship and co-operation to which he had sworn upon the Host—yet he kept that pledge with Luque and Luque's heirs. From the beginning to the end of their association, he distrusted and hated Diego Almagro and was hated in return. No distinctions can be made between those two; neither can be blackened at the other's expense.

If such be perfidy, Francisco Pizarro was perfidious, yet none can point to a single word or deed of his and say: "Herein he was disloyal to his king." From first to last he was a king's man. He thought of Peru only as a royal province and of himself only as a servant of the king to whom God—through Pope Alexander VI—had given the seas and the plains and the mountains of this western world.

The man must be judged by his times, and any characterization of Francisco Pizarro is a characterization of his brothers Hernando and Gonzalo, of Cortez, of Soto, of Vasco Nuñez de Balboa, of Valdivia, Ponce de León, Alvarado of Guatemala, Velasquez of Cuban infamy, Coronado, Ojeda, the mariners Cabrillo and Ruiz and Alarcon, and all those who marched and sailed with them. They were cruel, ruthless, and avaricious. They were ambitious.

They were superlatively courageous in a day when physical courage was the commonplace rather than the exceptional. They were of high but singularly elastic honor. They won the New World sixty years before Humphrey Gilbert and Walter Raleigh sailed and the ever-cautious English began to dream of empire. They were the Conquerors, and in their front rank will ever stand the humble man-at-arms who embarked with Ojeda in 1509 and who died thirty-two years later a Marquis of Spain, Governor and *Adelantado* of New Castile, and a Knight of the Order of Santiago.

Chapter Thirteen

FRANCISCO PIZARRO WAS DEAD, and but one of the Brothers of Doom remained in the western world. Gonzalo was far from Lima when the Men of Chile slew the marquis in the old palace of the governors. He was somewhere among the jungles which flank the Napo River in the region where Ecuador and Peru and Chile meet and where the delineation of national boundaries depends largely upon the political sympathies of the cartographer. He was not to learn of Francisco's death until a year had passed, but the events of that year determined to no small degree his own adventurous and tragic career.

For a few days after the assassination of Francisco Pizarro, the Almagristas had everything their own way. They rioted in the streets of Lima. They arrested and imprisoned the officers of the government they had overthrown. They looted the dead governor's palace and the home of his secretary, Antonio Picado, and they pried that unfortunate individual from the corner where he had hidden himself in the residence of the royal treasurer, Riquelme. They confiscated horses and arms and supplies wherever they could find those articles, of which they had so long been deprived. Then they discovered that money, too, was useful, so Picado was taken from his cell and put to the torture of the *garrucha* and the *escalera* to compel him to reveal the hiding place of the vast wealth which his master Pizarro had accumulated. Picado would not or could not—probably could not—answer. He was beheaded in the Plaza de Armas, and his severed head impaled on a pike. It was not necessary to bind his wrists when he was led to the block. Both arms had been completely dislocated at the shoulder by the torture of the hoist.

It is in connection with the death of Antonio Picado that Fray Vicente Valverde, now Bishop of Cuzco, appears for the last time in Peruvian history. He interceded vigorously, if in vain, for the unfortunate secretary. Shortly thereafter the friar was permitted to sail for Panamá. Velasquez, *Alcalde Mayor* of Lima, went with him. Both died when the entire ship's company was killed by the Indians of Isla Puná.

Within a very short time Almagro the Lad and his followers learned that their bloody *coup* did not meet with general approval and that the Spaniards in Peru refused to recognize a governor who had murdered his way into office. True, the Men of Chile were responding to the call from every section of the land, but only from those who had followed his father did El Joven find sympathy with his rebellious course.

It is unnecessary to trace the complete history of the next fourteen months. Juan de Herrada died—a severe blow to Almagro—and was succeeded in command by Cristobal de Sotelo and Garcia de Alvarado, two officers whose loyalty to the doomed cause was exceeded only

243

by their jealousy of one another. Alvarado killed Sotelo. Young Almagro settled the question by killing Alvarado and personally taking over the command. He was then in Cuzco, which he had captured by avoiding the forces of Pedro Alvarez Holgúin who had set out from the ancient capital to do battle with him. Holgúin let Cuzco go. He continued to the coast, joined his force of three hundred to the other loyalist detachments, and awaited the arrival of Don Cristobal Vaca de Castro, now Governor of New Castile.

Vaca did not rush matters. He was a stranger in the land where fate had catapulted him into the position of highest authority, and it behooved him to move slowly. Also, every day's reports indicated that the situation would develop into a shooting war, and Vaca was no soldier. Still, as a lawyer, he could unite soldiers and reconcile the jealousies of generals. This took some time, but by the late spring of 1542 he was at Jauja in nominal command of an "army" of seven hundred fairly well-equipped men. The Lad's headquarters by this time were at Vilcas where he received considerable aid from Manco, Inca-in-exile, who had moved his fugitive government to that point from Vitcos—to which he retreated swiftly enough before the shooting started.

Young Almagro's force amounted to some five hundred men, the majority of them veterans of the Chilean campaign. These were augmented by some Indians furnished by Manco, whose brother Paullu also fought under Almagro's banner. The rebels were better armed than the loyalist forces and were far superior in artillery strength, thanks to the ability and activity of Pedro de Candia, who, it will be remembered, had been named as Pizarro's chief of artillery in the original *capitulacion*. The veteran Man of Gallo had turned against his former chieftain and had thrown in his lot with the Almagristas.

The two armies—neither of them as large as one of today's battalions—met at Chupas, eight miles south of Huamanga, the present Ayacucho. The place is a narrow valley, its surface broken by ridges thrust out by the surrounding mountains. On the longest of those spurs, at the southern end of the valley, the Lad placed his sixteen pieces of artillery, relying upon Candia and his gunners to break the ranks of Vaca's strong cavalry detachments. The date was September 16, 1542, and the advancing loyalists did not make contact with the enemy until late afternoon, so late that Vaca required considerable urging to begin the action for which Almagro waited.

The battle was bloody and desperate. The loyalists charged—"*Santiago! El Rey y el gobernador!*"—and Candia's gunners retorted with "*El Rey y el Joven!*" and pressed their glowing matches to the primed touchholes of the *falconetes*. Smoke from the salvo obscured both friend and foe, but as the white clouds lifted it was seen that the shots had passed above the heads of the attackers. The range might have been overestimated, the clumsy pieces may have been improperly laid, but Almagro saw only treachery in the error. He slew Pedro de Candia on the spot and himself assumed command of the guns for the few moments which remained for their effective action; the few moments before the loyalist infantry charged under the inspiring leadership of Francisco de Carvajal.

Forget the battle of Chupas and the name of every man

who participated therein, but remember Francisco Carvajal, who here enters the history of Spanish conquest. Carvajal, the toughest, fiercest, most ribald old soldier who ever girded on sword. If the chroniclers are correct he was then at least seventy-five years old—a statement which is not easy to accept even if it cannot be refuted. Behind him, say those tellers of tales and embroiderers of reputations, were forty years of service in the Italian wars from which he emerged with nothing but military experience, the scars of a dozen or more wounds, and the price of a passage for himself and his wife, Catalina, to the New World where he arrived about 1532. He was first in Mexico, but the conquest of that land had been completed, and neither there nor in Central America was there brilliant opportunity for the impecunious fighting man. Only Peru was open territory for one who knew no trade other than fighting, no tools but the sword; and Carvajal was among those who sailed from Panamá when Pizarro appealed frantically for reinforcements for his scattered garrisons. He took an inconspicuous but undoubtedly valiant part in the fighting incident to the Manco revolt and was rewarded for his services with a small holding near Cuzco. There he remained until the Almagrista rebellion when he marched to the sea with Pedro Alvarez Holgúin and rose, as has been remarked, to command of one of the divisions of Vaca's microscopic army.

He was a huge man, standing well over six feet and weighing more than two hundred and fifty pounds, and the chroniclers tell that at Chupas he ran in front of the soldiers who wavered before the Almagristas' fire and shouted that he, who offered a better target than any of them, was not afraid. The infantrymen rallied, and their charge swept over and captured the rebels' guns.

Holgúin was killed in the fighting, along with thirteen other *caballeros*, but the attack was continued, and by late evening the Lad's force was crushed. Several of his officers, knowing well the fate which awaited them as prisoners, formed ranks for a suicidal charge and, shouting, "We killed Pizarro, the tyrant!" flung themselves on the lances of the victors.

The rebel dead were the more fortunate, for Vaca showed mercy to neither the wounded nor the captured enemy. All who were involved even indirectly in the plot against Pizarro were given summary trials, beheaded, and quartered. Retribution followed those who fled the field. They were hunted down in every city and hamlet where they sought refuge and there executed. The hacked quarters of the headless bodies were left on display to illustrate the fate awaiting those who took up arms against their king or his governor. Leniency was extended only toward those who could satisfy the judges that they had not joined the Lad until after he had occupied Cuzco. These were permitted to live, minus the right hands which had drawn sword against the lawfully appointed officers of the crown.

Young Almagro escaped in the darkness, which fell before the fighting ceased. His goal was Vitcos, where Inca Manco was awaiting news of the battle, but he passed through Cuzco in his flight and was arrested and imprisoned by the municipal officers whom he had appointed and who now knew on which side their political bread was buttered. He shared the fate of those who had enlisted in his hopeless cause. Only the last barbaric ignominy of quartering was spared him. He was executed in the same plaza which had witnessed the posthumous decapitation of his sire, and his body was buried beside that of his father.

There was, for a space, peace in the land, but the man who was to break that peace was now at Charcas (Potosí) sulking because Vaca had snubbed him when all others of military experience had been paid large sums or promised great rewards if they joined in the operations against the Lad. That man was the last of the Pizarros, Gonzalo, and he could look back upon a year as stirring, and adventures as amazing, as had ever befallen a Conquistador.

Gonzalo, it will be remembered, became his brother's lieutenant-governor in Quito at about the same time that Hernando Pizarro left Peru for Spain. He was especially charged with the task of exploring the unknown lands to the east and with discovering and conquering Canela, the Land of Cinnamon, the existence of which had been reported by Sebastián Benalcazar. Canela, of course, was a land of Indian dreams. It was Zenu and Dobayba and Cibola and Quivira, but the valor of the Conquistadores was matched only by their credulity. Gonzalo Pizarro was to hear many such stories of lands rich in gold, in jewels, and in fine spices. They are unnamed in the fragmentary accounts of his adventure, but they are one with Zenu and Quivira, ever receding before the explorer's advance.

It was no mean expedition which set out from Quito early in 1540. Gonzalo had heard from his brother of the suffering at San Sebastián and Puerto Hambre, and he knew of the perils which awaited an undermanned and poorly equipped party. He left Quito at the head of a force of 350 cavaliers and men-at-arms, 150 of whom were mounted. With them were 4,000 Indians—warriors, slaves, and porters—and upward of 1,000 dogs, the majority of which were of the Indian-fighting breed. Moreover, if we are to believe the chroniclers, that army was followed by an enormous drove of swine—5,000 of them, according to one account. The last item strains belief. Seven years had not passed since Atahualpa died, and stock raising could have made little progress throughout the long months of the Manco revolt when the Spanish colonists were under close siege in their scattered settlements. The peccary, the only wild hog native to America, is found in the temperate zones of Ecuador, but it was never domesticated by the Indians. It would appear impossible that the European hog would have reached the neglected northern province of Quito in sufficient numbers for so large a reserve to have been bred by the time Gonzalo Pizarro arrived in the land. Nor is the hog a creature which takes kindly to or thrives upon long marches. His feet are small, his body heavy, and the hooves of even the hardy "razorback" soon break down on rocky ground or in rough country. He is the poorest swimmer of all the domesticated animals, and much of the country over which the expedition marched abounds with streams which must be crossed by swimming. This writer has no substitute to offer for the hogs reported by the chroniclers, but he cannot believe that any number accompanied the expedition of Gonzalo Pizarro.

No historian was a member of the party, nor did Pizarro or any of his officers bequeath to posterity their journals or any personal memoirs of the most important geographical exploration of the South American continent. All records which have come down to us are second-hand, the interpretations of early historians of the accounts given by survivors or the narrations of those who had talked with survivors. Those tales lost nothing in the telling and the retelling, and in reading them one must follow only the main thread of the narrative and dismiss the lurid details, the stories of events which existed only in the imaginations of the veterans. The introduction of a few elements of truth does not detract in any way from the achievements of those men who were first of their race to descend the eastern face of the Andes, first to look upon the waters of the Amazon more than two thousand miles from the sea.

The route must have been south from Quito, then east to a crossing of the cordillera in the vicinity of the 19,000-foot peak of the volcano Cotopaxi, then in active eruption to judge from the tales of the severe earthquakes which terrified the explorers during their crossing of the mountains. The ground opened, they reported, and a village of five hundred houses vanished from sight. The vast opening of the earth is imaginary, of course, but a village may well have been swept into an existing ravine by an avalanche of mud and water similar to those which have destroyed many Andean hamlets within recent years.

The explorers discovered the Land of Cinnamon, indefinitely located east of the mountains, and there saw enormous forests of trees which bore the valuable bark. The actual identity of those trees is any man's guess, but there is no native cinnamon in South America. The weary searchers had been many weeks in reaching Canela, but spices were forgotten when they were told of far richer territories, abounding with gold, which lay only ten days' march to the east. That was enough for Gonzalo Pizarro and his men. Spurred on by dreams of new conquest they continued their journey by following the Napo River toward its mouth in the Amazon.

There is far more fiction than fact in the accounts of the march along the Napo. At no point does that stream narrow to twenty feet and plunge over a precipice twelve hundred feet high. A cataract which might answer that description —the naturalist Humboldt measured its descent as fifteen hundred feet in three leaps of the foaming waters—is to be found on the western slope of the volcano Tunguragua in the Ecuadorean province of that name, but Tunguragua is far south of Cotopaxi, and it is impossible to believe that Pizarro, after having once descended the mountains to the region he called Canela, should once more have climbed the sierra. The foregoing will illustrate the difficulty of reconciling the early accounts with present geography, for the chronicles, without exception, place the cataract found by Pizarro on the Napo where no such waterfall exists. The Napo is navigable over virtually all its course. Shallow-draft launches can ascend almost to the mouth of the Coca, principal tributary of the Napo, and the canoes of gold prospectors and collectors of cinchona bark and sarsaparilla make the trip from the mountain headwaters to the Amazon in five or six weeks.

The chroniclers believed the tales of cataracts and of gorges so narrow that they could be bridged by a single tree on which the entire company—hogs included, presumably—crossed to the further bank. The chroniclers

251

believed because they knew nothing to the contrary; others who should have known better have failed to look beyond the early accounts and have pictured both the Napo and the Amazon as abounding in hazardous rapids. Only after Pizarro and his followers were well down the Napo does truth begin to eclipse fiction in the accounts of the expedition. There the exhausted men heard again the old story of pleasant lands to the eastward, and there they built a boat which would transport to the new lands the weaker members of the company and the little which was left of the stores with which they had set out.

That ship has been described as "a tall and stately vessel." It was not. It has been called both brigantine and bark by those who knew nothing of nautical distinctions and who translated too freely the "*barca*" of the chronicles. *Barca* should be translated from early Spanish merely as "boat." A *barca* might be a skiff or a dory or even a larger craft in which oars were supplemented by mast and sail, but to translate the word as "bark"—a three-masted vessel square-rigged except for the mizzen—is wholly erroneous. No one who has passed the mouth of the Napo, which is less than five hundred feet wide where it enters the Solimoes-Marañon arm of the Amazon, could possibly believe that the stream could be navigated under sail. In 1851 an American naval officer, Lieutenant William L. Herndon, followed the Amazon from its most remote Peruvian headwaters to its mouth. He wrote: "I shall content myself with observing that if Pizarro built a brig or anything that carried a mast, he either embarked low down upon the Napo, or, what I rather suspect, the Napo was a much larger stream then than now."

There is neither geological nor historical evidence that the Napo, the Putamayo, or any of the Amazon affluents have decreased in size within the past five centuries, nor does one belittle the achievements of Gonzalo Pizarro in pointing out that the vessel which he built was a barge. This is attested by the chronicles. Nowhere in the early accounts does one find any mention of sails or masts, or anything to indicate that the crew of the craft did more than permit it to drop downstream with the Napo's rather gentle current while the shore party kept pace along the bank.

Francisco de Orellana, heretofore unmentioned in the chronicles, commanded the barge and those men whose condition entitled them to the more comfortable transportation. For a time the two parties, ship and shore, kept together and camped each night at the same point. The food supplies were close to exhaustion, however, and Pizarro ordered Orellana to proceed to the mouth of the Napo, survey the country there, and return with provisions, which could be obtained readily from the friendly natives of whom he had been told so much. Fifty men sailed with Orellana, and the remainder, already on starvation rations, waited. Neither time nor distance can be reconciled in the various accounts, but Pizarro and his men camped on the Napo long enough to learn well the food value of tropical fruits and herbs, of toads and of snakes, and of "other evil and disgusting things." Then, despairing, they resumed their march toward the river's mouth. There, or near there, they found Sanchez de Vargas, a cavalier with an excellent record as a fighting man and with a high sense of honor. He had been on the barge with Orellana and

253

had been put ashore when he refused to join in that navigator's ambitious project. The tale which Vargas told gives us one of the few instances of rank treachery in the field to be found in the annals of the Conquest. Spanish chicanery was usually of a political nature and was reserved for the council table or the court.

The sight of the broad, placid Amazon was too much for Francisco de Orellana. Somewhere that mighty stream must reach the sea, and he proposed to his crew that they follow the river to the Atlantic, proceed to Spain, and claim for themselves all the lands through which they passed. To their shame, the men upon the vessel agreed enthusiastically to desert their starving fellows in the jungle and to set out upon their own careers as conquerors. Vargas, the only dissenter, was left on the bank without food and with no weapons save the sword he had refused to sully. Let it be said at this point that Orellana succeeded. The perils of that first voyage upon the Amazon have been greatly exaggerated. The tales of rapids on that river are as fictional as those of the warrior women which the early travelers asserted dwelt along its banks. The mouth of the Napo is only 350 feet above the sea, and there can be no rapids in a stream which descends only 350 feet in a distance of 2,500 miles and which can be navigated by ocean-going steamers. As a matter of fact, over much of its course the Amazon is a decidedly sluggish river.

Strict justice would demand that Orellana and his fellows in treachery be slaughtered to the last man by hostile savages, but they were not. Fifty armed men, traveling by boat, found little trouble in beating off the tribesmen who from time to time disputed their passage. One such skirmish, however, earned for the great river the name it bears. Orellana noted that the women of the Taparu tribe fought shoulder to shoulder with the male warriors, and he promptly named the stream the River of the Amazons. By the time he reached Spain the skirmish had grown to a pitched battle, the men of the tribe had vanished, and the banks of the river had become populated by warrior women of demoniacal courage and remarkably quaint methods of reproduction.

At some point in the descent of the Amazon the barge must have been reconstructed and equipped with a mast and a sail, for Orellana reached the sea, cruised northward along the coast to Tobago, and eventually reached Hispaniola where he obtained passage to Spain. Charles I welcomed him as he did every man who brought tales of new lands and new sources of wealth. The coastal areas of Brazil fell within that portion of the New World which Pope Alexander VI had given to Portugal, but Orellana was authorized to equip an expedition to ascend the great river and to claim the interior of the continent for Spain. Backers were easily found, and the traitor sailed from Burgos with five hundred men in six ships. He died before the squadron sighted the Brazilian coast, and his leaderless men abandoned the project.

Gonzalo Pizarro knew only that the man whom he had trusted had proved a traitor. He and his companions were alone, their food exhausted, their horses dead, in a region hundreds of miles from the nearest settlement of their countrymen. In that hour of despair Gonzalo proved himself a worthy brother of him who had challenged the starving Men of Gallo to endure still greater privations. Return to Quito, he said, or perish miserably here in the wilderness. The way is long and toilsome, the perils many and great, but we must retrace our steps or die.

Thus began an anabasis as terrible as any ever recorded. From the mouth of the Napo to Quito, in an air line, is more than five hundred miles, and that distance is doubled by the tortuous route which must be followed along the meandering rivers and the arduous ascent of the eastern and central cordilleras to the interior plateau. In few regions is it more difficult for a large party to support itself, to obtain the food upon which life depends, than in the jungle. Contrary to general belief, animal life is not plentiful. The rivers abound with fish, but the land creatures have adapted themselves to the dense cover along the banks and to the semiaquatic existence which must be theirs in a region with an annual rainfall of more than eighty inches. The tapir, the capybara, the agouti, and the small deer of the *campos* are all shy creatures, largely nocturnal in their habits, and to be taken only by skillful and patient hunters. Indicative of the difficulties in obtaining animal food is the circumstance that nearly all of the Indian tribes of the region have developed the blowpipe and the poisoned dart. Man does not adopt the weapon of the adder in regions where game is plentiful and life is not a desperate struggle for existence.

Nor is vegetable food any more abundant. There are fruits of sorts in the jungle, and edible nuts, but they mature swiftly in the steamy heat, and the trees which bear them

256

are scattered and difficult to recognize. The natives of the region—and many of the tribes have changed little since the first white man entered the country—have small fields where a few crops are painfully cultivated: squashes and a species of hard, fibrous melon; an indigenous legume, plantains, and the bitter cassava, or manioc, the roots of which produce the coarse flour which we know as farina. It is quite possible that it was the manioc which killed those Spaniards who "died after the eating of poisonous fruits." The raw root contains a lethal quantity of hydrocyanic acid, which the Indians have learned to expel by repeated washings and dryings before the extracted farina is edible.

Pizarro and his men stripped those fields which they encountered on their march, and the tribesmen fled before the gaunt, ragged soldiers. Many of their Indians deserted, others struggled on with the white men in desperate hope that they might win through to their homes in the distant highlands. The sick, red man and white, died and were left behind in the jungle. The well retreated from the Napo's banks and made their way painfully to the westward along the slightly higher ground of the low divide between the waters of the Napo and those of the Putamayo to the north. No roster was kept of either the living or the dead. The survivors told afterward of living companions who were deserted by those able to struggle on. They told of men— three in one day—who died swiftly but in horrible agony from the bites of venomous serpents: the fer-de-lance, the coral snake, the jararaca, and the huge bushmaster, to give some of them the names by which they are known today. Men died in attempts to swim the jungle rivers, men weakened in the clinging mud of the frequent marshes and died in the slime. And some of those who survived the jungle died in the biting cold of the cordillera which had to be crossed before the central plateau was gained.

More than two hundred and fifty Spaniards were in the party which turned back from the Napo's mouth. In June of 1542 eighty of them reached Quito. There is the story of Gonzalo Pizarro's march. Small wonder that Garcilaso de la Vega wrote in later years that sheer strength of spirit had triumphed over disasters greater than any humans had ever endured.

In Quito, Lorenzo de Aldana told Gonzalo of the assassination of his brother, of the arrival of Vaca, and of all the other momentous events which had taken place during his long absence in the wilds, including the important news that Hernando Pizarro was now a political prisoner in La Mota fortress. Gonzalo must have set out for the south almost immediately, for he reached his estates in the Charcas before Vaca had completed the organization of the force which took the field against the Almagristas.

Pizarro offered his services, which were tactfully, though no less conclusively, rejected by the able diplomat who was now Governor of New Castile and who was not predisposed in favor of anyone of the Pizarro name. Gonzalo sulked, and after the Lad's defeat at Chupas it is very probable that he made some of the statements which his contemporaries attributed to him. He asserted, it is said, that he should have succeeded the murdered Francisco as governor, that the Spaniards whom Peru had made rich had forgotten the Pizarros who had led them to conquest;

and he hinted—it could have been no more than a hint designed to test popular reaction—that the time might now be ripe for another Pizarro to assert the rights of his clan and take in the land the position which he had earned.

Rebellious words, those. Words which would have hustled the speaker to the block had a governor less wise, less diplomatic, and less tolerant than Don Cristobal Vaca de Castro been supreme in New Castile.

Vaca listened to the reports which were brought him and formed his own opinion of Gonzalo Pizarro. He then summoned the man to Cuzco, where he had established his headquarters, and devoted several days to soothing the proud cavalier's ruffled feelings. He inquired at length into Gonzalo's adventures in the jungle, all of which, he said, would be reported to the crown. He asserted publicly his confidence in the honor and loyalty of this last of the Pizarros, and, finally, he urged Gonzalo to return to his estates and there enjoy the leisure to which his valiant services entitled him.

It was a dismissal, of course. It was tacit information to Gonzalo that his services in any capacity, military or civil, were not desired, but the coating of sugary compliments was so heavy that Gonzalo never tasted the bitter flavor of the pill beneath. He returned to La Plata, as the Potosí area was then known, and for nearly two years devoted himself industriously to the affairs of his encomienda, the chief of his duties being the development of the huge silver deposits on the property. He was accompanied into that voluntary exile by Francisco Carvajal, although the records are silent as to the capacity in which the old fighter served the younger. They may have thought, both of them, that at last there was an end to fighting and hardship, but events far across the sea were at that moment determining the destinies of Gonzalo Pizarro and Francisco Carvajal. On November 20, 1542, in the royal palace in Barcelona, Charles I of Spain placed his signature upon the revised code of colonial government which was to be known as the New Laws.

Chapter Fourteen

THOSE NEW LAWS were the direct result of the zeal and fervent oratory of Fray Bartolomé de las Casas, the apostle of the Indians. It is quite unnecessary here to trace the development of that movement, which basically was exalted, humanitarian, and altruistic, or of the ebb and flow of political sentiment in Castile. A different story might have been written if news from Peru had reached Charles more promptly. Of his province of New Castile the monarch knew only that Francisco Pizarro had been assassinated and that Vaca de Castro was waging war against a strong revolutionary if not rebellious faction. Spain and Spain's king were quite ignorant of the defeat of the Almagristas or of the excellent progress which Vaca was making in stabilizing the colonial government. Circumstances pointed to a need for vigorous and radical reforms—and here at court was Fray Bartolomé, widely traveled in the Indies, wholly unselfish, preaching and writing of the exact manner in which those reforms should be made.

The New Laws were drastic; they represented a complete turnabout from all previous policies of colonial administration, an overthrow of established precedents and privileges.

There was to be no more exploitation of native peoples, no more slavery. The Indians, one and all, on the islands and the main, were declared free men and subjects—not vassals—of the king. Their rights in law were those of any citizen. That in itself was enough to end the system of encomiendas and *repartimientos,* but the New Laws went further and were specific in regard to the huge land grants with which the conquerors had been rewarded. Many of them were to be materially reduced in size, and hence in potential income. The Indians now held in slavery were to be released unconditionally. Indian labor was henceforth to be contracted for and paid for, and religious instruction was to be given to all at the encomendado's expense. Further, title in the land grants was to pass to the crown upon the death of the original grantee; ownership was not to continue "throughout two lives," as heretofore—which meant that the holder's widow and children were automatically made homeless and perhaps penniless upon his death.

Those regulations were extended to all the New World colonies, but there was a particular—and extremely ill-considered—paragraph which applied to Peru alone. Anyone who had taken part in the Almagro-Pizarro quarrel, on either side, was automatically and immediately deprived of all his holdings in New Castile. No distinction was made between the most loyal follower of the governor and him who had fought for the Almagros at Salinas and Chupas. This, naturally, stripped virtually every landowner in Peru of his estates.

Civil and criminal jurisdiction in Peru was vested in four *oidores*—"hearers"—who formed a newly created body known as the Royal Audience of Peru, which was to be established in Lima. From the decisions of those judges there should be no appeal, either to the high courts of Spain or to the king. Those appointed as the first *oidores* were the Licentiates Diego de Cepeda, Pedro Ortiz de Zárate, Juan Jerónimo Alvarez, and Miguel Lisón de Tejada. All were rather able men, with considerable experience in the law and in political administration, and there is some chance that they might have brought order out of Peruvian chaos if a man of even mediocre ability had been placed in the supreme post. That was not to be. The office of governor-general was abolished, Peru was made a viceroyalty, and Charles I appointed to the exalted post of viceroy one Don Blasco Nuñez Vela. He was a Knight of Avila and had held various political and quasi-political positions but none of sufficient importance to warrant his appointment to a position where he was answerable only to the king. He had seen some military service, but little real fighting, in Italy and was now to command in a country which, literally, had been hacked by the sword into a Spanish province. No man less fitted for the post could have been found in all of Charles's European domains, and before the voyage to the New World was well under way he "revealed himself to be the possessor of a mentality like that of a lunatic hyena!"

Thus does Means, a master of biting phrase, characterize the first of the viceroys, who was, in truth, to prove himself a shrieking scavenger. Vain, like any incompetent elevated suddenly far above his proper station, he surrounded himself with a personal staff of sycophants, maintained fifty servants in attendance, and established a viceregal court with all the ceremony and punctilio of royalty itself. The

263

flotilla on which he sailed from San Lucar on November 3, 1543, numbered 49 vessels, and among the 915 colonists were the first upper-class Spanish women who had ever set out for the distant land of Peru. Eighty-seven were unmarried girls. The Virgins of the Sun, at long last, were to have some competition.

The four *oidores* sailed with the viceroy. The harmony of the relations between them and Nuñez Vela is best shown by the fact that the viceroy described the Judges of the Audience as a boy, a lunatic, a simpleton, and a fool. Before the end of their adventure the judges probably applied all those epithets to the viceroy, for, from the arrogant beginning to the bloody end of his career in the New World, the king's appointee acted with childish petulance and insane incompetence. He refused to wait at Nombre de Dios until one of the *oidores* had recovered from an illness contracted on the long voyage but assembled his escort, crossed the isthmus to Panamá, and entered that city with all possible viceregal pomp. There he gave the residents a taste of what they might expect under the New Laws. He declared some three or four hundred Peruvian Indians—slaves, but quite contented with their lot—to be free men and women, and directed that they be returned forthwith to their homeland at the expense of their masters. He slapped a restraining order upon a vessel then at Nombre de Dios and forbade it to sail for Spain because the Peruvian silver included in its lading was the product of slave labor.

The Judges of the Audience and such officials as dared offer advice to a viceroy urged him to act less impetuously and to learn something of the political and economic situation in the colonies before interpreting the New Laws so literally. Nuñez Vela replied—"with asperity," says the chronicler—to the effect that he had come to the New World for no other purpose than to execute those ordinances and that execute them he would in every last detail and without delay.

Again he refused to wait for the *oidores*, here detained by necessary business. He sailed from Panamá on February 10 and reached Tumbez before the end of that month after one of the quickest trips ever recorded for the voyage. He learned there that the Spaniards in Peru were in a state of extreme unrest, to put it mildly, over the laws the enforcement of which promised to ruin them all. Governor Vaca de Castro was in Lima and had persuaded the residents of that city to wait and see what happened before believing all the rumors which reached their ears. At Cuzco, however, was Gonzalo Pizarro, who had taken the field at the demand of the *vecinos* and encomendados and was now hailed as captain-general, the title under which his brother had entered and conquered the land. At Gonzalo's right hand was the hardy, shrewd, and ever-ribald Francisco de Carvajal. The old soldier must have been well paid for his duties at Potosí. He was ready to retire and to return with Catalina to Spain where he could live comfortably for those years which remained to him on the wealth he had amassed. Then came the rumors and finally the definite information of the New Laws and the severity with which the king's viceroy was enforcing them. The worried landowners turned to Gonzalo Pizarro—who stood to lose as much or more than any of them—and that cavalier called upon the veteran Carvajal to ride once more to the wars. "I was not eager to put my

265

hands into the warp of this cloth," said the old warrior, "but with things as they are now I promise to be the principal weaver."

Together, he and Gonzalo formed a tough team for any man to oppose, a team which a politic administrator might profitably have appeased, but Nuñez Vela was not politic. Such advances as he did make, including rather vague hints of amnesty to all those who laid down their arms, were distrusted by Pizarro and Carvajal. Rumor quoted Vela as having said that the two rebels would suffer the same fate as the Almagros if he could lay his hands on them.

One is entitled to ask whether Gonzalo Pizarro, at the beginning of this last stage of his adventurous career, was driven by personal ambition. Lust for power has been read into his demand upon the citizens of Cuzco that they name him captain-general instead of to the less important post of procurator-general, which would designate a leadership more political than military; but there is considerable factual evidence that the man sincerely believed that Nuñez Vela would be impressed only by a show of force and that the head of the opposition party must have military command. There is much in the chronicles to confuse the student who desires only to brush aside the web of politics and see clearly the man who for nearly four years was to be the most prominent individual in the New World, but this writer believes that Gonzalo Pizarro was both candid and sincere when he said that he "wished nothing for himself but only that which was best for all." He overruled those who urged that he march upon Lima, oust Vaca, and anticipate Nuñez Vela by declaring himself governor. That would be rebellion, and Gonzalo was not yet ready to rebel against his king.

The shedding of much blood would have been spared had he reconsidered that decision while Nuñez Vela was advancing overland from Tumbez to the capital, where he arrived with all the panoply of his exalted rank on May 17, 1544. Some words of Vela's were interpreted by the anxious landowners as indicating that he purposed to administer the New Laws judicially and to suspend for the present their more onerous provisions. The Viceroy Antonio de Mendoza in Mexico—whose little finger held more of wisdom than was contained in all of Vela's body—had done just that thing and thereby averted a revolution in the land he governed. The encomendados took heart. Gonzalo Pizarro announced that he was ready to relinquish his new title and return to Potosí—and then the "lunatic hyena" snarled! Governor Vaca was arrested and imprisoned, first in a cell in the palace, then upon a ship in the harbor at Callao. Gonzalo Pizarro was ordered to surrender and to disband his army. The command was not obeyed, and he was declared a rebel. Anyone who spoke favorably of Gonzalo or against the New Laws, said Vela, would be given a hundred lashes at the pillory in the Plaza de Armas. A sentence of two hundred lashes, let it be said, was considered equivalent to the death penalty. The man who lived after receiving one hundred lashes was a twisted, broken cripple for all of his days.

The New Laws, the Viceroy continued, would be enforced to the last paragraph, and he immediately issued manifestos freeing all slaves, wherever held, and confiscating much of the property awarded to citizens by Francisco Pizarro and Vaca de Castro. Those who opposed him, said Vela in another manifesto, would be hanged—sixty and seventy at a time, if need be.

267

It was at this juncture, in July of 1544, that the four *oidores* arrived in Lima. Within the short space of two months, Nuñez Vela had antagonized virtually every citizen of Peru. There were few who were not affected personally by the New Laws, but the population of Lima included many minor officials and other citizens who held no property aside from their homes and who possessed no slaves. Even those were openly critical of the viceroy, while the country sections and the inland cities were openly in revolt. From Cuzco, Gonzalo Pizarro addressed a personal appeal to his king in behalf of the citizens of Cuzco, La Plata, Arequipa, Huamanga, Huánuco, and Quito, and of the owners of property. He humbly beseeched that the New Laws be repealed or at least be amended so as to provide for appeal to the high courts of Spain from the decisions of the Audience. Humbly—for he was speaking to his king—but with soldierly bluntness Gonzalo informed Charles I of the acts of his viceroy since arriving in the New World. He asked respectfully that Nuñez Vela be replaced by a more able administrator—and on August 23, 1544, three of the four *oidores* placed their signatures upon a letter to Gonzalo which expressed their approval of the course he had taken. The only judge who failed to sign was Alvarez.

We do not know if Charles ever saw that letter, although it reached Spain. It indicates, however, that even at that late date Gonzalo Pizarro was at least making a gesture toward a legal settlement of the crisis in Peruvian affairs. He may have realized that events were moving far more swiftly than the slow communications between Peru and Spain and that Nuñez Vela would be deposed long before that letter reached Castile, but he dispatched the letter and thereby put himself on record as a loyal subject. It is quite certain that Nuñez Vela was either sublimely ignorant of the hatred which his maladministration had engendered or that he fatuously ignored the many ominous portents. On September 14, 1544, in the viceregal palace, he murdered with his own hand the *factor* Illán Suárez de Carvajal. Vela summoned the minor official—no kin to the redoubtable Francisco—to his office and there accused him of having joined one of the numerous cabals which had been formed in Lima. Suárez denied the charge, a quarrel developed, and the testy Nuñez Vela drew a dagger and stabbed the other man. The corpse was secretly buried, but servants in the palace gossiped of the circumstance, and friends of the murdered man opened the grave the next day and found Suárez wrapped in his bloodstained cloak.

That was the last straw so far as the *oidores* were concerned. The perquisites of a viceroy did not include murder, and within three days of the killing of Suárez the judges filed with their own body, the Royal Audience, an indictment including fifty-nine assorted charges against Nuñez Vela. How they purposed to handle so delicate a matter is a mystery, but coincident with their action the report reached Lima that Gonzalo Pizarro had left Cuzco and was advancing toward the coast. The viceroy promptly lost his head. He talked of leading an army against Gonzalo, of defending Lima, and finally proposed that the city be abandoned and the capital moved to Trujillo. At the last suggestion the *oidores* raised the highly technical point that they were required by law to hold their sessions in Lima and that the move to Trujillo was a violation of the New Laws under which the viceroy held his office. Nuñez Vela was placed

269

under arrest, held for a time on one of the small islands off Callao, and finally confined on a ship in the harbor. Cepeda, Zárate, and Tejeda may have wished to get rid of their colleague Alvarez, for they designated him to escort the deposed viceroy to Spain and make full report upon the action taken. That selection was not well considered. None of the four *oidores* were strong men, but Alvarez was the weakest of the weak lot. The ship was scarcely squared off on its northern course before he yielded to the arguments—or bribes—of Vela and repledged his allegiance to that officer as lawful viceroy of Peru. The captain of the ship was under Alvarez' orders and obeyed when directed to make a landing at Tumbez. There Nuñez Vela established what might be termed a viceroyalty in exile, and there—for the present—he remained.

The triumvirate of Cepeda, Zárate, and Tejeda was in control of Lima and the government. Then, if ever in its history, the land needed strong men, but none of the three was equal to the task they had collectively undertaken, especially in regard to Gonzalo Pizarro and Francisco Carvajal. Those leaders, at the head of a considerable force, had advanced from Cuzco to Jauja and there received the embassy sent by the worried *oidores* to treat with them. Gonzalo may have placed no more trust in the Audience than in Nuñez Vela. He may have been influenced by the bold but never prudent Carvajal. It is equally possible that he had succumbed by that time to the ambition which was first to lead him, then drive him to glory and disaster. He dismissed the ambassadors with the curt word that the people of Peru had called him to govern the country. Let the Audience recognize him forthwith as governor-general and confirm him in that position.

If the *oidores* had been worried before, they were now panicky. They had sought conciliation and peace; they received a haughty ultimatum and an unmistakable threat of war. They turned hurriedly to Vaca de Castro, whose prison ship still lay at Callao. That gentleman declined to advise them. They were the Royal Audience, he was merely the governor who had been deposed by the viceroy they had themselves deposed. Since they had elected to govern the land, let them do so. All in all, it was a most distressing situation for Cepeda, Zárate, and Tejeda, nor did they sleep more tranquilly after the demonstration staged by Francisco Carvajal. That tough old hellion marched to Lima at the head of a small force of picked fighters and dragged from their beds a number of encomendados whom he regarded as deserters from Gonzalo's cause. The three most prominent were set astride of mules, taken to the outskirts of the city, and hanged. To that one highest in rank, Carvajal extended the boon of permitting him to select the branch from which he would presently dangle.

The *oidores* asked for no further demonstration of Pizarro-Carvajal power politics. Possibly they remembered that they too were three in number and that there were other trees along the Rimac's banks. They hastily capitulated to the youngest of the Pizarros, who entered Lima in triumph on October 28, 1544, and on the same day was declared Governor and Captain-General of Peru. Cannons boomed in salute, bells pealed, and thousands cheered as the last of the Pizarros flung down the gauntlet to Fate.

Gonzalo's administrative policy was a simple one. He sought only the restoration of government as it had existed under his brother Francisco and the extension and strengthening of Pizarro rule until even a king would hesitate before ordering him deposed. He had already gone so far, Carvajal warned him, that he need expect nothing from Charles of Spain if he humbled himself before the throne. He must place himself in a position to demand royal favors. By a margin little wider than the blade of the headsman's ax did Francisco Carvajal escape taking his place among the king-makers of history.

The New Laws were brushed aside. All owners of estates were confirmed in their holdings save those who had openly allied themselves with Nuñez Vela. Those found their lands confiscated, themselves banished. A few were condemned to death, but the sentences were commuted—to the openly expressed disapproval of Carvajal. Vaca de Castro may have saved his neck when he bribed the captain of his prison ship to leave Callao harbor and sail for Panamá, whence the ex-governor returned to Spain and another prison. He was made the scapegoat for all the royal errors and was a political prisoner for five years before he was cleared of the various unjustified charges brought against him.

The Royal Audience was never formally dissolved; it simply ceased to exist. Tejeda and Zárate—he must not be confused with the historian Augustín de Zárate—vanish from history, Diego de Cepeda climbed on the bandwagon and was rewarded by Gonzalo with appointment as Lieutenant General and Chief Justice of Peru. Pizarro-rule was extended even to Panamá by the bold—and utterly lawless—exploits of one Hernando Bachicao, dispatched by Gonzalo to the

272

isthmus late in 1544. Bachicao built up a navy for his master by the simple method of stealing every vessel which came into port and replacing its crew with his own cutthroats. He learned that Nuñez Vela was at Tumbez and sailed thither, thereby driving the viceroy to Quito, high in the mountains, from which safe retreat he entered into correspondence with Sebastián Benalcazar, one-time commander of the city. That cavalier had returned from Spain, allied himself with Gonzalo Jiminez de Quesada, and was now at Popayán in Quesada's province of New Granada—the name by which the Republic of Colombia was known until 1861. He had little love for any Pizarro and promised to support Nuñez Vela in any move against the usurper. Thus encouraged, the viceroy assembled a small force and set out for San Miguel, on the Peruvian coast south of Tumbez. He left Quito on March 4, 1545, the very day upon which Gonzalo Pizarro sailed from Lima for Trujillo, whither he had already sent Francisco Carvajal and six hundred men, far more experienced in warfare and better equipped than Vela's little army. Gonzalo could not be secure in Peru while Nuñez Vela was in the land.

There is no need to trace here the story of the long months of guerrilla fighting which followed. It would prove the repetitious account of one rear-guard action after another in desert and in mountain over all the distance from San Miguel to the Colombian frontier. Again and again the advance force under Carvajal established brief contact with the enemy; again and again Nuñez Vela effected a withdrawal. Pizarro pledged himself to chase the retreating viceroy to the Caribbean, if necessary; he forgot that boast when Vela crossed the frontier into New Granada. Gonzalo retired to Quito and remained in that city while the viceroy recruited and trained new troops in Popayan before marching again to the south—this time accompanied by Benalcazar.

There was considerable sparring, considerable of feint and counter-feint, before the two foes came to grips in the only battle of the campaign, which had dragged on for nearly a year; but on January 18, 1546, the Pizarro-Carvajal team met that of Vela and Benalcazar on the field of Añaquito, some five or six miles north of the city. The area is now the Panagra Airport, and the big Pan-American transports flying north over the densely forested mountains from Guayaquil to the Ecuadorean capital first touch their wheels on the site of the battle which determined, temporarily, the ruler of all western South America.

Pizarro held the advantage both in position and numbers, counting some seven hundred men to the four hundred under the viceroy's command. The issue between forces so unevenly matched was not long in doubt—brief and bloody will serve as a description of virtually any hand-to-hand conflict. Cabrera, Benalcazar's lieutenant, was killed; Alvarez, one-time *Oidor* of the Royal Audience, was mortally wounded. His former colleague Cepeda, fighting under the Pizarro banner, was also wounded but recovered. Nuñez Vela was among the last to fall. Supported by a few of his officers, he held a position on a low knoll until struck from his saddle by one of the attacking soldiers. Badly wounded and trampled into the mire of the battleground, he was recognized by the Licentiate Benito Suárez de Carvajal, brother of the *factor* whom the viceroy had stabbed in Lima. That cavalier promptly avenged his brother's death. His Negro

274

slave struck off the viceroy's head, which was stuck on a pike and paraded among the victors, some of whom tore the hairs from the beard as the grisly trophy passed them.

Pizarro, let it be said, was far more generous in victory than Vela would have been. The wounded Benalcazar, after pledging never again to take up arms against the victor, was given leave to return to Popayán. The dead viceroy's head and body were brought together and buried in Quito's cathedral where they rest today. Pizarro marched as chief mourner behind the bier, nor must we sneer and condemn that gesture as hypocritical. The Conquistadores died blithely, but death itself and the solemn pageantry which followed was a grave business. Pizarro could afford to kneel humbly while the requiem was chanted over the poor dead incompetent who once had been a royal viceroy. Save for the crown upon his head, this youngest of the four brothers was King of Peru.

Even the crown was his, we are assured, if he had expressed a willingness to take it. The historian must guard against accepting unreservedly all that was recorded by the chroniclers. Antiquity of the written word is in itself no guarantee of accuracy—but Diego Fernandez tells a tale which might well be true; the gorgeous story of a brawling celebration at which Francisco Carvajal and his drunken cronies planned a kingdom and a dynasty for the western world. Gonzalo Pizarro, their leader, was to wear the crown and to have as his consort a princess of the royal line founded by Manco Capac. To themselves the revelers allotted duchys, marquisates, and other patents of nobility, which would be hereditary and thus assure the permanence of the Hispano-Incaic dynasty. The Doña Catalina Leytón de Carvajal broke up the party and shattered the dreams of empire, Fernandez continues, but the doughty old Francisco never wholly relinquished the bottle-born idea.

Whether the Spaniards of Peru would have accepted so revolutionary a move is wholly a matter of speculation. Their quarrels among themselves were invariably regarded as local affairs, and every rebel against the Lima government swore allegiance to his faraway king and went into battle under the banners of Castile. They were Spaniards all, those colonists, but no monarch returning in triumph from wars which had saved the state could have been greeted with more tumultuous acclaim than was Gonzalo Pizarro.

He came by land, riding in bright armor and red velvet cap at the head of his veterans, and over all the long route he was welcomed as a conqueror and a savior. In Lima it was seriously proposed to destroy a number of buildings of the city so as to open a new, broad street which would lead directly to the palace and which would bear forever the name of the "victorious prince"—he was so acclaimed!—who had been first to ride over it. Gonzalo declined that particular honor, but not the triumphal entry into his capital. He rode in state over streets strewn with flowers and between houses hung with garlands. Two captains led his horse; the Archbishop of Lima and the Bishops of Cuzco, Quito, and Bogotá, splendid in mitres and vestments, rode at his side. Overhead was the crimson and gold banner of Spain. Thus did the last of the Brothers of Doom return to his land and his people.

Only one figure was missing from the pageant, that of Francisco Carvajal. That fighting man had ridden from Quito to Cuzco and there organized a force which would know no rest—so Carvajal promised every officer and soldier—until it had put down what Francisco was pleased to call the rebellion of Diego Centeno. When Pizarro had set out for the north he had left that officer in command of the Charcas area with headquarters at Gonzalo's own encomienda at La Plata. Centeno had turned against his chief and had rallied many of the landholders of southern Peru to fight for the king and to recognize only that governor or viceroy whom Charles I might send to rule. Now Francisco Carvajal was sent to liquidate the rebel.

He is a character out of legend, that huge, roistering old Demon of the Andes, who feared neither God, man, nor devil and had no particular reverence for any of the three. Even in 1546 he was an atavism: an unbelievable creature who had been born four centuries or a score of centuries after his time. The saga of his deeds should have been sung by troubadours; it should have come down to us in fragments of Homeric verse. He was Attila and Timur the Lame; he was Goliath and Magog and that David who slew his tens of thousands; he was Gargantua and Antæus; he was a ribald Galahad whose Grail was the wine rather than the cup. He was a fighting man who recognized but one policy for warfare—extermination of the enemy. To that end he pursued Centeno and his followers over all the mountains of southern Peru. There were no pitched battles. Centeno's forces were scattered almost from the outset of the campaign, and the leader did not dare pause in his own flight while he rallied them for a stand against the demon who rode so hard on his trail. His men were captured, many of them, but none—regardless of station—was sent as a prisoner to Lima. Nor were there any trials for treason. Carvajal had no time, nor

277

did he see the reason, for such political flubdub. He conducted his own trials from the saddle where those who rode in his train aver that he ate, drank, and slept. "Hang them!" quoth Francisco Carvajal. "*El muerto no morde!*" And they were hanged forthwith, in couples and in dozens and in scores, until "the trees were peopled with corpses." Such was Francisco Carvajal. There is a place for him in today's world.

He followed Centeno from the mountains to the sea and back once more to the cordillera. Every rebel who fell into his hands was hanged, and Carvajal mocked them as they died, but he failed in the principal object of his bloody campaign. The rebel commander, Centeno, escaped. He and the few men who remained of his band scattered, each for himself, and the leader found a hiding place in a cave somewhere near Arequipa where he was fed by friendly Indians. It would have been well for Gonzalo Pizarro if Carvajal had found that cave before calling off the chase. Diego Centeno, alive, could still bite.

None can say why, in this hour when his career was at its zenith, Gonzalo Pizarro did not declare Peru an independent monarchy and—crowned as its king—challenge Charles I and all of Charles's officers in the New World. He was supreme from Panamá to Chile; he commanded a fleet stronger than any Charles could send to the western coast; he had the men and the money, and—for, when all is said, he governed wisely and generously—he probably would have been supported in that bold move. It is inconceivable that Gonzalo was not aware of the manner in which the Spanish court would receive the news of Vela's overthrow and death and the complete abrogation of the New Laws. Charles

278

would not accept supinely such flouting of the royal authority, and Gonzalo Pizarro, in Lima, must have known that Nuñez Vela would inevitably be succeeded.

As King of Peru he might have conquered, but he refused the crown and rode into Lima as a self-appointed captain-general and, paradoxically, a loyal subject of Charles I. That was in September of 1546, six weeks after the shrewd, patient diplomat who was to crush him had landed at Nombre de Dios and entered into negotiations with Pizarro's own officers in Panamá.

Chapter Fifteen

CHARLES OF SPAIN, to put matters very mildly, was in a stew. Word of Vela's death at Añaquito had not yet reached the court, but the king knew that his viceroy had proved a complete failure and had been thrown out of office, that the encomendados had rallied behind Gonzalo Pizarro, now governor-general, and that Spain faced the threat of a monarchy in Peru—and the loss of all revenue from that richest of her colonies. Many men were willing to accept the post of viceroy, but Charles was illy disposed toward all politicians, political aspirants, and courtiers who possessed few qualifications other than ancient lineage. He was deaf to all their urgings as well as to those men who shouted for the full weight of Spain's military power to be thrown against the usurper. A blustering soldier would fail as surely as an incompetent courtier. Charles sought a man equal to the delicate task at hand, a man who was capable of employing force but who was wise enough to keep the sword sheathed until victory was assured. He found that man in Pedro de la Gasca, a priest, who held at that time a rather important civil post in the city of Valencia.

What manner of man was this one who was to prove the

Nemesis of Gonzalo Pizarro? Let us go first to Peru where Gonzalo, in today's histories, is regarded as a rebel but, withal, a somewhat lovable one. Time has tempered the heinousness of his crimes, and he has become a bold gambler who cast the dice for a glorious stake and lost the main. He is a swashbuckling privateer rather than a Benedict Arnold in Peruvian history, yet he is not exalted at the expense of the man who broke him, body and soul. In the land which he saved for Spain, Pedro de la Gasca is regarded as a great man and a truly saintly character.

Others, writing in another tongue, have committed to print less friendly opinions. "Pitiless cruelty and cunning and an ugly and deformed body were conjoined in Pedro de la Gasca." "The Licentiate Pedro de la Gasca, an able ecclesiastic who was to prove an unscrupulous conspirator." ". . . the new envoy [Gasca] was a wily spider. During a brilliant career in Spain in the fields of scholarship, theology, warfare, and administration, Gasca had displayed astuteness, bravery, and considerable histrionic ability. Possessed of a saintly and ingratiating exterior, he had an inner self of finely tempered steel."

Let it be said here that the first of those citations is wholly unjustified. Gasca proved that he could be merciful where mercy was merited, he could be stern and unrelenting toward the guilty, but he was incapable of the savage cruelty of a Pedro de Alvarado or a Carvajal. To lack comeliness is not necessarily to be ugly or deformed. In his *History of the Conquest*, Prescott reproduces as frontispiece to Volume II a portrait of the man, which hangs, or which once hung, in the sacristy of the church of Santa Maria Magdalena in Valladolid. The painting was made as Gasca's life was drawing to a close, for it shows him, in armor, seated at a table which bears the bishop's mitre which was his sole reward for his services in the New World. True, the artist may have wished to flatter his subject, but the portrait is that of a rather handsome and straight-backed soldier-churchman. Garcilaso de la Vega, who saw him often, has described Gasca as an awkward man with long legs and arms and a disproportionately short body, but a man whose physical shortcomings were speedily forgotten by those who met him and were conquered by his personality.

"Pedro de la Gasca, a name which, brighter by contrast with the gloomy times in which it first appeared, still shines with undiminished splendor after the lapse of ages." Thus wrote Prescott in 1847, exactly three centuries after Gasca's career in Peru. The half-blind, pedantic scholar, whose translations are monumentally inaccurate, was as ready to criticize as to praise, but he could find not a single malicious word to direct toward the man to whom was assigned a diplomatic mission as delicate as any in history. Pedro de la Gasca succeeded in that mission. Had he failed—but he did not fail, and therein is the stature of the man.

He was a true patriot, that modest priest, in a day when patriotism bore a price tag, plainly marked. He asked nothing for himself, neither salary nor perquisites, neither present honors nor promises of future rewards. That in itself was a miracle in Spain at that day, but Gasca went further. If his king called, he said, he would serve, but he would be answerable only to the throne, not to courts or courtiers or any royal council. He declined courteously but firmly to sail for Peru unless his hands were free from the fetters of diplomatic precedent and established policy. He and he alone should make what decisions might be necessary and should execute them.

In short, that inconspicuous priest asked for dictatorial powers, and he got them. Charles I saw to that last. The king-emperor overruled his ministers and gave Gasca everything he demanded. So far as the record was concerned, the priest was named President of the Royal Audience. That was no mean position, but Gasca was fortified therein by privately granted authority which placed him at the head of every branch of government in the province. He was lord of the high justice, the middle, and the low; he could punish, and he could pardon. He could repeal any or all of the New Laws, which had been primarily responsible for Peruvian political chaos, and could grant amnesty to anyone, however rebellious, who had been involved in the disorders. He bore letters to every officer of the crown from Mexico to the limits of Peru which ordered those officials to co-operate with the king's envoy in whatever manner he might direct, to furnish him with arms and men, and to permit him to draw at will upon royal funds within their jurisdiction. And if all those powers were not sufficient, Gasca was given a number of sheets of paper which were blank except for the royal signature and seal. He could fill in above that signature as he desired.

No man in Spain's history had ever held such unlimited powers, yet the man who sailed from San Lucar on May 26, 1546, was in no wise different from the young priest who had been made a Master of Theology from the seminary of Alcalá de Jenares more than thirty years before. He wore his clerical habit—he had said he wished no other badge of rank—and was accompanied by only a small staff of men whose loyalty was beyond question. Among them was Alonso de Alvarado, who had been *Maestro del Campo* under Francisco Pizarro.

Landing first at Santa Marta (Colombia), Gasca learned of the battle of Añaquito and of the death of Nuñez Vela, no word of which had reached Spain prior to his departure. The news was not particularly distressing, we may believe. Vela, alive, would undoubtedly have made himself obnoxious. More serious was the information that Gonzalo Pizarro's rule was now supreme and that ships for passage to Peru could be obtained only by the favor of one Hinojosa, who had succeeded the energetic and rascally Bachicao as Pizarro's lieutenant in Panamá. Command at Nombre de Dios had been entrusted to Hernán Mexia, yet Gasca crossed to the Caribbean port and—a humble if indeed wily priest—presented himself to that officer as the new President of the *Audiencia Real*.

Gasca was a borer from within. If wiliness be the winning of men by mild words and skillful arguments, he was indeed wily. He told Mexia, among other things, that he had come to repeal the hated New Laws and that he was empowered to grant amnesty without loss of position to all those who had rebelled against Nuñez Vela. It sounded reasonable, very reasonable, to Hernán Mexia. He accepted the pardon which Gasca offered, renewed his allegiance to his king, and joined Alonso de Alvarado as ambassadors who would inform Hinojosa in Panamá of the nature of the priest's mission. Gasca followed them within a few days.

Even one who has come to admire him as a man of signal ability among many incompetent royal appointees must admit that Gasca was a wily diplomat and a spider who patiently spun one web after another. Small webs at first, webs of inconspicuous strands through which any man might break, nor notice that the thread of counter-intrigue had checked him for a moment. They were designed to trap only small game, those Spaniards in Panamá who were not too sure within their hearts that Pizarro was not riding to a fall. Gasca talked with those men. He explained his mission to them as he had to Hernán Mexia, and to some of them he granted amnesties and secretly pledged them to support King Charles rather than the uncrowned Gonzalo.

None of them learned the full extent of the priest's powers. Gasca was not yet ready to expose his hand. Hinojosa was wary, and the new president gave him no opportunity to refuse the use of the ships. Instead, he seemed perfectly willing to remain indefinitely in Panamá, but every ship which sailed to the south bore his secret agents, who were instructed to circulate news of Gasca's arrival, of his power to revoke the New Laws, and his promised amnesty to all who were loyal to the king.

Wearisome, perhaps, this recital of diplomatic intrigues, but of such is history made. All wars are political, and the generals who take the field do so upon the orders of political leaders or because of the success or failure of a politician's plans. France fell long before Leopold of Belgium surrendered and the *Wehrmacht* pierced the lines at Sedan; those Londoners who died at the Great Blitz were sentenced to death at Munich and at Berchtesgaden. So was the fate of Gonzalo Pizarro and the destiny of Spain in the New World determined during the months from July to November of 1546 when Pedro de la Gasca waited and plotted in Panamá.

Gasca's tactics were Hitlerian—the parallel is inescapable.

285

His "tourists" were missionary priests journeying to Peru where they broadcast throughout the land the doctrine of the "new order" of full pardon for political offenses. Nor was economic pressure ignored. Crown officers in Mexico and Guatemala were told secretly of the real power held by the humble priest and were ordered, in the king's name, to have no commercial or political relations with Peru so long as Gonzalo Pizarro was in power. Not until all that groundwork had been laid did Gasca enter into direct communication with his enemy in the yet undeclared war.

Hinojosa had begun to suspect that he might be perched on a volcano, and he granted permission for an envoy of Gasca's to sail to Peru. That ambassador, a cavalier named Paniagua, was entrusted with various missions. He bore two letters addressed to Gonzalo Pizarro. One was from the king. At least it bore the royal signature, but one cannot help asking if the hand which penned it was not that of the adroit Gasca and if the paper used was not one of the blank sheets which Charles had signed for just such a purpose. The second was from Gasca as President of the Royal Audience. Both communications were in much the same vein. Gonzalo was neither warned nor threatened—in fact, his rebellion against the incompetent and unpopular Nuñez Vela was tacitly approved as the only course possible for a gentleman of honor and abdominal investiture—but no promises were made that he would be sustained in his high office or in any position at all. Both letters included, of course, the implication that Gonzalo would share with his followers in the amnesty which Charles guaranteed to all who would lay down their arms.

There were other letters, hundreds of them in all, sent to

Peru. They were addressed to cavaliers and commoners, to landholders and parish priests, to municipal officers of high and low station. One was to Diego de Cepeda, that *oidor* of the defunct Audience whom Gonzalo had appointed Chief Justice of Peru and who was one of his principal advisors. Cepeda was given many a verbal pat on the back, he was reminded that he was still an officer of the highest tribunal under the crown, and he was asked to present the names of those who in his judgment were qualified for appointment to that body. Gasca's interest in or solicitude for Diego Cepeda was no greater than the reader's, but small fish must be caught before the hook can be baited for larger quarry.

The cumulative effect of those insidious attacks upon Gonzalo's power was great, but the last of the Pizarros remained contemptuous of the mild-mannered priest, who, he argued, was merely the President of the Audience. He decided to go over Gasca's head and to send his own embassy to the court of Charles I. The ambassadors were to ask that Pizarro be confirmed in the office he now held. He was the choice of the people, the petition stated, "greatly loved by all for his virtues and regarded as the father of Peru." To carry that word of first in war, first in peace, and first in the hearts of his countrymen, Gonzalo selected several distinguished hidalgos and the Bishop of Lima, and placed at the head of the mission Don Lorenzo de Aldana, who had secret instructions, it is hinted, to offer Gasca a bribe of fifty thousand gold pesos if he would return to Spain with Pizarro's envoys. The story of that bribe is apocryphal, but the money was never offered to Pedro de la Gasca. Don Lorenzo talked with the awkward, thin-faced President of the Audience and immediately sold out to him. Hinojosa, Governor of Panamá, followed that example. Gasca, at last, had netted the bait for which he had angled so long and so patiently.

He must have been a swift and amazingly accurate judge of men, that Pedro de la Gasca. Not once during the months from July to early November had he revealed to anyone the full extent of the power which he held, yet in his first meeting with Lorenzo de Aldana he spread all his cards on the table and informed that cavalier of the fate to be expected by those who persisted in their opposition. Aldana was given his choice between ending his days on the scaffold where traitors died and receiving an immediate grant of amnesty and appointment to high office under the Audience. Gasca, too, had a bribe to offer, and Aldana accepted it. He reaffirmed his allegiance to the crown and wrote to Gonzalo Pizarro and advised him to do likewise.

That was enough for Hinojosa. The volcano on which he sat was rumbling, and he scampered to safety before the explosion. On November 19 he and all his officers capitulated to Gasca. The fleet was surrendered to him, and he promptly recommissioned Hinojosa and the ship commanders in his own service. He had taken the outer bastion of Pizarro's defenses; he was now ready to move, in his own good time, upon the main citadel.

The first realization that Gasca was an enemy to be feared —and most certainly respected—dawned on Gonzalo Pizarro when Lorenzo de Aldana arrived off Lima with a small squadron. The traitor, as his former chief must have regarded him, sent a bulky pouch to the governor. The diplomatic mail included another letter from Gasca, but the accompanying documents were certified copies of the priest's various patents of authority. The cards which had been shown to Aldana and Hinojosa were now laid before the eyes of the man whose cause they had deserted. The offer of amnesty was repeated. The last of the Pizarros was given a last chance.

There followed a momentous conference within the walls of the old Palace of the Governors on Lima's plaza. The chroniclers have told us much of what was said there, but the picture they draw is a very inadequate description of what must have been a most dramatic scene. We can see, if we wish, a long room hung with arms, with bright tapestries, and with the red and gold banners of imperial Spain. Its only furniture is a large table about which a number of men are seated in high-backed chairs. At the table's head is Gonzalo Pizarro, Governor and Captain-General, a brilliant figure in crimson and gold-embroidered velvets—for this youngest of the brothers was a lover of color and of gaudy self-adornment. On his one hand is the huge figure of Francisco Carvajal, seated on a bench unless a chair could be found which would accommodate his three-hundred-pound frame. He is soberly, even carelessly dressed. He was eighty years old and had left any sartorial vanities far behind him. Clothes either covered one's nakedness or—if made of good steel—protected one in battle. Beyond that the old warrior did not know the difference between silk and cotton, and his garments were as coarse as his speech. Across from him, on the other hand of the governor-general, is Diego de Cepeda, thin-faced, slightly stooped, whose long fingers drum the table or caress his forked beard as he listens to the secretary's reading of the documents which have come from Pedro de la Gasca. There are other men about that table, men who had followed the aegis of the Pizarros since Cajamarca and earlier, and others who were more recent arrivals in the land. The Licentiate Benito Suárez de Carvajal, he who had slain Nuñez Vela, may have been present. So might Garcilaso de la Vega, father of the historian of the same name, and Juan de Acosta, a gallant hidalgo and intrepid soldier, who was to prove faithful to the last. Decision, however, rested with the three first named: with the arrogant Gonzalo, who had won for himself a kingdom and had gone so far on the road of ambition that he could see no turning; with Cepeda, fearful of the fate which Gasca might have in store for him and trusting the priest not at all; and with the foul-mouthed old Demon of the Andes, Francisco Carvajal.

Only Carvajal, surprisingly enough, advised the course dictated by prudence. Capitulate, he told his leader. Recognize this Gasca for what he is, an ambassador with powers as great as Charles's own. Open the gates of the city to him, vow allegiance to your king, and accept gratefully the amnesty offered. Were the decision mine alone, he continued, I would welcome the royal pardon and would "pave the path of its bearer with bars of silver and plates of gold."

So spoke Carvajal, a fighter of such proven courage that he could sheathe his sword without disgrace—even if Cepeda did hint that the old man was trying to save his own skin. Cepeda's advice was diametrically opposed to that given by the soldier. The lawyer professed distrust of all of Gasca's pledges. The President of the Audience, he said, would make promises only to break them as soon as he arrived in Peru. Gasca was no simple and ingenuous priest but a man of great cunning and finesse, of lies and frauds.

The chroniclers have not recorded the words of Gonzalo Pizarro. What need, when his decision spoke for him? He voted with Cepeda and declared for outright rebellion. He would rule Peru without interference from Charles of Spain or Charles's ambassadors. War! Saint James and Pizarro! The die was cast. Gonzalo had been offered one last opportunity and had sealed his fate by rejecting that final chance. The reckless men about him cheered and vowed they would stand fast to the end, but the cheering did not drown out the biting words of Francisco Carvajal. "So be it," he said. "But a few years remain to me at the best, and I have as long a neck for the hangman's noose as any of your honors!" There was bitter prophecy in that speech.

For a short time all went well. Gonzalo was a gallant, colorful figure, as leaders of lost causes have ever been, and he drew to his banners many who believed that they would have lost their lands and possibly their lives save for his spirited defiance of Nuñez Vela and the New Laws. Also, he was tremendously wealthy. Old Carvajal had returned to Potosí after the Centeno campaign, and under his management the mines there had begun to yield their fabulous store of silver. A well-lined purse is a vital asset to any revolutionary movement, and Gonzalo dipped lavishly both into his own funds and those of the royal treasury, which he now confiscated. He spent half a million *pesos de oro* in hiring and equipping the thousand men with which he would meet Gasca whenever that skillful diplomat set foot on Peruvian soil. Never in the history of the Spanish wars had soldiers been so well paid or had cavaliers been promised such huge rewards in the hour of victory. The army included the largest force of arquebusiers ever assembled in the New World.

So far, good, but there is more to the trade of a soldier than the enlistment of men or the wearing of gleaming armor. Gonzalo Pizarro was a sorry military tactician and a worse diplomat. He listened to Diego Cepeda and approved the lawyer's suggestion that the ships now in Callao Harbor be burned so as to prevent their being used by any of the citizens of Lima who might wish to escape the conflict which was now inevitable. Carvajal, absent at the time, expressed in unmistakable terms his opinion of that folly. "Your Lordship," he said, "you ordered the burning of the five angels which protected the coast of Peru!" The loftiness of the pinnacle upon which Pizarro had placed himself by that time is indicated by the fact that even old Carvajal, no respecter of persons, addressed him as *"Vuesa Señoria"*—Your Lordship.

That was but one of many errors, some of them ludicrous. Cepeda, the legal quibbler, prepared indictments under which Gasca, Aldana, and Hinojosa were solemnly tried for treason against the lawful government of Peru, convicted, and sentenced to death. The process, the lawyer explained, made legal the immediate execution of any of the three who might be captured. Carvajal bellowed with laughter when the technicality was explained. The old warrior could see no need for such devious circumlocutions. He would personally guarantee, he roared, that there would be no delay if he made a prisoner of any of the three!

The old rascal mocked every one of the bungling political moves made by the inefficient combination of Pizarro and Cepeda, yet he remained loyal when scores of others were deserting and either joining Gasca in Panamá or fleeing to one of the northern cities from which they could safely proclaim their loyalty to the crown. Benito Suárez de Carvajal fled to Trujillo and announced that he had accepted the amnesty which Gasca offered. His example was followed by many who thought rightfully that they need fear nothing from the man who granted pardon to the slayer of Nuñez Vela.

Gasca remained in Panamá, and war seemed far away, yet already Pizarro had lost the northern cities, including Quito, where his lieutenant Puelles had been assassinated, and held Lima only by force and terrorism. Cuzco, too, had gone over to the king's side. Diego Centeno had emerged from the cave near Arequipa where he had hidden for more than a year, had rallied a small force, and had marched upon the ancient Incan capital where Pizarro's officers had offered only half-hearted resistance. Other towns and villages in the mountain area raised the royal banner, and Centeno presently controlled all the territory from Cuzco to the Vilcañota Pass and on southward to Lake Titicaca and the Charcas area. He had approximately a thousand men under him while desertions had reduced Gonzalo's force to about half that number.

It was then, as the summer of 1547 ended, that Gonzalo reached the realization that there could be no victory for him on Peruvian soil. Gasca was already at Jauja, having landed at Tumbez on June 13 and marched to Cajamarca and on to the south over precisely the same route which Gonzalo himself had followed with his brother Francisco fifteen years before. Jauja, the soldier-priest announced, was to be his headquarters, and he would receive there all who were loyal to their king.

Gonzalo abandoned Lima—which immediately surrendered happily to Lorenzo de Aldana—and led his men toward

Arequipa. His little army was excellently equipped, and the sagacious Carvajal had brought along all those arquebuses which the deserters had left behind. Gonzalo may have thought he was beaten, but he kept his head high before his men and told them that if only ten remained loyal he would reconquer Peru. For the present they would withdraw beyond the Chilean frontier where they would remain until the insidious plotter Gasca had revealed himself for what he was and the people of Peru called again upon Gonzalo Pizarro. A proud speech; the speaker may even have believed it himself.

He halted for a time at Arequipa, that most pleasant of all the cities of Peru, then marched inland more than two hundred miles to a position near Lake Titicaca. We are asked to believe that Centeno held the passes through which Pizarro must pass if he was to reach Chile and that the long detour to Titicaca was undertaken for no other purpose than to request that commander to stand aside and permit Pizarro to leave Peru. It would be difficult to imagine a more ridiculous explanation, and it is here that the entire legend of the Chilean adventure collapses; contradicted by the very chroniclers who made it and whose word has been accepted without question.

While Arequipa is some seven thousand feet above the sea there are neither mountains nor mountain passes between it and the coast; the barren hills can be crossed at any point. Further, Centeno was camped near Titicaca and had with him his entire force of about a thousand men—leaving exactly none to guard the nonexistent passes south of Arequipa. The Chilean myth was probably invented by Pedro Pizarro, who had no love for his cousin Gonzalo. What is far

294

more likely is that Gonzalo hoped to induce Centeno, once his lieutenant, to join the revolt and launch an attack upon Gasca, who at that time could not have mustered a third of the combined Pizarro-Centeno force.

If such were the scheme, it failed. Centeno was a royalist, and he declined to receive his former commander except as a prisoner. Tell your chief to surrender, he told Pizarro's messenger, and I promise to plead with Father Gasca that he be granted the pardon which already has been extended to all who bore arms against Nuñez Vela. Surrender—or fight.

Pizarro elected to fight. No other decision was possible if he had any intention of seeking a refuge in Chile. There on the western shore of Titicaca, Centeno actually was between the rebel chief and the passes. The two former comrades met on October 26, 1547, at Huarina, a village on the *altiplano* south of Puno. Less than five hundred men marched against a thousand, but God fought then, as ever, on the side of the heaviest artillery. It was the first battle in the history of the New World to be decided by reserve fire-power, for stout Carvajal's men went into action bearing, many of them, two loaded arquebuses.

The old Demon was a magnificent infantry leader. Two centuries before Bunker Hill he issued an order equivalent to "don't fire until you see the whites of their eyes!" He permitted a few shots at long range to provoke a charge over ground highly favorable to mass attacks by either horse or foot, but the main body of his arquebusiers were ordered to hold their fire until the packed ranks were within a hundred paces. That is the distance mentioned in the chronicles. The actual range was probably little more than half as far since fifty or sixty yards was about the limit at which the clumsy, smooth-bored pieces could be fired with even approximate accuracy. Aim low, Carvajal ordered; aim no higher than their belts. A shot falling short may still ricochet and inflict damage, but one which passes over the enemy's head is wasted.

The whites of his foes' eyes must have been visible when the veteran shouted the order to fire. *Fuego!*—and from the steady ranks a volley of lead and jagged iron bullets and the terrible chain shot tore at point-blank range into the advancing troops. A hundred men were killed in that first blast, as many more wounded; and, before the shattered attackers could be rallied, Carvajal's troopers dropped the fired weapons, picked up the reserve arms which lay ready to their hands, and poured another withering hail upon Centeno's ranks. Those of the enemy footmen who still lived broke and fled. Carvajal made no attempt to pursue them. Not all of the battle was upon his immediate front, and he ordered his men to stand firm and to recharge their pieces.

It was well for the fortunes of Gonzalo Pizarro that he did so. Gonzalo, on Carvajal's right, elected to receive the charge of Centeno's cavalry rather than initiate the attack with his inferior forces. So many *caballeros* had deserted his cause that he now mustered less than a hundred horsemen against more than double that number. Had he charged first the advantages of speed and impact would have been his; but he chose the defensive, and Centeno's squadrons smashed through him and over him and turned to charge again. Many men and horses were killed, and the survivors, including their leader, fled in a hopeless rout. Centeno was so certain of victory that he ordered the trumpets to sound the signal that the field had been won—a challenge which his old foeman Carvajal answered with a victory blast from his own field-music. He had turned back both infantry and cavalry attacks, his ranks were unbroken, his weapons were loaded in readiness for another charge. "Come on, Centeno! I chased you over all these mountains only a year ago; let us see now if you can fight as well as you can run!"

Centeno charged. To be accurate, he ordered the charge, for he had been severely ill for several days and was unable to mount a horse or take any active part in the fighting. His infantry had been shattered, but his cavalry squadrons were still intact and flushed with their easy victory over Pizarro. Carvajal's steady men received that charge with cold steel, upon an abattis of pikes and spears which yielded not an inch to the smashing impact of horse and rider. The few cavaliers who broke through were disposed of by the daggers of the pikemen who stood in reserve within the square. Behind the reserves were the arquebusiers who fired above their companions' heads to drop chain shot and other varieties of hot lead into the charging troopers. When the attack recoiled from the unyielding spears the gunners stepped into the front rank and poured their fire into the retreating squadrons.

The cavalry circled and smashed from the opposite side, but the square turned with them, its formation unbroken, and again the horses and riders were received on pikes, which were now reddened to the hand guards. A third charge was made, but the men who made it had little spirit for further fighting, and their retreat was a rout. Of a thousand men, Centeno had lost—in killed, wounded, and a few prisoners—fully eight hundred. The dead alone numbered three hundred and fifty, say the chroniclers, and more than that number of wounded were left on the field. The victory cost Pizarro about a hundred men, nearly all of them from the cavalry which had been under his personal command.

"Jesús, que una victoria!" he exclaimed as he rode about the field, and he crossed himself piously and, doubtless, thanked God rather than the quite ungodly Francisco Carvajal, who wasted no time in gloating but called for horses and rode in pursuit of Centeno. The sick and beaten leader escaped once more, to his own good fortune. There are no trees in that region to be used as gallows, so Carvajal ordered the garroting of every cavalier who fell into his hands. None was spared because of wounds. Only the common soldiers were offered life in exchange for an oath of allegiance to Pizarro. An enormous booty was taken in the Centeno camp. Its value exceeded 1,400,000 pesos, according to Fernandez —a figure which probably includes about 300 per cent of exaggeration but which indicates that Centeno had been far more industrious in looting than in guarding the mountain passes into Chile.

With the victory at Huarina, Gonzalo Pizarro was free to enter Chile by any route he might choose. He was free to march to the southeast, if he desired, to round Lake Titicaca and enter the deep valley occupied by the Indian village of Choqueyapu, which Alonso de Mendoza, a year later, was to name the City of Our Lady of Peace—La Paz. He could have set up his own government there or could have continued to the eastward and been first of his race to enter the rich lands which we now call the *Oriente* of Bolivia. He could have done any of those things, and it is quite possible that Pedro de la Gasca would have made peace with him and granted him a pardon on terms no more severe than that he keep his meddling fingers out of Peruvian affairs. The news of Centeno's crushing defeat at Huarina was a severe blow to Gasca, who had underestimated both Pizarro's popularity and Carvajal's generalship.

Gonzalo chose to do none of those things which might have assured him a normal span of life and death in his bed. Instead, he marched north and east for more than two hundred miles directly to the "navel" of Peru. He marched to Cuzco and announced that the Holy City of the Incas was now his headquarters and capital. No more fatal decision was ever made by a leader of a lost cause.

Chapter Sixteen

GONZALO PIZARRO occupied Cuzco late in November of 1547. He was welcomed enthusiastically by the fickle citizenry, who throughout all the civil wars cheered loudly for whatever leader who demonstrated by his presence that he was for the moment on top of the heap. The victor of Huarina chose to enter the city humbly and on foot. He laid aside his bright armor and fine raiment. Clad in plain garments and bareheaded, he ignored the cheers and walked directly to the cathedral where he knelt in prayer and listened to the singing of a *Te Deum Laudamus*. The pose of humility, however, was a temporary one. He speedily assumed all the attributes of a conqueror: he was contemptuous toward Gasca, he displayed little active interest in the securing of his own position, and showed in every way that his head had been turned completely on the field of Huarina and that he expected Gasca to sue for peace.

Gasca was willing to do so, for on December 16, while still at Jauja, he wrote Gonzalo a most temperate and conciliatory letter: a letter which could not conceivably have been written prior to Centeno's defeat. The last of the Pizarros was given still another chance to restore himself to favor. There was no outright promise of pardon for him and those others who persisted in rebellion, but the way was opened for them to sue for that pardon.

Your excellency would have little to fear from me [Gasca wrote], if I had not on my side God and the king, justice and fidelity, and all the good vassals who serve His Majesty; but fighting against all those things, your excellency has good reason to quail; and, if you do not repent and return to the service of both Majesties, divine and human, you will lose both body and soul, as you will shortly see.[1]

There is steel in that letter, but it is well cushioned with soft words. The course of wisdom would have been to accept the priest's offer, but this last Pizarro was the most hot-headed and reckless of the clan. He may not have authorized the reply, but he permitted the forwarding of a letter from Francisco Carvajal under date of December 29. "It is scurrilous, blasphemous, and vulgar, but most amusing," says Means, who has been privileged to examine the original. It is regrettable that after such a promising introduction the historian quotes only the final sentence:

"May the Lord preserve your reverend personality by permitting, through His most holy clemency, that your sins should bring you into my hands, that you may once and for all cease to do so much harm in the world."

The hand of the reckless Carvajal is visible in every word of that letter, but Pizarro must have known of its contents and approved its sending. Such defiance might be excused

[1] The above extract, together with that from the letter of Francisco Carvajal which follows, are from the original documents in the Huntington Memorial Library, San Marino, California. The above citations are as given by Philip Ainsworth Means, from whose *Fall of the Inca Empire* they are lifted bodily and gratefully.

301

in an arrogant leader if it had been coupled with earnest preparation for a vigorous offensive whereby that leadership could be asserted, that arrogance justified, but Gonzalo's military vocabulary did not include the word preparedness. He must have known that since Huarina his priestly opponent had been preparing almost frenziedly for war. Gasca made a hurried trip to Lima and borrowed eighty thousand gold pesos from the merchants of that city. The royal treasury in the City of Kings was empty—Gonzalo had attended to that—but there was still plenty of gold in this richest of Spain's colonies. The loan, backed by the unquestionable authority granted to Gasca, enabled him to return to the mountains at the head of a force of two thousand fighting men, including five hundred cavalry and eight hundred arquebusiers. The President of the Audience did not regard his meager military experiences in Spain as qualifying him to command. He placed Hinojosa at the head of the army, Alonso de Alvarado second, with the title of Master of the Camp, and never once interfered with either of his generals. The roster of the subordinate officers included the names of many of the most skillful soldiers in the New World, among them Pedro de Valdivia, who had returned from the first of his Chilean expeditions and joined the royalist force.

Many of those men were old friends and associates of Gonzalo Pizarro. He knew them all, he knew that they were allied against him; yet he personally did nothing and showed only casual interest in the strenuous efforts of Francisco Carvajal to drill and equip more men. It seems impossible that two men so different in temperament could have remained in such close association, yet Carvajal was ever loyal to the chief who was only half his own age and Gonzalo

302

never resented the bullying interference of the military commander who worked day and night to prepare for a battle far more decisive than Huarina. It must be said, however, that Diego Cepeda was higher in Gonzalo's confidence and was listened to more attentively than the veteran soldier.

The occupation of Cuzco was an error, and Carvajal knew it. No settlement save that of the battlefield was possible so long as Pizarro remained in the Incan capital. Carvajal urged that the often looted city be stripped once more of its movable wealth and abandoned to Gasca and the royalists, who might be willing to make concessions rather than face months or years of guerrilla warfare in the eastern Andes. Neither Pizarro nor Diego Cepeda had such long-range vision. The victory at Huarina had convinced Gonzalo—God knows why!—that he was invincible in battle and that Gasca feared him. Too, he had no wish to leave Cuzco. There he had a palace as his headquarters. There he had women, both brown and white. There he could obtain good food; he could drink deeply of wine and of maize beer. He had undergone more than his share of hardship in jungle and mountain, and he was unwilling to exchange his pleasant life as a conqueror for what promised to be a repetition of the grim experience on the Napo.

Cepeda supported him in that decision. Carvajal did not. The Demon of the Andes did not break with his leader, nor did he relax in his intense military activities, but there was a rift between Gonzalo and the man who had been his principal adviser and both men knew it. Gasca was now at Andahuaylas, a city within the Apurimac drainage and only a hundred miles directly west of Cuzco. To reach the Incan capital the royalists must cross the Apurimac, too swift and too deep to ford, by the famous Apurimac Bridge near the hamlet of Curahausi. The first bridge at that site had been erected by Inca Capac Yupanqui, and the present span was of the same construction. Fiber cables slung between stone piers supported a six-foot "roadway" that was 250 feet long and hung at its midpoint 150 feet above the mad waters. Exactly similar bridges span the deep Andean ravines today, and the crossing of any one of them is an adventure which is not soon forgotten.

Pizarro ordered the bridge destroyed. The act, he reasoned, rendered Cuzco impregnable so long as Gasca remained at Andahuaylas, and he maintained only a few scouts in scattered outposts to protect the frontier he had thus established. A messenger from one of those detachments arrived in Cuzco with the news that Gasca had moved a short distance up the river and there, near Cotabamba, had succeeded in making a crossing and was building another bridge.

Carvajal instantly applied for field service. Let him pick a hundred men, he asserted, and he would guarantee to turn back the vastly superior enemy force and to make a prisoner of Gasca—"this chaplain who calls himself president." The bold challenge was not accepted. Carvajal could not be spared from the more important task of defending Cuzco, said Pizarro, and he assigned the mission to Juan de Acosta and two hundred arquebusiers. The younger captain failed to reach the Apurimac in time. The bridge was completed, and Gasca's entire force was in Pizarro's territory before Acosta even sighted the river. He returned to Cuzco at a much better speed and reported that the enemy was already advancing on the capital. The date was April 1, 1548.

Carvajal made a final appeal that the city be abandoned and a strategic withdrawal made to the mountains. Both Pizarro and Cepeda declined to consider it, and the veteran asked to be relieved of his command and granted permission to fight as an ordinary trooper in the cavalry ranks. Pizarro agreed. The rift between the two had become a ravine as deep and as wide as that of the Apurimac.

The army which Gonzalo Pizarro led out of Cuzco included nine hundred excellently equipped men. He mustered at least four hundred arquebusiers, a dozen *falconetes,* or other pieces of artillery, and perhaps a hundred and fifty horsemen. Pikemen and other infantry fighters made up the remainder. He faced at least two thousand, but if there was fear in Gonzalo's heart he did not betray it. He had seen much fighting since his arrival in Peru fifteen years before, and he had never—he boasted—lost a battle. Fatalism has no place in military philosophy.

Strategy dictated his choice of the ground on which he would meet Gasca, but Fate was there as well. Gonzalo camped upon the eastern edge of the Plain of Xaquixahuana, the modern Sacsahuana or Zúrite, at no great distance from the present town of Anta. Peruvian history knows no more famous battleground than that beautiful vale surrounded by the towering snowclad peaks of the Eastern Cordillera. The warriors of Manco Capac and of Sinchi Roca, the War Chief, had fought there. On that level terrain the young prince Hatun Tupac—the Inca Viracocha—had met and defeated the Chanca hordes in the battle of Yahuarpampa and had thereby saved the empire. There Huáscar, great-grandson of Viracocha, had been vanquished by the usurper Atahualpa. Francisco Pizarro had halted there long enough to burn Atahualpa's general Chalchuchima and to negotiate with that Manco whom he made Inca. And here, again, the destiny of a nation and the fate of many men were to be decided.

Gasca, if some of the accounts are correct, felt none too certain of the result of the battle now in prospect. He had made prisoners of two friars whom Gonzalo had sent to meet him with a demand that he forward copies of the various authorities which he claimed to hold. The men were undoubtedly spies, and Gasca held them. They gave him such an account of Pizarro's strength and of the host of Indian warriors which fought under his banner that the president sent one of his own friars to the rebel camp with still another appeal that Gonzalo surrender and accept a full pardon for all his misdeeds. The incident is unmentioned by all who wrote from first-hand knowledge but is presented as factual by Gomara and by Augustín de Zárate, the latter of whom was in Peru at the time.

Unmentioned also by the chroniclers is the lowering of morale which must have followed the demotion of Francisco Carvajal. The soldiers whom he drove so relentlessly may have hated the old martinet, but they trusted him as a leader. Now they knew that the man who had saved the day at Chupas, who had turned possible defeat into decisive victory at Huarina, was reduced to the ranks. They did not know why —generals do not take common soldiers into their confidence—but rumors started and were magnified as they spread from campfire to campfire through the long and sleepless night which might be the last which many of those men would know. They faced double their own number; the price of victory would be heavy.

There was some skirmishing between scouts on April 8 when the royalist force entered the valley from the northwest, but issue was not joined until the following day. Mass was sung in both camps. The priests heard confession and granted absolution to those about to die. Gonzalo Pizarro, as at Huarina, took command of the cavalry, and no more gaily attired knight ever prepared to lead a charge. He was clad from head to foot in gleaming armor heavily ornamented with gold, and he rode a fiery chestnut stallion famous for its speed and courage. Command of the pikemen and arquebusiers had been given—since Carvajal's demotion—to Diego Cepeda, and it is easy to believe that the lawyer-soldier had crouched in his tent through the night and pondered on what the coming day might bring forth. At Huarina a rapier stroke had laid open his face from brow to lip, splitting his nose and scarring him so horribly that he was compelled to hide the mutilation beneath a cloth mask. His fate this day might be worse, and by the time the ranks had formed he had determined upon the course he would follow. Even before the bugles sounded the order for assembly an incident occurred which may have clinched that decision in the minds of Cepeda and many others. Pizarro's soldiers had been told that the enemy lacked artillery, but as they girded on their mail and primed their weapons they heard the bellow of a cannon and saw its smoke puff up above the royalist lines. The ball was so accurately aimed that it killed Pizarro's own orderly and the horse he was holding.

Pizarro mounted his charger and spurred the beast up and down in front of his ranks in a flashy exhibition of superb horsemanship, then called his officers for a final word on the disposition of their commands and the orders for the day.

Diego Cepeda rode away from the conference as though to rejoin his infantry in the center of the front, then suddenly wheeled the horse and galloped madly toward Gasca's lines. Several cavaliers, better mounted, spurred after him but were turned back by a detachment of Gasca's troopers which charged out to receive the deserter. One, however, was close enough to cast his spear. The weapon pierced the coward's thigh and wounded his horse, but he was picked up by the enemy and carried to the rear. Gasca placed him under arrest and—later—sent him to Spain to be tried for his various crimes against the crown. The licentiate died in prison before the trial was ended, thereby denying a fee to the executioner at Toledo.

Diego Cepeda was not the only deserter. Many others had decided that Pizarro's cause was lost and speedily followed the example set by the cowardly licentiate. One who thus saved his own skin was Garcilaso de la Vega, father of the youth who in after years was to devote considerable space in his history to an attempt to condone his sire's action. A dozen arquebusiers threw down their pieces and ran toward the enemy. As many pikemen followed. Pizarro, courageously enough, shouted for the trumpets to sound the order for an immediate charge. As though that were the signal for which they waited, an entire company of arquebusiers marched directly into Gasca's lines, their loaded weapons on their shoulders. The majority of the gunners had once been soldiers of Diego Centeno. Virtually impressed into Pizarro's forces after Huarina, they deserted now to their former commander.

That was the battle of the Zúrite Plain. Thus, without a shot's being fired or a blow's being struck, crumbled the ambitions of Gonzalo Pizarro. The close-packed ranks broke. The men flung down their arms and fled—some across the plain to the foe, some back along the great road which the Incas had built to Cuzco, others into the mountains. At the last Gonzalo Pizarro was alone save for eight or ten cavaliers, who could die but who could never be cowards. Francisco Carvajal was not among them. Pizarro raised the vizor of his helmet and spoke—gently, for they all were men already dead—to Juan de Acosta.

"What shall we do, Juan, my brother?"

"Let us charge," replied Acosta, "and die like the ancient Romans."

Gonzalo Pizarro shook his head.

"It is better," he said, "to die like Christians."

He raised the bridle reins and turned the chestnut stallion toward the Gasca lines. His companions—it is in such moments that the words *caballero* and hidalgo assume their true significance—followed. Pizarro announced his name to the first officer they met and surrendered his sword.

Francisco Carvajal was no coward, but neither was he an hidalgo. Life was still sweet to the old Demon of the Andes, who had drunk so deeply of life and who knew only too well the fate that would be his at Gasca's hands. He was among the last to leave the field, but when he saw Pizarro's squadrons scatter in flight he joined the rout. A number of small streams cross the Plain of Zúrite, and at the ford of one of them the horse fell and pinned the rider. Before he could pull himself free Carvajal was seized and disarmed by some of his own men, who hustled him to the Gasca camp.

He was recognized, of course. There was no man in Peru who did not know the huge old veteran at first sight, but an officer rode up and scattered those who were threatening immediate death to the man whose hands had been reddened with the blood of their comrades at Huarina and during the year-long warfare in the Charcas. Carvajal, courteously enough, asked the name of his rescuer. The officer bowed.

"I am Diego Centeno."

Carvajal, ever irrepressible, shook with laughter.

"By God, señor," he roared, "I have looked so often upon your back that now when I behold your face I do not recognize it!"

The common soldiers, ever pawns in the game of life and death, were not punished, but the prisoners of rank were tried by drumhead court martial upon that very day. Andres de Cianca, recently appointed *Oidor* of the Royal Audience, prepared the indictments and with Alonso de Alvarado composed the court which decided the fate of Pizarro, Carvajal, Juan de Acosta, and several others. There is nothing in the chronicles to indicate that any testimony was taken or that the accused men appeared in their own defense. There was no defense; there was no doubt either of guilt or the degree of sentence.

É como á tal condenamos al dicho Gonzalo Pizarro . . . and therefore we condemn the said Gonzalo Pizarro to punishment by death, which we declare shall be inflicted as follows: He shall be taken from the prison and, bound hand and foot, set upon a mule and be brought publicly before the Army of His Majesty; the crier shall there declare his guilt; he shall bear a placard which proclaims this sentence to the army; he shall then be taken down and his head shall be struck from off his neck.

And we command that after his death the said head be borne to the City of the Kings, the principal city of this province, and nailed upon the gallows there with an inscription in large print which shall say: "This is the head of the traitor Gonzalo Pizarro, who has been brought to justice in the Valley of Sacsahuana where victory in battle was given to the royal standard against those who sought to defend his treachery and tyranny; no one shall dare remove it from here on pain of death."

We do further decree that the house which the said Gonzalo Pizarro owns in the city of Cuzco shall be destroyed to its foundations and sown with salt, and that where the door now stands there shall be placed a post bearing a placard which shall say: "Here was the house of Gonzalo Pizarro, which was ordered destroyed for his treachery, and no person shall dare to restore it or to build here without special permission of His Majesty on pain of death."

And we further sentence him to the loss of all property of whatever nature which belongs to him, the which are to revert to the Treasury of His Majesty . . . and this we find to be our final sentence, and we so declare and pronounce and affix thereto our hands and seals.

ALONSO DE ALVARADO [*rubrica*]
THE LICENTIATE CIANCA [*rubrica*]

The sentences imposed upon the others were identical except that Carvajal, for his greater infamies, was to be drawn and quartered after decapitation. The traitors were to die upon the following day, April 10, 1548, upon the field where their cause had been lost. Priests were sent to the condemned men to tell them of their fate, to hear their confessions, and to prepare their souls for death.

The good father who visited the tent where Francisco Carvajal was confined faced a problem for which none of his ecclesiastical experience had prepared him. The old hellion had lived for more than eighty years without God's saving grace, he wanted none of it in his last hours. "*Basta matar!*" he said to the cleric, which may be translated as "I die—so what?" He thrust the priest aside and continued to bandy ribaldries with the many soldiers who crowded about the entrance to the tent to view the famous prisoner. Even some of those urged him to recall the father, to confess his many sins, and to receive absolution therefor.

"Sins?" snorted Carvajal. "I have no such burden except the debt of half a *real* which I owed to the keeper of a grog shop in Seville, near the Arenal Harbor, when I sailed for the Indies."

An officer asked if he could perform any last services for the doomed man, saying that Carvajal had once spared his life and that he considered himself indebted thereby.

"Service?"' the old fellow sneered. "What do you mean? The only service anyone can do is to set me free. You owe me nothing. If I ever spared your life—which I do not remember doing—it was because I did not think you worth killing!"

That clause in the death sentences which provided that the condemned be borne to the place of execution on a mule was an added refinement of mental torture and public shame for a *caballero*—a man who always rode a horse. Mules were for women and priests and eunuchs, not for men. No mule could be found in the camp, however, which could bear Carvajal's weight. Two mules were necessary, and the veteran's three-hundred-pound frame was wedged into what appears to have been some sort of large wicker basket slung on poles between the animals. That incident, too, amused him.

"A baby in a cradle and an old man in a cradle!" he chuckled.

The priests were aghast at his repeated blasphemies, but they followed the improvised conveyance to the platform which had been erected on the field. One more insistent than the others implored Carvajal to commend his soul to God by repeating, at least, a *Pater Noster* and an *Ave Maria*. At the foot of the scaffold the grinning Carvajal flung the priest's words back at him.

"*Pater noster!*" he gibbered mockingly. "*Ave Maria. Pater noster. Ave Maria.*"

It was a final defiance of God and man. Awkwardly, for his hands were bound, he clambered to the scaffold and laid his head on the block. The ax rose and fell. The executioner lifted the grinning head from the basket and held it aloft that all men might see that the king's justice had been inflicted upon Carvajal, the traitor. Then, methodically, he completed the horrid task. The headless body was chopped into four parts, which were borne to Cuzco, painted with tar to preserve them the longer, and placed one upon each of the principal highways entering that city. The head was taken to Lima.

In Gonzalo Pizarro was none of Carvajal's callousness. He refused all visitors and spent his last night pacing up and down within his tent. At dawn he sent for a priest, confessed, received absolution, and knelt in prayer until it was time to dress himself for the final ordeal. Those who were accustomed to see Gonzalo Pizarro in all his finery should not be disappointed in his final appearance. He wore red shoes of soft leather, his finest hose and doublet, and flung over all an army cloak of yellow velvet almost entirely covered with plates of gold—the chronicler's description of what may have been gold ornaments which bore the intertwined G-P

313

adopted by Gonzalo as his insignia. A yellow velvet hat with the same device was on his head.

He submitted with dignity to the last infamies, to the placard which branded him as a traitor and to the mule. His hands, however, were not bound, and he bore in them an image of the Virgin, whom, we learn suddenly, he had always adored. The priests who escorted him chanted the prayers for the dying. In his last hour Gonzalo Pizarro was suddenly mindful of his soul, for he stood upon the platform beside the block and reminded all within sound of his voice that he was now penniless and could bequeath no money to pay for masses for that soul's repose and its speedy release from Purgatory. Would they—many of whom owed their wealth to the Pizarros—grant him that last charity after his death? He prayed, then put aside his cloak and cap and asked the executioner to do his duty "with a firm hand." Then, his eyes unbandaged, his hands unbound, he laid his head upon the block. The ax fell. One blow was enough. The head of the youngest of the Brothers of Doom fell into the basket placed to receive it.

Their God—the grim and terrible God of the sixteenth century—has judged those brothers. Their deeds, good and evil, speak for them. This earth has never known their like, it can never know their like again.

INDEX

INDEX

A

Acla: replaces Antigua, 64; ships built at, 66; scene of Balboa's execution, 70; today, 72

Acosta, Juan de, 304, 309, 310

Aguilar, Geronimo de, 39

Alcántara, Francisco Martín de, 4, 96-7, 166, 236; death of, 237

Aldana, Lorenzo de, 233, 258, 287, 293

Alfonso V [of Portugal], 9

Almagro, Diego: partner of Francisco Pizarro, 75; obscure history of, 75; loses eye, 77; at Tacamez, 82; returns to Panamá, 82; made hidalgo, 93; his quarrels with Pizarro, 94, 98; reaches Cajamarca, 164; tries Atahualpa, 174; aids Soto, 181; negotiates with Alvarado, 190-91; governor of Cuzco, 195; *adelantado*, 196; Chilean expedition, 198, 211; negotiates with Manco, 212; at Urcos, 213, 214; imprisons Hernando and Gonzalo Pizarro, 215; Battle of Abancay, 216; at Mala, 218 ff; Battle of Salinas, 221; captured, 221; trial and execution, 222 ff

Almagro El Joven [Diego, Jr.]: birth, 76, 220; captured, 222;

in Lima, 234; takes command of forces, 244; defeat, trial, execution, 247-48

Alvarado, Alonso, 199, 216, 284, 302, 310, 311

Alvarado, Beatriz de la Cueva de, 191

Alvarado, Diego, 226, 231

Alvarado, Garcia de, 243-44

Alvarado, Pedro de, 41, 190; paid with rubber check, 191; death of, 191; widow succeeds, 191

Alvarez, Juan Jeronimo, *Oidor de Audiencia*, 263; reaches Lima, 268; with Nuñez Vela, 270; killed at Añaquito, 274

Andagoya, Pascual de, expedition to Biruquote, 74

Arguello, Hernando de, execution of, 71

Atahualpa, Inca, 10, 117 ff; deposes Huáscar, 120; receives Soto, 137; captured, 146; offers ransom, 149 ff; orders Huáscar killed, 151; pays ransom, 164; trial of, 173; baptism and execution, 176-7; burial, 177

Aurea Chersonesus, 13

Ayllon, Lucas Vasquez de, 32

Ayorra, Juan de, crosses isthmus, 60

317

319

hualpa, 175; takes mistress, 176; occupies Cuzco, 183; made marquis, 196; treaty with Almagro, 220; civil war, 221 ff; approves Almagro execution, 223; treatment of Almagristas, 225, 234; assassinated, 238; burial, 238; character of, 239 ff

Pizarro, Gonzalo: birth, 3; enlists with brother, 95; share in ransom, 166; *regidor* of Cuzco, 188; prisoner, 215; escapes, 218; army leader, 220; campaigns in Peru, 228; sent to Quito, 229; Napo expedition, 248-258; interview with Vaca, 259; at Potosí, 259; takes field against Nuñez Vela, 265; protests to king, 268; declared Governor-General, 271; campaign against Vela, 273-75; triumphant return, 275-76; letters from Gasca, 286; organizes army, 291; abandons Lima, 293; battle of Huarina, 295 ff; occupies Cuzco, 300; at Sacsahuana, 305-309; trial and execution of, 310, 313, 314

Pizarro, Gonzalo, Sr., sire of brothers, 3. [*See* Morales, Francisca]

Pizarro, Hernando: birth, 3; education, 5; appearance, 6; service in Italy, 19; enlists with Francisco, 95 ff; wounded, 125; at Atahualpa's camp, 136 ff; expedition to Pachacamac, 156 ff; returns to Cajamarca, 160; share in ransom, 166; returns to Spain, 169; again in Peru, 195; governor of Cuzco, 200; besieged, 204 ff; captured

by Almagro, 215; released, 219; army leader, 220; captures Almagro, 221; executes Almagro, 223; return to Spain, 230; imprisoned, 231; marries niece Francisca, 231; death of, 231

Pizarro, Isabel de Vargas de, wife of Gonzalo, Sr., 3

Pizarro, Juan: birth, 3; enlists with Francisco, 95; share in ransom, 166; *regidor* of Cuzco, 188; captures Manco, 201; fights at Yucay, 202-03; at Sacsahuamán, 207; death of, 209; eulogies of, 209; burial place, 210

Pizarro, Pedro: 95, 124, 187, 205, 295

Platerriayoc, "lost city," 154

Polo, Marco, 13

Ponce de Leon, Hernan, 207

Ponce de Leon, Juan, 15

Poncel, Juan, 199

Poncra, cacique, defeated, tortured, killed, 53

Portobello, named, 13

Prester John, 13

Pulgar, Hernando de, quoted, 9, 10, 11

Q

Quaraquá, cacique, 48

Quevedo, Juan de, Bishop of Darien, 59, 65

Quivira: sought by Coronado, 32; survives on maps, 33

Quizquiz, Inca general, 180, 188

R

Roca, Inca, 114

Rojas, Gabriel de, 207

Roldan, Francisco, 16

Ruiz de Estrada, Bartolomé, pilot, 80, 84, 93, 163

322

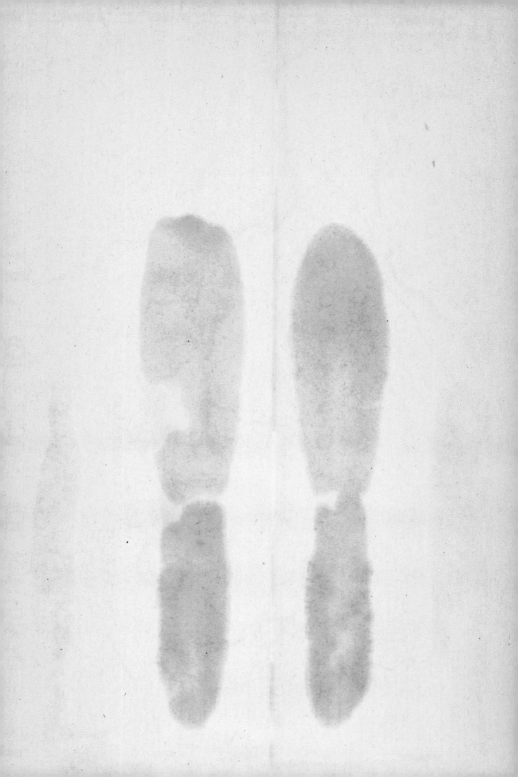